HOW
TO
USE
FRENCH
VERBS

HOW TO USE FRENCH VERBS

By Laura W. Fleder
Department of French and Romance Philology
Columbia University

Diane Wolfe Levy
Assistant Professor
Department of French
State University of New York at Albany

Barron's Educational Series Inc.
NEW YORK

All inquiries should be addressed to:
Barron's Educational Series, Inc.
250 Wireless Boulevard
Hauppauge, New York 11788

Library of Congress Catalog Card No. 75-22441

Library of Congress Cataloging in Publication Data

Fleder, Laura W.
    How to use French verbs.

    1. French language—Verb. I. Levy, Diane Wolfe,
joint author. II. Title.
PC2271.F55   445   75-22441
ISBN 0-8120-0599-6

International Standard Book No. 0-8120-0599-6

PRINTED IN THE UNITED STATES OF AMERICA

23   510   11 10 9

Table of Contents

Introduction

This book is intended to help students over two of the toughest hurdles in learning French: the use of prepositions and pronouns with verbs.

Prepositions are troublesome because they are governed by usage, not by systematic rules. No grammar rule will tell you, for example, why "J'essaye *de* finir mon travail" (I am trying to finish my work) uses *de* rather than some other preposition or no preposition at all. The use of *de* is completely arbitrary. Moreover, the use of prepositions is not consistent from one language to another. The student cannot rely on English usage as a model for his French sentence. In English, you wait *for* the bus; in French, "vous attendez l'autobus"—no preposition. Even more perplexing problems arise because many verbs can have different meanings with different prepositions.

Compare: Je réponds *à* Georges. I answer George.
and: Je réponds *de* Georges. I vouch for George.

The VERB LIST of this book helps you with this problem area. It lists 1500 verbs, the various prepositions each verb can take, and the meaning of each verb-preposition combination.

The second problem area, pronoun use, is tackled in the REVIEW and VERB CATEGORIES sections. Pronouns do follow systematic rules, but their usage is tricky: there are many more pronouns in French than in English and each pronoun in French has a very specific function. The REVIEW provides the basic concepts and rules necessary for understanding and using pronouns: it defines direct and indirect objects and explains the various types of personal pronouns. The REVIEW also outlines the basic verbal structures: the difference between transitive and intransitive verbs, the use of reflexive verbs, the rules for using *être* and *avoir* in compound tenses, the agreement of the past participle in compound tenses, and the use of infinitives. The REVIEW identifies and explains the various elements of verb usage. The VERB CATEGORIES section shows how to put these verbs and pronouns into use.

How to use this book

The VERB LIST goes hand in hand with the VERB CATEGORIES section. Suppose, for example, that you want to use the verb *penser* in the sentence, "I am thinking about my sister." How do you know what preposition to use after the verb, if any at all?

1. Check in the VERB LIST. You will find the following entry:

penser

1. _____ à Qn ou Qch*(to think about . . .) III
2. _____ Qch de Qn ou Qch (to think . . . of, about . . . ; in questions, to have an opinion about . . . Ex: *Que pensez-vous du nouveau professeur?* What do you think of the new professor?) VI
3. _____ *Inf.* (to intend to . . . ; to think that . . . Ex: *Il pense pouvoir le faire.* He thinks that he can do it.) VII-A
4. _____ à *Inf.* (to think about, to consider ---*ing*) VIII-A

---

*Qn stands for *quelqu'un* (someone) and Qch stands for *quelque chose* (something). For other abbreviations see KEY TO VERB LIST, p. 67.

The first entry, "penser à Qn ou Qch," is what you need: You can substitute "ma soeur" for "quelqu'un" and you have, "Je pense à ma soeur."

2. Suppose you want to substitute a pronoun for "ma soeur," to say, "I am thinking about her." If you are not sure which pronoun to use or how to incorporate it in the sentence, turn back to the Category indicated by the roman numeral after the definition. You will find Category III (p. 44): VERBS WHICH TAKE *À* BEFORE A NOUN BUT WHICH CANNOT USE AN INDIRECT OBJECT PRONOUN TO SUBSTITUTE FOR THAT NOUN. You find that **penser** does not work like most verbs which take *à*, such as *parler, e.g.,* "Je parle *à ma soeur*" → "Je *lui* parle." Category III tells you that when the noun is a person, you keep the preposition *à* and replace the noun with a *tonic pronoun.* The category gives you an example of this type of substitution:

Je m'habitue *à mon nouveau patron.*	I'm getting used to *my new boss.*
Je m'habitue *à lui.*	I'm getting used to *him.*

Using the example as a model, make the same kind of substitution:

Je pense *à ma soeur.*	I'm thinking *about my sister.*
Je pense *à elle.*	I'm thinking *about her.*

3. If you are unsure of a grammatical term used in the Category entry, such as "tonic pronoun" or "indirect object pronoun," check in the REVIEW for a more detailed definition and explanation.

This book serves students at all levels of proficiency. Advanced students can use the VERB LIST exclusively, as a quick reference to check the preposition required by a verb. The less advanced student can use the VERB LIST along with the VERB CATEGORIES section to find out how to make a pronoun substitution. Beginners will need the REVIEW in addition to the VERB CATEGORIES as a reference for terms and as a basic grammar and guide to verb usage. In short, this book will show you step-by-step, **How to Use French Verbs.**

PART ONE

Review

A. Verbs: Basic Concepts

There are two kinds of verbs: Intransitive and Transitive.

Intransitive Verbs

Intransitive verbs do not take a direct or indirect object. This means that the subject of the verb directs no action at another person or thing. Most intransitive verbs are complete in themselves:

Je pars.	I am leaving.
Il dort.	He is sleeping.
Nous travaillons.	We are working.

SUBJECT $\longrightarrow$ **VERB**

Some intransitive verbs do take a noun after the verb: this noun is called a predicate noun.* The predicate noun is not, however, the object of the verb. The predicate noun is always the same person or thing as the subject, and the verb serves as a kind of equal sign, linking the subject to the predicate noun:

Mon frère est *médecin*.   My brother is a *doctor*.

SUBJECT $\xrightarrow[=]{\textbf{VERB}}$ **PREDICATE NOUN.**

Intransitive verbs can also take a predicate adjective after the verb. The predicate adjective simply modifies the subject of the sentence. The verb acts as a link between the subject and the predicate adjective which describes it.

Vous semblez *fatigué*.   You seem *tired*.

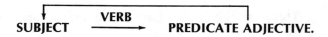

SUBJECT $\xrightarrow{\textbf{VERB}}$ **PREDICATE ADJECTIVE.**

The most common intransitive verbs which take predicate nouns and adjectives are *devenir* (to become), *être* (to be), *paraître* (to seem, to look), *rester* (to remain), *se montrer* (to appear), *se sentir* (to feel), and *sembler* (to seem).

---

*The term *predicate* refers to the "verb" part of the sentence and includes the verb and anything which completes the sense of the verb.

SUBJECT	PREDICATE	
We	walked.	
(*subject*)	(*verb*)	
The boys	walked	to the store.
(*subject*)	(*verb*)	(*adverbial phrase*)
Einstein	was	a genius.
(*subject*)	(*verb*)	(*predicate noun*)

Transitive Verbs

Transitive verbs can take a direct object, an indirect object, or both a direct object AND an indirect object.

1. *Transitive verbs which take a direct object*

A noun is a direct object if it receives the action of the verb directly, without the help of a preposition.

J'ouvre *la porte.*	I open *the door.*
Je vois *mes amis.*	I see *my friends.*
Elle amène *sa fille* chez le dentiste.	She takes *her daughter* to the dentist.

$$\text{SUBJECT} \xrightarrow{\text{VERB}} \text{DIRECT OBJECT.}$$

The direct object always answers the questions "What?" or "Whom?"

J'ouvre *la porte.*	(What do I open?)
Je vois *mes amis.*	(Whom do I see?)

Be careful not to confuse the direct object, which answers the questions "What?" or "Whom?" with nouns telling "Where", "When", "How", or "Why". In the following sentences, there are NO direct objects. The phrases *au Mexique* and *avant le professeur* are simply adverbial phrases telling "Where" and "When".

Je vais au Mexique.	I am going to Mexico.
Les élèves arrivent avant le professeur.	The students arrive before the teacher.

Many verbs can be either transitive or intransitive, depending on how they are used.

(*Intransitive*)	Elle écrit bien.	She writes well.
(*Transitive*)	Elle écrit une lettre.	She is writing a letter.
(*Intransitive*)	La cheminée fume.	The chimney is smoking.
(*Transitive*)	Il fume des cigares.	He smokes cigars.

2. *Transitive verbs which take an indirect object*

In English, an indirect object is rarely used without a direct object (see Section 3 on following page).

In French, an indirect object is a noun that is linked to the verb by the preposition *à*.

Je parle à *Jean*.	I speak to John.
J'écris à *ma mère*.	I write to my mother.
Nous obéissons à *la loi*.	We obey the law.*

$$\text{SUBJECT} \xrightarrow{\quad\overbrace{\text{VERB}}\quad} \overset{\frown}{\text{à}} \longrightarrow \text{INDIRECT OBJECT.}$$

Many verbs in French take prepositions other than *à* before a noun (for example, *se moquer de*—to make fun of; *lutter avec*—to struggle with; *protester contre*—to protest against). The nouns following these prepositions are not technically indirect objects. Only nouns following the preposition *à* are indirect objects in French; and only these nouns can be replaced by indirect object pronouns.

---

*Note that the French verb *obéir* takes an indirect object, whereas the English verb *to obey* takes a direct object.

3. *Transitive verbs which take a direct* AND *an indirect object*

While the direct object receives the action of the verb, the indirect object can be said to "receive" the direct object.

In English, an indirect object is commonly used with a direct object. It is a noun or pronoun placed between the verb and the direct object. The indirect object answers the question "To whom?" or "For whom?"

She brought *him* the book.	Elle *lui* a apporté le livre.
I loaned *my friend* ten dollars.	J'ai prêté dix dollars à *mon ami*.

In French, the indirect object can be used alone—as in the examples in Section 2 above—or with a direct object. It is most often linked to a direct object.

J'ai posé + *une question* + à *l'agent.*
     (*direct object*)   (*indirect object*)
I asked the policeman a question.

J'ai envoyé + *une lettre* + à *mon sénateur.*
     (*direct object*)   (*indirect object*)
I sent my senator a letter.

$$\text{SUBJECT} \xrightarrow{\text{VERB}} \text{DIRECT OBJECT} \rightarrow \overset{\frown}{\text{à}} \leftarrow \text{INDIRECT OBJECT.}$$

4. *Reflexive verbs*

A reflexive verb takes a pronoun object which "reflects" back to the subject of the sentence; that is, the subject and the object of the verb's action are the same person or thing. In English, the reflexive pronoun (*myself, himself, yourself, etc.*) is usually only implied.

Je *me* lave.	I get washed. ("I wash *myself*.")
Nous *nous* dépêchons.	We are hurrying. ("We hurry *ourselves*.")
Il *se* couche.	He goes to bed. ("He puts *himself* to bed.")

```
┌────────────────────────────────────────────────┐
  SUBJECT     REFLEXIVE PRONOUN     VERB │
└────────────────────────────────────────────────┘
```

The French reflexive pronouns are:

SINGULAR	PLURAL
me	nous
te	vous
se (masculine & feminine)	se (masculine & feminine)

These pronouns may be direct or indirect objects, depending on whether or not the verb takes the preposition *à*.

Il *se* réveille.	He wakes up. ("He wakes *himself*.")
	se = direct object
Elle *se* parle.	She talks to *herself*.
	se = indirect object

In the plural, the reflexive pronoun can have a reciprocal sense, meaning "each other."

| Ils *se* regardent tendrement. | They look at *each other* tenderly. |
| Elles *se* parlent tous les jours. | They talk to *each other* every day. |

The context of the sentence tells you whether the pronoun has a reciprocal or a reflexive meaning. In the above two sentences, for example, *"Ils se regardent"* and *"Elles se parlent"* could conceivably mean "They look at themselves" and "They talk to themselves"; but in light of the context, these latter meanings seem very unlikely.*

Reflexive verbs are often used in French where the passive form is used in English:

Cela *ne se fait pas* en   That *isn't done* in
    bonne société.   polite company.

Ce médicament *se vend*   That medicine *is sold* at
    à la pharmacie.   the pharmacy.

Most transitive verbs can be reflexive or not, depending on whether the object of the verb is the same person or thing as the subject.

Je lave ma robe.   I wash my dress.
Je *me* lave.   I wash (*myself*).

Elle habille sa fille.   She dresses her daughter.
Elle *s'*habille.   She gets dressed. ("She
                         dresses *herself*.")

Some verbs, however, are ALWAYS reflexive, even though the action of the verb is directed at someone or something other than the subject. For these verbs the reflexive pronoun has no true reflexive or reciprocal meaning.

---

*In order to avoid ambiguity, and if the meaning intended is "at each other," or "to each other," the following can be added to make the thought clear: *l'un l'autre* in the first sentence or *l'une à l'autre* in the second sentence.

Il *se* moque de son petit frère.	He makes fun of his little brother.
Je ne *me* souviens pas de votre nom.	I don't remember your name.
Elle *s'*aperçoit de son erreur.	She realizes her error.

Position of Reflexive Pronouns

Reflexive pronouns, like other personal pronouns, normally **precede** the verb:

Il *se* lève.	He gets up.
Il ne *se* lève pas.	He doesn't get up.
Se lève-t-il?*	Is he getting up?
Ne *se* lève-t-il pas?	Isn't he getting up?

In compound tenses, the reflexive pronoun **precedes** the AUXILIARY verb:

Il *s'*est levé.	He got up.
Il ne *s'*est pas levé.	He didn't get up.
*S'*est-il levé?	Did he get up?
Ne *s'*est-il pas levé?	Didn't he get up?

---

*Be careful of the position of the subject pronoun and the reflexive pronoun in questions using the inverted form: The reflexive pronoun keeps its position directly preceding the verb and the subject pronoun swings around *after* the verb. The verb and the subject pronoun are then joined with a hyphen:

Tu *te* leves.   Vous *vous* levez.
Te lèves-tu?   *Vous* levez-vous?

EXCEPTION: Note the following changes that occur in the affirmative imperative (command form):

(1) The reflexive pronoun goes AFTER the verb.

(2) The stressed pronoun *toi* replaces *te*.

Levez-*vous!*	Get up!
Lève-*toi!*	Get up! (familiar)
Levons-*nous!*	Let's get up!

There is no change in the negative imperative form. The reflexive pronoun remains **in front** of the verb:

Ne *vous* levez pas!	Don't get up!
Ne *te* lève pas!	Don't get up! (familiar)
Ne *nous* levons pas!	Let's not get up!

Use of Auxiliary Verbs AVOIR and ÊTRE in Compound Tenses

1. *Verbs conjugated with* AVOIR

Most verbs in French are conjugated with AVOIR in compound tenses:

Avez-vous reçu ma lettre?	Did you receive my letter?
Ils *ont* acheté une nouvelle maison.	They bought a new house.

2. *Verbs conjugated with* ÊTRE

All Reflexive Verbs

Elle s'*est* couchée tard.	She went to bed late.
Nous nous *sommes* promenés aujourd'hui.	We went for a walk today.

The Following Verbs:

aller	to go
venir	to come
entrer	to enter, go in
sortir	to go out
arriver	to arrive
partir	to leave
revenir	to come back
retourner	to return, go back
rentrer	to go in again, go back
monter	to go up
descendre	to go down
tomber	to fall
passer	to go by, pass by
rester	to remain
devenir	to become
naître	to be born
mourir	to die

Thinking of these verbs as "verbs of movement" is a handy way to remember them. NOTE, however, that while all these verbs which take **être** are verbs of movement (literal or figurative), not all verbs of movement take **être**. There are many verbs of movement that do NOT take **être**. For example, *courir* (to run) and *marcher* (to walk) take **avoir**.

J'*ai* marché vite.	I walked quickly.
Nous *avons* couru pour attraper l'autobus.	We ran to catch the bus.

The verbs of movement which take **être** are all intransitive verbs—that is, they do not take a direct or indirect object. Five of these verbs—*monter, descendre, sortir, rentrer,* and *passer*—can also be used in a transitive sense and take a direct object. When they take a direct object, they are conjugated with **avoir**. Compare the following examples:

1. Il *est* monté au premier étage.	He went up to the second floor.
Le porteur *a* monté les valises.	The porter took the suitcases up.
2. Je *suis* descendu à la gare St-Lazare.	I got off at the St. Lazare station.
J'*ai* descendu l'escalier en vitesse.	I went down the stairs quickly.
3. Elle *est* sortie à huit heures.	She went out at eight o'clock.
Elle *a* sorti un livre de la bibliothèque.	She took a book out of the library.
4. Il *est* rentré tôt.	He came home early.
Il *a* rentré les chaises avant la pluie.	He took in the chairs before the rain.
5. Je *suis* passé chez vous cet après-midi.	I came by your house this afternoon.
J'*ai* passé un examen de biologie ce matin.	I took a biology exam this morning.

Agreement of the Past Participle in Compound Tenses

AGREEMENT WITH SUBJECT	— VERBS CONJUGATED WITH **ÊTRE**
AGREEMENT WITH PRECEDING DIRECT OBJECT	— ALL VERBS CONJUGATED WITH **AVOIR** AND ALL REFLEXIVE VERBS

1. The past participle of verbs conjugated with *être* agrees in gender and number with the SUBJECT.

Il est sorti.	He went out.
Ils sont sortis.	They went out.
Elle est allée en classe.	She went to class.
Elles sont allées en classe.	They went to class.

2. The past participle of verbs conjugated with *avoir* agrees in gender and number with the DIRECT OBJECT, if the direct object PRECEDES the verb.

Study the following examples:

(a) Quelle robe avez-vous *portée*   What dress did you
      hier soir?   wear last night?

AGREEMENT: The past participle agrees with the PRECED-ING direct object, which is feminine singular.

(b) Les légumes que j'ai *achetés*   The vegetables that I
      sont délicieux.   bought are delicious.

AGREEMENT: The past participle agrees with the PRECED-ING direct object, the relative pronoun *que,* whose antecedent is *les légumes. Les légumes* is masculine plural.

(c) Où sont mes clés?   Where are my keys?
      Je les ai *perdues!*   I've lost them!

AGREEMENT: The past participle agrees with the PRECED-ING direct object pronoun *les; les* stands for *les clés,* which is feminine plural.

BUT:

(d) J'ai *acheté* des ⎡légumes⎤   I bought some vegetables
    au supermarché.   at the supermarket.

NO AGREEMENT: The direct object comes AFTER the verb.

NOTE: The past participle **does not agree** with **en** when **en** is
the PRECEDING direct object:

Avez-vous acheté des disques?   Did you buy any records?
Oui, j'en ai *acheté.*   Yes, I bought some.

3. The past participle of reflexive verbs agrees with the
DIRECT OBJECT, if the direct object PRECEDES the verb.

(a) Jeanne ⎡s⎤'est *levée* de   Jeanne got up early.
    bonne heure.

AGREEMENT: The past participle agrees with the PRECED-
ING direct object, *se; se,* like the subject, is feminine singular.

(b) Les enfants ⎡se⎤ sont *lavés.*   The children got washed.
                              ("washed themselves")

AGREEMENT: The past participle agrees with the PRECED-
ING direct object, *se; se,* like the subject, is masculine plural.

BUT:

(c) Les enfants se sont *lavé*   The children washed
    les mains.   their hands.

NO AGREEMENT: The direct object (*les mains*) comes
AFTER the verb. When a reflexive verb is followed by a
noun direct object, the reflexive pronoun is considered to
be the indirect object.

(d) Elles se sont *parlé* au   They talked to each other
     téléphone.   on the telephone.

NO AGREEMENT: There is no direct object in this sentence. The reflexive pronoun *se* is an indirect object: the verb *parler* takes the preposition *à*.*

B. Verbs and Pronouns

Introduction to Pronouns

A pronoun is a word that is used to replace a noun. It can perform all the functions that nouns perform: subject, direct object, indirect object, or object of a preposition. Pronouns are less specific than nouns, but we usually use these "shorthand" forms within a context which avoids confusion. You wouldn't say "*He* came" or "I saw *her* yesterday" or "I put *it* there" if you didn't know who, or where, or what you were talking about.

The general pronouns we use to substitute for persons or things are called personal pronouns. They change form depending on their function. In English, there are only two forms: one for subject pronouns and one for object pronouns. For example, we say "*She* is ready" (subject); "I spoke to *her*" (object); "Where are *they*?" (subject); "The letter is for *them*" (object).

---

*If you are not sure whether a verb takes a direct or an indirect object, check the verb in the **VERB LIST**.

The Personal Pronouns

English Personal Pronouns

SUBJECT	OBJECT
I	me
you	you
he, she, it	him, her, it
we	us
you	you
they	them

The object form of English pronouns is used for all objects—direct, indirect, or object of a preposition:

I heard *them*. (*direct object*)

I brought *them* some wine. (*indirect object*)

I spoke with *them*. (*object of a preposition*)

In French, however, there is a special form for each kind of object pronoun:

I heard *them*.	Je *les* ai entendus.
I brought *them* some wine.	Je *leur* ai apporté du vin.
I spoke with *them*.	J'ai parlé avec *eux*.

French Personal Pronouns

SUBJECT	DIRECT OBJECT	INDIRECT OBJECT	TONIC OR STRESSED PRONOUNS (OBJECT OF PREPOSITION)
je	me	me	moi
tu	te	te	toi
il, elle, on	le, la	lui	lui, elle
	(se)	(se)	
nous	nous	nous	nous
vous	vous	vous	vous
ils, elles	les	leur	eux, elles
	(se)	(se)	

Notice that although some forms are identical, the context clearly determines what kind of pronoun you are dealing with:

Nous partons. (*subject*)　　　　*We* are leaving.

Il est venu avec *nous*.　　　　He came with *us*.
　　(*object of preposition*)

Elle *lui* parle.　　　　She is speaking *to him*.
　　(*indirect object*)

Elle parle de *lui*.　　　　She is speaking about *him*.
　　(*object of preposition*)

Subject Pronouns

Subject pronouns represent persons or things. They generally precede the verb.

Il can mean "he" or "it" and *elle* can mean "she" or "it", depending on whether the noun replaced by the pronoun is a person or a thing.

Voilà ma petite soeur.	There is my little sister.
Elle a neuf ans.	*She* is nine.
Voilà ma voiture.	There is my car.
Elle est neuve.	*It's* new.

On is an indefinite subject pronoun which has various meanings in English. The most common are the vague or indefinite "you" or "they". Other translations for *on* are "one" or "people".

On ne devrait pas parler pendant un concert.	You (*one*) shouldn't talk during a concert.
On le dit très riche.	They (*people*) say he's very rich.

On is also used as a substitute for *nous* in spoken French:

Si *on* allait au cinéma?	Shall *we* go to the movies?
On s'est disputé hier.	*We* had a quarrel yesterday.

French people generally avoid using the passive form. *On* is often used as an active subject where a passive would be used in English.

Ici *on* parle français.	French *is spoken* here.
On a libéré le prisonnier.	The prisoner *was freed*.

Direct Object Pronouns

Direct object pronouns represent either persons or things. Unlike noun direct objects, which follow the verb, pronoun direct objects PRECEDE the verb in French, except in the affirmative imperative (command form).

Il connaît *cette femme.*	He knows *that woman.*
Il *la* connaît.	He knows *her.*

Il ferme *la porte.*	He is closing *the door.*
Il *la* ferme.	He is closing *it.*

Fermez *la porte.*	Close *the door.*
Fermez-*la.*	Close *it.*

Le can mean "him" or "it" and *la* can mean "her" or "it", depending on whether the noun replaced by the pronoun is a person or a thing.

Indirect Object Pronouns

Indirect object pronouns are used to substitute for persons, animals, or animate objects, and ONLY when the preposition following the verb is *à*.* Unlike noun indirect objects, which follow the verb, pronoun indirect objects PRECEDE the verb in French except in the affirmative imperative (command form). The indirect object pronoun replaces both the preposition *à* and the noun group following it.

---

*See p. 43 for a list of verbs which take indirect objects in French and direct objects in English.

Il a téléphoné *à son amie.*	He called *his girlfriend.*
Il *lui* a téléphoné.	He called *her.*

Ecrivez *à vos parents.*	Write *to your parents.*
Ecrivez-*leur.*	Write *to them.*

Le médecin *me* défend de fumer.	The doctor forbids *me* to smoke.

Elle parle *à ses plantes* tous les jours!	She talks *to her plants* every day!
Elle *leur* parle tous les jours!	She talks *to them* every day!

Tonic Pronouns

Tonic, or stressed pronouns, have several functions. They are used:

1. after prepositions
2. for emphasis, to reinforce a subject, direct object or indirect object
3. after *c'est* or *ce sont*
4. in a compound subject, direct object, or indirect object
5. in comparisons
6. when there is no verb in the sentence

1. *After Prepositions*

Since indirect object pronouns are used only when a verb takes the preposition *à*, a different set of pronouns is used with other prepositions: *the tonic pronouns.*

Like the indirect object pronouns, *tonic pronouns* used as the object of a preposition replace nouns representing people, animals, or animate objects. Tonic pronouns are placed AFTER the preposition, just like the noun they replace.

On s'est révolté contre *le dictateur.*	They rebelled against *the dictator.*
On s'est révolté contre *lui.*	They rebelled against *him.*
Il compte sur *ses amis.*	He is counting on *his friends.*
Il compte sur *eux.*	He is counting on *them.*

2. *For Emphasis*

In English, subject or object pronouns can be stressed by the inflection of the voice. For example, you could say "You invited *him*?!" or "*I* did it!" In French, however, *tonic pronouns* are added to the sentence for emphasis. They are used in addition to the unstressed subject or object.* The tonic pronoun can be added at the beginning or at the end of the sentence.

---

*All tonic pronouns except *moi* and *toi* can be used alone as an *emphatic* subject, without a subject pronoun:

Lui ne parle jamais.	*He* never speaks.
Il ne parle jamais, *lui.*	*He* never speaks.

Tu l'as invité, *lui*?	You invited *him*?
Je l'ai fait, *moi*!	*I* did it!
Moi, j'y vais tous les jours.	*I* go there every day.

3. After *C'est* or *Ce Sont*

The subject or object can also be stressed by using the expression *c'est* or *ce sont* + tonic pronoun. *C'est* is used with *moi, toi, lui, elle, nous* and *vous*. *Ce sont* is used only with the pronouns *eux* and *elles*. This construction is often followed by a relative clause.

C'est Pierre qui téléphone?	Is it Peter calling?
Oui, c'est *lui*.	Yes, it's *he*.
C'est *lui* que j'ai vu.	I saw *him*.
C'est *moi* qui ai raison et ce sont *eux* qui ont tort!	*I'm* right and *they're* wrong!

4. In Compound Subjects and Objects

Tonic pronouns are used in compound subjects, direct objects or indirect objects:

Georges et *lui* viennent demain.	George and *he* are coming tomorrow.

They are also used to make a subject or object more explicit:

Nous restons à la maison,
   elle et *moi.*

We are staying at home,
   she and *I.*

5. *In Comparisons*

Tonic pronouns (NOT subject pronouns) are used as the second element of a comparison in French:

Tu es plus aimable qu'*eux.*

You are nicer than *they.*

Il mange moins vite que
   nous.

He eats less quickly than
   we.

6. *When There Is No Verb*

Tonic pronouns are used in sentences where the verb is merely implied:

Qui est là? *Moi.* (*C'est moi.*)

Who's there? *Me.*

Tu n'aimes pas l'art
   moderne? *Lui* non plus.

You don't like modern
   art? Neither does *he.*

The Adverbial Pronouns Y *and* En

As we have seen above, indirect object pronouns and tonic pronouns are used only to represent people, animals, or animate objects. What pronoun do you use if the indirect object or the object of a preposition is a THING? The adverbial pronouns **y** and **en** are used in this case:

Je réponds *à la question.*	I answer *the question.*
J'y réponds.	I answer *it.*
Elle se souvient *de l'adresse.*	She remembers *the address.*
Elle s'*en* souvient.	She remembers *it.*

These useful pronouns have other functions as well. They can help you out of many awkward grammatical situations. Read on!

The Adverbial Pronoun Y

The pronoun **y** has two major functions. It can replace:

1. *à* + noun (thing)
2. a prepositional phrase of location

1. À + noun (thing)

Y is used as an indirect object pronoun to substitute for THINGS. Like indirect object pronouns used to substitute for people, **y** replaces both the preposition *à* and the noun group following it. **Y** normally precedes the verb, except in affirmative imperative sentences:

Nous obéissons *à la loi.*	We obey *the law.*
Nous *y* obéissons.	We obey *it.*

Pensez *à ce problème!*	Think about *this problem!*
Pensez-*y!*	Think about *it!*

2. Prepositional Phrases of Location

Y is also used as a pronoun of place. It can replace any prepositional phrase of location or position (except those using the preposition *de*) when the noun following the preposition is a THING. In this case, **y** means "there."

J'ai laissé les clés *dans la voiture.*	I left the keys *in the car.*
J'*y* ai laissé les clés.	I left the keys *there.*

Nous allons *à Moscou.*	We are going *to Moscow.*
Nous *y* allons.	We are going *there.*

Va *à la poste!*	Go *to the post office!*
Vas-*y!*	Go *there!*

Il a jeté des cailloux *contre la fenêtre.*	He threw some pebbles *at the window.*
Il *y* a jeté des cailloux.	He threw some pebbles (*there*) *at it.*

The Adverbial Pronoun En

The various uses of *en* are not hard to remember if you keep in mind that this pronoun is usually associated in some way with the preposition *de*. You can use **en** to replace the word or group of words following:

1. a partitive article (*du, de la, de l', des, de, d'*)
2. an expression of quantity (*beaucoup de, trop de, etc.*)
3. The preposition *de*

1. Partitive Articles

When the noun direct object of a verb is introduced by a partitive article, *you cannot replace the noun direct object with a direct object pronoun*. **En** is used to replace the partitive article AND the direct object, PERSON or THING. **En** normally precedes the verb.

Il connaît *des gens importants.*	He knows *some important people.*
Il *en* connaît.	He knows *some* (people).
Je veux *du gâteau.*	I want *some cake.*
J'*en* veux.	I want *some.*

but:

Elle gronde *les enfants.*	She scolds *the children.*
Elle *les* gronde.	She scolds *them.*
J'ai perdu *ma montre!*	I've lost *my watch!*
Je *l'*ai perdue!	I've lost *it!*

2. *Expressions of Quantity*

Similarly, you cannot replace the noun direct object of a verb with a direct object pronoun when the noun direct object is introduced by an expression of quantity. **En** is used to replace the direct object, PERSON or THING. Notice that **en** normally precedes the verb, while the word of quantity stays after the verb.

Ce médecin a guéri *beaucoup de malades.*	This doctor has cured *many patients.*
Ce médecin *en* a guéri *beaucoup.*	This doctor has cured *many* (*of them*).

J'ai *tant de travail!*	I have *so much work!*
J'*en* ai *tant!*	I have *so much!* (*of it*)

Elle a *trois enfants.*	She has *three children.*
Elle *en* a *trois.*	She has *three* (*of them*).

Le chef a mis *trop de sel* dans la soupe.	The chef put *too much salt* in the soup.
Le chef *en* a mis *trop* dans la soupe.	The chef put *too much* (*of it*) in the soup.

The same sequence is used with certain indefinite pronouns like *quelques-uns, quelques-unes* (some, a few); *plusieurs* (several); *certains, certaines* (certain ones); and *aucun, aucune* (none).

Il a invité *quelques amis.*	He invited *a few friends.*
Il *en* a invité *quelques-uns.*	He invited *a few* (*of them*).

J'ai cassé *plusieurs verres.*   I broke *several glasses.*

J'*en* ai cassé *plusieurs.*   I broke *several (of them).*

3. The Preposition de

A. Many verbs* take the preposition *de* before a noun. **En** can replace *de* + noun when the noun following *de* is a THING:

Elle a besoin *d'argent.*	She needs *(some) money.*
Elle *en* a besoin.	She needs *some.*

Je me moque *de l'examen.*	I don't care about *the test.*
Je m'*en* moque.	I don't care about *it.*

When the noun following *de* is a PERSON, keep *de* and replace the noun with a *tonic pronoun.*

Je me méfie *de cet homme.*	I don't trust *that man.*
Je me méfie *de lui.*	I don't trust *him.*

B. *De* can introduce a prepositional phrase modifying an adjective. **En** replaces *de* + noun when the noun following *de* is a THING.

Nous sommes contents *de notre progrès.*	We are happy with *our progress.*
Nous *en* sommes contents.	We are happy with *it.*

---

*And verbal expressions such as *avoir besoin de, avoir envie de, avoir peur de.*

Il était surpris *de votre réponse.*	He was surprised by *your answer.*
Il *en* était surpris.	He was surprised by *it.*

When the noun following *de* is a PERSON, keep *de* and replace the noun with a *tonic pronoun.*

Il est fier *de son fils.*	He is proud of *his son.*
Il est fier *de lui.*	He is proud of *him.*

C. *De* can introduce a prepositional phrase modifying a noun. **En** replaces *de* + noun when the noun following *de* is a THING.

Il a mangé la moitié *du gâteau.*	He ate half *of the cake.*
Il *en* a mangé la moitié.	He ate half (*of it*).

J'ai oublié la fin *de l'histoire.*	I've forgotten the end *of the story.*
J'*en* ai oublié la fin.	I've forgotten the end (*of it*).

When the noun following *de* is a PERSON, *de* + noun is usually replaced by a *possessive adjective.*

Sais-tu le nom *de cette femme?*	Do you know *that woman's* name?
Sais-tu *son* nom?	Do you know *her* name?

Je n'aime pas les films   I don't like *that actor's*
    de cet acteur-là.   films.

Je n'aime pas *ses* films.   I don't like *his* films.

D. *De* is sometimes used as a preposition of place, meaning "from." **En** can be used to replace *de* + the noun of place, and means "from there."

Il est arrivé *de Paris* ce matin.	He arrived *from Paris* this morning.
Il *en* est arrivé ce matin.	He arrived (*from there*) this morning.

Elle vient *du bureau.*	She is coming *from the office.*
Elle *en* vient.	She is coming *from there.*

Position of Personal Pronouns

All personal pronouns in French—except tonic pronouns—are normally placed BEFORE the verb. This can create a problem of order when there is more than one pronoun in the same sentence.

The sequence of personal pronouns is not determined by function. Direct objects do not always precede indirect objects, for instance. Compare the order of the pronouns in the following two sentences:

Je *le lui* donne.   I am giving *it to him.*

le = direct object

lui = indirect object

Il *me le* donne.   He is giving *it to me.*

me = indirect object

le = direct object

The direct object pronoun precedes the indirect object pronoun in the first sentence, but the order is reversed in the second.

The order of the personal pronouns is simply a matter of usage. There are many ways of learning the proper order. One helpful way to remember the order of *y* and *en* is to think of having a "yen" for something. Another device is to think of the sound of a braying donkey, *y-en!* But the easiest way to be sure of these pronouns is to memorize the following chart. Once you have learned this order, certain combinations will become automatic and you will no longer have to think consciously of the sequence.

The following sequence of pronouns is used for all kinds of sentences (declarative, negative, interrogative) with one exception: affirmative imperative sentences. (*See Table I on following page.*)

TABLE I

SUBJECT	(ne)	me te se nous vous	le la les	lui leur	y	en	VERB (or auxiliary verb)	(pas)	(past participle)

Note that pronouns of the first and second persons precede pronouns of the third person. When there are two pronouns of the third person, the direct object precedes the indirect object.

Notice that *ne* and *pas* enclose the pronoun(s) and verb, like bookends. In a compound tense, *ne* and *pas* enclose the pronoun(s) and the AUXILIARY verb; the past participle goes after *pas*.*

Some examples with more than one object pronoun in a sentence will illustrate this sequence.

Elle a rendu *sa bague à son financé*.	She returned *her ring to her fiancé*.
Elle *la lui* a rendue.	She returned *it to him*.
Nous ne donnons pas *de chocolats aux enfants*.	We don't give *the children chocolates*.
Nous ne *leur en* donnons pas.	We don't give *them any*.
As-tu parlé *à Georges de son projet?*	Did you speak *to George about his project?*
Lui en as-tu parlé?	Did you speak *to him about it?*
N'avez-vous pas pris *les billets?*	Didn't you get *the tickets?*
Ne *les* avez-vous pas pris?	Didn't you get *them?*

Affirmative imperative sentences alter this order somewhat.

**ne pas is usually placed as a unit BEFORE an infinitive. For example:

Elle préférerait *ne pas* aller *au concert*.	She would rather *not* go *to the concert*.
Elle préférerait *ne pas* y aller.	She would rather *not* go (*there*).

A brief review of this verb form might be useful. The imperative is used for exclamations and commands. It exists in the *tu*, *nous* and *vous* forms. To form the imperative, drop the subject pronoun.*

Tu parles.	You are talking.
Parle!	Talk!
Nous commençons.	We are beginning.
Commençons!	Let's begin!
Vous sortez.	You are going out.
Sortez!	Get out!

Three changes occur when personal (or reflexive) pronouns are used with the affirmative imperative, one of form and two of position:

1. First, all pronouns are placed AFTER the verb, and the verb and pronoun(s) are joined by hyphens.

2. Secondly,

le		me
la	PRECEDE	te
les		nous
		vous

The rest of the sequence of pronouns is unchanged.

---

*The final *s* in the *tu* form of -er verbs is dropped in imperative sentences, except before *y* and *en*, where it facilitates pronunciation, *e.g.*, *Vas-y! Manges-en!*

3. Finally, for added emphasis, the pronouns *me* and *te* take the tonic forms *moi* and *toi*. (*Nous* and *vous* are already tonic forms.) This change DOES NOT occur if *me* and *te* precede *y* or *en*.

Thus, the order of the personal pronouns in **affirmative imperative** sentences is:

VERB	le	moi	lui	y	en
	la	toi	leur		
	les	nous			
		vous			

For example:

Tu mets *les fleurs sur la table.*	You are putting *the flowers on the table.*
Mets-*les-y*!	Put *them there*!

Tu *te* tais.	You are quiet.
Tais-*toi*!	Be quiet!

Vous *me* donnez *de l'eau.*	You are giving *me some water.*
Donnez-*m'en*!	Give *me some*!

Tu rends *le livre à Suzanne.*	You are giving *the book* back *to Susan.*
Rends-*le-lui*!	Give *it* back *to her*!

| Vous *me* passez *le pain.* | You are passing *me the bread.* |
| Passez-*le-moi!* | Pass *it to me!* |

There is NO CHANGE from the normal form and order of personal pronouns in a NEGATIVE imperative sentence, nor are hyphens used between the elements.

NE	me	le	lui	y	en	VERB	PAS
	te	la	leur				
	nous	les					
	vous						

For example:

| Tu ne mets pas *les fleurs sur la table.* | You are not putting *the flowers on the table.* |
| Ne *les y* mets pas! | Don't put *them there!* |

| Vous ne *me* donnez pas *d'eau.* | You are not giving *me any water.* |
| Ne *m'en* donnez pas! | Don't give *me any!* |

| Tu ne *te* tais pas. | You don't stop talking. |
| Ne *te* tais pas! | Don't stop talking! |

| Vous ne *me* passez pas *le pain.* | You aren't passing *me the bread.* |
| Ne *me le* passez pas! | Don't pass *it to me!* |

Tu ne rends pas *le livre*
    à Suzanne.
	You aren't giving *the book*
	    back *to Susan.*

Ne *le lui* rends pas!	Don't give *it* back *to her!*

C. Verbs and Infinitives

The Present Infinitive

An infinitive is the "pure" form of the verb that expresses the idea of a verb without regard to person, number, or tense. In English, infinitives are prefaced by "to": *to swim, to rain, to leave.* We frequently use infinitives after another verb.

> I like *to swim.*

> It's beginning *to rain.*

> He decided *to leave.*

The preposition "to" in English is actually part of the infinitive, a kind of "marker." The main verb in English never takes another preposition before an infinitive.

In French, however, infinitives need no external marker, since the endings **-er, -ir**, and **-re** clearly identify them. Moreover, the main verb can take the prepositions *à, de, par,* or no preposition at all before the infinitive:

J'aime nager.	I like to swim.
Il commence *à* pleuvoir.	It's beginning to rain.
Il a décidé *de* partir.	He decided to leave.

The use of prepositions in French is completely arbitrary. You must simply try to learn what preposition, if any, a verb uses before an infinitive when you learn the verb; or check in the VERB LIST.

The use of the infinitive in French is more extensive than in English. French uses an infinitive where English might use an infinitive or another construction, such as a gerund* or a subordinate clause:

	I like *to swim.*
J'aime *nager.*	OR
	I like *swimming.*

	He continues *to work.*
Il continue de *travailler.*	OR
	He continues *working.*

	She asked me *to stay.*
Elle m'a demandé de *rester.*	OR
	She asked *that I stay.*

FRENCH	ENGLISH
VERB + (preposition) + Infinitive	VERB + $\begin{cases} \textbf{Infinitive} \\ \textbf{Gerund} \\ \textbf{Subordinate} \\ \textbf{Clause} \end{cases}$

---

*In English, when the present participle (the *-ing* form of the verb) is used as a noun, it is called a *gerund.* The present participle form in French (the *-ant* form) is NEVER used as a verbal noun; an infinitive is used instead. For example, the saying, "Seeing is believing" is translated, *"Voir, c'est croire."*

Of course, in some cases in English one form is clearly correct. We would never say "He finished to eat" but rather, "He finished eating."

Two prepositions, *sans* and *avant de*, which take an infinitive in French, never take an infinitive in English:

Il est parti sans *payer*.   He left without *paying*.

Pensez-y avant de *répondre*.   Think about it before
                                                            answering (*before
                                                            you answer*).

The Past Infinitive

A past infinitive is simply the infinitive of the appropriate auxiliary verb (*être* or *avoir*) plus the past participle:

avoir parlé	to have spoken
être parti	to have left

French uses a past infinitive where English usually uses a gerund or a subordinate clause:

On l'accuse d'*avoir volé*   He is accused of *robbing*
la banque.   the bank.

Je m'excuse d'*être venu*   I'm sorry *that I'm late*.
en retard.

Verbs that usually take a past infinitive in French are indicated in the VERB LIST.

Note that the preposition *après* takes a past infinitive.

Je suis sorti après *avoir* dîné.	I went out after *I ate* (*after eating*) dinner.

Ils ont regardé la télévision après *avoir fini* leurs devoirs.	They watched television after *they finished* (*after finishing*) their homework.

It is considered bad style in French to use a subordinate clause when the subject of the subordinate clause is the same person as the subject of the main clause. French uses an infinitive (past or present) to avoid this repetition.

Je regrette d'*avoir gaspillé* mon temps.	I'm sorry *that I wasted* (*to have wasted*) my time.

Je pense *pouvoir faire* le travail.	I think *that I can do* the work.

PART TWO

Verb Categories

Verbs and Nouns

I. *Direct object verbs: These verbs take* **NO** *preposition before a noun.*

Examples:

Je connais le chef.	I know the chef.
Je connais le restaurant.	I know the restaurant.

Substitutions:

1. Use direct object pronouns to replace most DIRECT OBJECT NOUNS, people or things.

Je connais *le chef*.	I know *the chef*.
Je *le* connais.	I know *him*.
Je connais *le restaurant*.	I know *the restaurant*.
Je *le* connais.	I know *it*.

2. Use *en* to replace a DIRECT OBJECT NOUN introduced by a partitive article (*du, de la, de l', des, de, d'*)
or an expression of quantity (*beaucoup de, trop de, etc.*).

La reine a *des ennemis.*	The queen has *enemies.*
La reine *en* a.	The queen has *some* (enemies).
La reine a *des bijoux.*	The queen has *jewels.*
La reine *en* a.	The queen has *some* (jewels).
Elle a *beaucoup d'ennemis.*	She has *many enemies.*
Elle *en* a beaucoup.	She has many (*of them*).
Elle a *beaucoup de bijoux.*	She has *many jewels.*
Elle *en* a beaucoup.	She has many (*of them*).

Most verbs in French, as in English, are DIRECT OBJECT
VERBS. They present no problems and, therefore, are not
listed in the VERB LIST.

Reflexive verbs fall in this Category when the reflexive pronoun is the direct object of the verb. For example, **se coucher,**

to go to bed (to put *oneself* to bed). See REFLEXIVE
VERBS, p. 5.

Note: The following common verbs take a DIRECT OBJECT
in French, whereas their English equivalents take a preposition
before a noun.

Example:

Il demande l'addition.   He asks *for* the check.

approuver	to approve of	**mettre**	to put on
attendre	to wait for	**opérer**	to operate on
chercher	to look for	**payer**	to pay for
demander	to ask for	**pleurer**	to cry over,
écouter	to listen to		about
envoyer chercher	to send for	**prier**	to pray to
essayer	to try on, out	**puer**	to stink of
habiter	to live in, on	**regarder**	to look at
ignorer	to be unaware of	**sentir**	to smell of
marchander	to haggle with, over	**soigner**	to take care of

II. *Verbs which take* À *before a noun*

Examples:

Les soldats obéissent *au*
   capitaine.

The soldiers obey the cap-
   tain.

Les soldats obéissent *à*
   l'ordre.

The soldiers obey the
   order.

Substitutions:

1. For people, use indirect object pronouns to replace *à* and the noun.

Les soldats obéissent *au capitaine*.	The soldiers obey *the captain*.
Les soldats *lui* obéissent.	The soldiers obey *him*.

2. For things, use *y* to replace *à* and the noun.

Les soldats obéissent *à l'ordre*.	The soldiers obey *the order*.
Les soldats *y* obéissent.	The soldiers obey *it*.

Note: The following common verbs take the preposition *à* before a noun, whereas their English equivalents take a direct object.

Example:

Ils assistent *à* la conférence.	They attend the lecture.

assister à	to attend	**obéir à**	to obey
s'attendre à	to expect	**s'opposer à**	to oppose
déplaire à	to displease	**plaire à**	to please
désobéir à	to disobey	**résister à**	to resist
se fier à	to trust	**ressembler à**	to resemble
goûter à	to taste	**survivre à**	to survive
jouer à	to play (a game)	**téléphoner à**	to telephone
nuire à	to harm		

III. *Verbs which take À before a noun but which cannot use an indirect object pronoun to substitute for that noun.*

Examples:

> Je m'habitue *à* mon nouveau patron.
>
> I'm getting used to my new boss.

> Je m'habitue *à* mon nouveau poste.
>
> I'm getting used to my new job.

Substitutions:

1. For people, keep the preposition *à* and replace the noun with a tonic pronoun.

> Je m'habitue *à mon nouveau patron.*
>
> I'm getting used to *my new boss.*

> Je m'habitue *à lui.*
>
> I'm getting used to *him.*

2. For things, use *y* to replace *à* and the noun, as in II, 2 above.

> Je m'habitue *à mon nouveau poste.*
>
> I'm getting used to *my new job.*

> Je m'y habitue.
>
> I'm getting used to *it.*

This category includes the following verbs and expressions:

être à	to belong to
faire attention à	to pay attention to
penser à	to think about
tenir à	to be fond of

And all reflexive verbs which take *à* before a noun, *e.g.*, **s'habituer à**, to get used to.

IV. *Verbs which take DE before a noun*

Examples:

Je me souviens *de* la chanteuse. I remember the singer.

Je me souviens *de* la chanson. I remember the song.

Substitutions:

1. For people, keep the preposition *de* and replace the noun with a tonic pronoun.

Je me souviens *de la chanteuse.* I remember *the singer.*

Je me souviens *d'elle.* I remember *her.*

2. For things, use **en** to replace *de* and the noun.

Je me souviens *de la* chanson.	I remember *the song.*
Je m'*en* souviens.	I remember *it.*

Note: The following common verbs take the preposition *de* before a noun, whereas their English equivalents take a direct object.

Example:

Le millionnaire ne manque pas *d'*argent.	The millionaire does not lack money.

s'apercevoir de	to notice	**hériter de**	to inherit
approcher de	to approach	**jouer de**	to play (an instrument)
changer de	to change		
douter de	to doubt	**jouir de**	to enjoy
se douter de	to suspect	**manquer de**	to lack
goûter de	to taste, try	**partir de**	to leave

V. *Verbs which commonly take a preposition other than À or DE before a noun*

Examples:

L'ambassadeur s'incline *devant* le roi.	The ambassador bows *to* the king.

J'entre *dans* le café.   I go *into* the café.

Substitutions:

1. For people, keep the preposition and replace the noun with a tonic pronoun.

> L'ambassadeur s'incline   The ambassador bows *to*
>   *devant le roi.*   *the king.*

> L'ambassadeur s'incline   The ambassador bows *to*
>   *devant lui.*   *him.*

2. For things:

   (a) When the preposition indicates position or location (*contre, dans, en, sous, sur*) **y** (meaning loosely, "there") is often used to replace the preposition and the noun:

> J'entre *dans le café.*   I go *into the café.*
>
> J'*y* entre.   I go in (*there*).

   The prepositions *dans, sous,* and *sur* have special forms which are more precise and emphatic than *y*: *là-dedans* (in, into it), *là-dessous* (under it), and *là-dessus* (on, about it). These forms may be used to replace the preposition and the noun. They are placed AFTER the verb.

L'archéologue a pénétré *dans la tombe égyptienne.*	The archeologist broke *into the Egyptian tomb.*
L'archéologue a pénétré *là-dedans.*	The archeologist broke *into it.*

(b) When the preposition does not indicate position or location, the noun following the preposition is usually kept.

Le prisonnier languit *après sa liberté.*	The prisoner longs *for his liberty.*

In colloquial French, however, the noun is sometimes omitted after the prepositions *contre* and *avec.*

Il a lutté *contre sa peur.*	He struggled *against his fear.*
Il a lutté *contre.*	He struggled *against (it).*

Note: Some French verbs take a preposition before a noun, whereas their English equivalents take a direct object. For example:

Anne se marie *avec* Georges.	Anne is marrying George.

VI. *Verbs which take a direct object plus a noun introduced by À, DE or another preposition*

A. Direct Object Plus À + NOUN

Step 1: To replace the DIRECT OBJECT, person or thing, use a direct object pronoun or **en** (See Category I, p. 40).

Step 2: To replace $\boxed{\text{À + NOUN}}$

    (a) When the noun following *à* is a person, replace $\boxed{\text{À + NOUN}}$ with an indirect object pronoun.

    (b) When the noun following *à* is a thing, replace $\boxed{\text{À + NOUN}}$ with *y*.

Step 3: To replace both the DIRECT OBJECT AND $\boxed{\text{À + NOUN}}$ combine Steps 1 and 2 above.*

Examples:

    Le serpent offrit *la pomme à Eve.*   The serpent offered *the apple to Eve.*

1. Le serpent *l'*offrit à Eve.   The serpent offered *it* to Eve.

2a. Le serpent *lui* offrit la pomme.   The serpent offered *her* the apple.

3. Le serpent *la lui* offrit.   The serpent offered *it to her.*

---

*For order of personal pronouns, see REVIEW, p. 29.

Il a prêté *du sucre à son voisin.*	He loaned *his neighbor some sugar.*
1. Il *en* a prêté à son voisin.	He loaned his neighbor *some.*
2a. Il *lui* a prêté du sucre.	He loaned *him* some sugar.
3. Il *lui en* a prêté.	He loaned *him some.*
La faim a poussé *le pauvre au vol.*	Hunger drove *the poor man to theft.*
1. La faim *l'*a poussé au vol.	Hunger drove *him* to theft.
2b. La faim *y* a poussé le pauvre.	Hunger drove the poor man *to it.*
3. La faim *l'y* a poussé.	Hunger drove *him to it.*

B. Direct Object Plus DE + NOUN

Step 1: To replace the DIRECT OBJECT, person or thing, use a direct object pronoun or **en** (See Category I, p. 40).

Step 2: To replace DE + NOUN

(a) When the noun following *de* is a person, keep *de* and replace the noun with a tonic pronoun.

(b) When the noun following *de* is a thing, replace *de* and the noun with **en.**

Step 3: To replace both the DIRECT OBJECT AND
$\boxed{\text{DE } + \text{ NOUN}}$ combine Steps 1 and 2
above.*

Example:

Le cambrioleur a rempli *ses poches d'argent.*	The burglar filled *his pockets with money.*

1. Le cambrioleur *les* a
   remplies d'argent.

   The burglar filled *them*
   with money.

2b. Le cambrioleur *en* a
    rempli ses poches.

    The burglar filled his
    pockets *with it.*

3. Le cambrioleur *les en* a
   remplies.

   The burglar filled *them*
   with it.

C. Direct Object Plus Prepositions Other Than À or DE

Step 1: To replace the DIRECT OBJECT, person or thing, use a direct object pronoun or **en** (See Category I, p. 40).

Step 2: To replace $\boxed{\textbf{PREPOSITION} + \textbf{NOUN}}$

---

*For order of personal pronouns, see REVIEW, p. 29.

(a) When the noun following the preposition is a person, keep the preposition and replace the noun with a tonic pronoun.

(b) When the noun following the preposition is a thing, there are several possibilities:

When the preposition indicates position or location (*contre*, *dans*, *en*, *sous*, *sur*), **y** (meaning loosely "there") is often used to replace the preposition and noun.

The prepositions *dans*, *sous*, and *sur* have special forms which are more precise and emphatic than *y: là-dedans* (in, into it), *là-dessous* (under it), and *là-dessus* (on, about it). These forms may be used to replace the preposition and noun. They are placed AFTER the verb.

When the preposition does not indicate position or location, the noun following the preposition is usually kept.

Step 3: To replace both the DIRECT OBJECT AND PREPOSITION + NOUN combine Steps 1 and 2 above.

Examples:

Le vieillard a partagé *sa fortune entre ses trois filles.*	The old man divided *his fortune among his three daughters.*

1. Le vieillard *l*'a partagée
   entre ses trois filles.

   The old man divided *it*
   among his three
   daughters.

2a. Le vieillard a partagé sa
    fortune *entre elles*.

    The old man divided his
    fortune *among them*.

3. Le vieillard *l*'a partagée
   entre elles.

   The old man divided *it*
   among them.

L'ouvrier a planté *l'échelle*
contre le mur.

The workman set *the lad-*
der against the wall.

1. L'ouvrier *l*'a plantée
   contre le mur.

   The workman set *it*
   against the wall.

2b. L'ouvrier *y* a planté
    l'échelle.

    The workman set the lad-
    der *there*.

3. L'ouvrier *l'y* a plantée.

   The workman set *it there*.

La police a interrogé
l'accusé sur le crime.

The police questioned *the*
suspect about the
crime.

1. La police *l*'a interrogé
   sur le crime.

   The police questioned
   him about the crime.

2b. La police a interrogé
    l'accusé *là-dessus*.

    The police questioned the
    suspect *about it*.

3. La police *l*'a interrogé
   là-dessus.

   The police questioned
   him about it.

Verbs and Infinitives

VII. *Verbs which take* NO *preposition before an infinitive*

A. Verbs which take an Infinitive but which do not take a Direct or Indirect Object

Examples:

Nous devons partir tout de suite.	We have to leave immediately.
J'aime lire.	I like to read.

If the *infinitive* is followed by a noun, the noun can be replaced by a pronoun. If you are uncertain of what pronoun to use, refer to Categories I-VI, VERBS AND NOUNS, pp. 40–53.

All personal pronouns, except tonic pronouns, directly PRECEDE the infinitive.

Les singes adorent manger *les bananes.*	Monkeys love to eat *bananas.*
Les singes adorent *les* manger.	Monkeys love to eat *them.*
Tout le monde aime recevoir *des cadeaux.*	Everyone likes to get *presents.*

Tout le monde aime *en* recevoir.	Everyone likes to get *them.*
Je veux parler *au directeur*!	I want to speak *to the manager*!
Je veux *lui* parler!	I want to speak *to him*!
Elle espère gagner *à la loterie.*	She hopes to win *the lottery.*
Elle espère *y* gagner.	She hopes to win *(it).*
Il n'ose pas se disputer *avec sa femme.*	He doesn't dare argue *with his wife.*
Il n'ose pas se disputer *avec elle.*	He doesn't dare argue *with her.*

B.   Verbs which take a Direct Object Plus an Infinitive

The most common of these verbs are *amener*, to bring (someone); *emmener*, to take (someone); *envoyer*, to send (someone); and *mener*, to lead (someone).

Example:

Il emmène *les enfants* nager.	He is taking *the children* swimming.

Substitutions:

1. To replace the direct object of the main verb, use a direct object pronoun.

Il emmène *les enfants* nager.	He is taking *the children* swimming.
Il *les* emmène nager.	He is taking *them* swimming.

2. If the *infinitive* is followed by a noun, the noun can be replaced by a pronoun. If you are not certain what pronoun to use, refer to Categories I-VI, VERBS AND NOUNS, pp. 40–53.

All personal pronouns, except tonic pronouns, directly PRECEDE the infinitive.

Elle a emmené les écoliers voir *l'exposition de Picasso.*	She took the students to see *the Picasso exhibit.*
Elle les a emmenés *la* voir.	She took them to see *it.*

J'ai envoyé Marie acheter *du pain.*	I sent Marie to buy *some bread.*
Je l'ai envoyée *en* acheter.	I sent her to buy *some.*

Note: The following verbs take an infinitive followed by a noun:

faire	to make, to do
laisser	to let, to allow

And certain verbs of perception:

écouter	to listen to
entendre	to hear
regarder	to look at, to watch
sentir	to feel, to smell
voir	to see

The noun, however, is not the direct object of the infinitive; it acts as the direct object of the main verb. Therefore, when the noun direct object is replaced by a pronoun, the pronoun precedes the main verb.

Examples:

J'entends tomber *la pluie*.	I hear *the rain* falling.
Je *l'*entends tomber.	I hear *it* falling.
On a fait venir *le médecin*.*	They had *the doctor* come.
On *l'*a fait venir.	They had *him* come.

---

*When the noun following the infinitive is a *thing*, the verb **faire** can take an indirect object as well as a direct object. For example:

VIII. *Verbs which take the preposition À before an infinitive*

A. Verbs which take NO Direct or Indirect Object before

```
À + INFINITIVE
```

Example:

Il hésite à parler.   He is reluctant to speak.

Substitutions:

If the *infinitive* is followed by a noun, the noun can be replaced by a pronoun. If you are not certain what pronoun to use, refer to Categories I-VI, VERBS AND NOUNS, pp. 40–53.

All personal pronouns, except tonic pronouns, directly PRECEDE the infinitive.

J'ai fait réparer *la voiture.*	I had *the car* repaired.
Je *l'*ai fait réparer.	I had *it* repaired.
J'ai fait réparer *la voiture au garagiste.*	I had *the car* repaired *by the mechanic.*
Je *la lui* ai fait réparer.	I had *him* repair *it.*

In the above example, the subject of the verb *faire, je,* causes the repairs to be made; the indirect object of *faire, le garagiste,* actually makes the repairs. The direct object of *faire, la voiture,* is the thing being repaired. This construction is called the *faire causatif.* (Note that when the past participle—in this case *fait*—precedes an infinitive, there is no agreement between the past participle and the preceding direct object.)

Un peintre célèbre a consenti à faire *mon portrait*.	A famous painter has agreed to paint *my portrait*.
Un peintre célèbre a consenti à *le* faire.*	A famous painter has agreed to paint *it*.
Mon père persiste à fumer *des cigares*.	My father won't give up smoking *cigars*.
Mon père persiste à *en* fumer.	My father won't give up smoking *them*.
Nous tenons à assister *au concert*.	We are eager to attend *the concert*.
Nous tenons à *y* assister.	We are eager to attend (*it*).
Elle hésite à sortir *avec cet homme*.	She is hesitant to go out *with that man*.
Elle hésite à sortir *avec lui*.	She is hesitant to go out *with him*.

B. Verbs which take a Direct or Indirect Object before
   [À + INFINITIVE]

Verbs which take [À + INFINITIVE] usually take a
DIRECT OBJECT.

---

*Note that when *le* and *les* are pronouns, there is no contraction with *à*.

Example:

J'ai décidé *mon ami* à venir.   I persuaded *my friend* to
                                        come.

A few verbs, however, take INDIRECT OBJECTS.

Example:

Elle apprend *aux enfants* à patiner.*	She is teaching *the children* to skate.

Substitutions:

1. To replace the DIRECT OBJECT of the main verb, person or thing, use a direct object pronoun.

J'ai décidé *mon ami* à venir.	I persuaded *my friend* to come.
Je *l'*ai décidé à venir.	I persuaded *him* to come.
Elle met *le linge* à sécher.	She is hanging *the laundry* up to dry.
Elle *le* met à sécher.	She is hanging *it* up to dry.

2. To replace the INDIRECT OBJECT of the main verb, use an indirect object pronoun.

---

*Other verbs which take an INDIRECT OBJECT plus
   &boxed{À + INFINITIVE} are: **enseigner** (*to teach*) and **montrer** (*to show*).

Elle apprend *aux en-fants* à patiner.	She is teaching *the children* to skate.
Elle *leur* apprend à patiner.	She is teaching *them* to skate.

3. If the *infinitive* is followed by a noun, the noun can be replaced by a pronoun. If you are not certain what pronoun to use, refer to Categories I-VI, VERBS AND NOUNS, pp. 40–53.

Le scout aide la vieille à traverser *la rue*.	The boy scout helps the old lady across *the street*.
Le scout l'aide à *la* traverser.	The boy scout helps her across *it*.
Le garçon encourage son client à prendre *des huîtres*.	The waiter urges his customer to have *some oysters*.
Le garçon l'encourage à *en* prendre.	The waiter urges him to have *some*.
On a autorisé le journaliste à parler *aux otages*.	They allowed the journalist to speak *to the hostages*.
On l'a autorisé à *leur* parler.	They allowed him to speak *to them*.

Il a invité ses amis à aller *au théâtre*.	He invited his friends to go *to the theatre*.
Il les a invités à *y* aller.	He invited them to go (*there*).

IX. *Verbs which take the preposition DE before an infinitive*

A. Verbs which take NO Direct or Indirect Object before
   ☐ **DE + INFINITIVE** ☐

Example:

Le bébé refuse de manger.	The baby refuses to eat.

Substitutions:

If the *infinitive* is followed by a noun, the noun can be replaced by a pronoun. If you are not certain what pronoun to use, refer to Categories I-VI, VERBS AND NOUNS, pp. 40–53.

All personal pronouns, except tonic pronouns, directly PRECEDE the infinitive.

J'ai oublié de rendre *le livre*.	I forgot to return *the book*.
J'ai oublié de *le* rendre.*	I forgot to return *it*.
Il a offert d'apporter *du vin*.	He offered to bring *some wine*.

---

*Note that when *le* and *les* are pronouns, there is no contraction with *de*.

Il a offert d'*en* apporter.	He offered to bring *some.*
Elle a promis d'assister *à la réunion.*	She promised to attend *the meeting.*
Elle a promis d'*y* assister.	She promised to attend (*it*).
Le chien essaye de plaire *à son maître.*	The dog tries to please *his master.*
Le chien essaye de *lui* plaire.	The dog tries to please *him.*

B. Verbs which take a Direct or Indirect Object before
     DE + INFINITIVE

Examples:

On a persuadé *le fugitif* de se rendre.	They persuaded *the fugitive* to give himself up.
J'ai dit *à mon ami* d'attendre.	I told *my friend* to wait.

Substitutions:

1. To replace the DIRECT OBJECT of the main verb, person or thing, use a direct object pronoun.

On a persuadé *le fugitif* de se rendre.	They persuaded *the fugitive* to give himself up.
On *l'*a persuadé de se rendre,	They persuaded *him* to give himself up.
L'orage a empêché *le bateau* de partir.	The storm prevented *the ship* from leaving.
L'orage *l'*a empêché de partir.	The storm prevented *it* from leaving.

2. To replace the INDIRECT OBJECT of the main verb, use an indirect object pronoun.

J'ai dit *à mon ami* d'attendre.	I told *my friend* to wait.
Je *lui* ai dit d'attendre.	I told *him* to wait.

3. If the *infinitive* is followed by a noun, the noun can be replaced by a pronoun. If you are not certain what pronoun to use, refer to Categories I-VI, VERBS AND NOUNS, pp. 40–53.

Elle a grondé l'enfant d'avoir perdu *ses moufles.*	She scolded the child for having lost *his mittens.*

Elle l'a grondé de *les* avoir perdues.*	She scolded him for having lost *them*.
Le gardien a permis au touriste de prendre *des photos*.	The guard allowed the tourist to take *pictures*.
Le gardien lui a permis d'*en* prendre.	The guard allowed him to take *some*.
Le professeur interdit aux étudiants de dormir *en classe*.	The professor forbids the students to sleep *in class*.
Le professeur leur interdit d'*y* dormir.	The professor forbids them to sleep *there*.
J'ai persuadé mon frère de se raccomoder *avec sa femme*.	I persuaded my brother to make up *with his wife*.
Je l'ai persuadé de se raccomoder *avec elle*.	I persuaded him to make up *with her*.

X. *Verbs which take prepositions other than À or DE before an infinitive.*

Example:

Il a fini par réussir.	He finally succeeded.

---

*Note that when *le* and *les* are pronouns, there is no contraction with *de*.

There are very few verbs in this category. The most common are:

commencer par	to begin by
débuter par	to start (one's career) by
finir par	to end by, to finally
insister pour	to insist on
terminer par	to end (something) by

Substitutions:

If the *infinitive* is followed by a noun, the noun can be replaced by a pronoun. If you are not certain what pronoun to use, refer to Categories I–VI, VERBS AND NOUNS, pp. 40–53.

All personal pronouns, except tonic pronouns, directly PRECEDE the infinitive.

Le conférencier a commencé par exposer *sa théorie.*	The speaker began by stating *his theory.*
Le conférencier a commencé par *l'*exposer.	The speaker began by stating *it.*
J'ai fini par me résigner *à la situation.*	I finally resigned myself *to the situation.*
J'ai fini par m'*y* résigner.	I finally resigned myself *to it.*

PART THREE
Verb List

- - - - - - - - - - - - - - - - -

Key To Verb List

ROMAN NUMERALS indicate Verb Categories (pp. 40–66). Refer to the appropriate Category for detailed explanation of verb type and usage. No Category is indicated for idiomatic expressions when a pronoun substitution is not possible.

I	(p. 40)	VI	(p. 48)
II	(p. 42)	VII	(p. 54)
III	(p. 44)	VIII	(p. 58)
IV	(p. 45)	IX	(p. 62)
V	(p. 46)	X	(p. 65)

ARABIC NUMERALS at the left-hand margin are included for easy reference to verb entries. They do not indicate order of importance of the definitions.

ABBREVIATIONS:

Qn	*Quelqu'un*	(People or animate objects)
Qch	*Quelque chose*	(Things or inanimate objects)
Inf.	*Infinitif*	(Infinitive)
Inf. passé	*Infinitif passé*	(Past Infinitive)
Coll:	Colloquial Expression	
Lit:	Literary Expression	

The ending ---*ing* appears frequently in the English definition of a verb and corresponds to the French abbreviation *Inf.* For example, for the verb **cesser** we find:

cesser
1. _____ Qch. (to stop . . .) I
2. _____ de *Inf.* (to stop ---*ing*) IX-A

The "---*ing*" in number 2 indicates that the present participle is used in English where French employs the infinitive, *e.g.*, "cesser de *fumer*"—"to stop *smoking*."

A

abaisser
1. ———— Qn ou Qch (to lower . . .) I
2. s'———— (to sink, subside; to lower oneself, humble oneself) I
3. s'———— à, jusqu'à *Inf.* (to stoop to, condescend to . . .) VIII-A

abandonner
1. ———— Qn ou Qch (to abandon . . .) I
2. s'———— (to let oneself go) I
3. s'———— à Qch (to give oneself up to . . .) III
4. ———— Qn ou Qch à Qch (to abandon, give up . . . to . . .) VI

abattre
1. ———— Qch (to knock down, bring down, slaughter . . .) I
2. s'———— (to fall down, crash down; to abate) I
3. s'———— sur Qch (to fall down on, swoop down on, pounce upon . . .) V

abîmer
1. ———— Qn ou Qch (to spoil, damage, ruin . . .) I
2. s'———— (to get spoiled, to spoil) I
3. s'———— *dans la douleur, dans le chagrin; dans ses pensées* (to be sunk in sorrow; in one's thoughts) V

abonder
1. ———— en Qch (to abound in . . .) V

abonner
1. s'———— à Qch (to subscribe to . . .) III
2. ———— Qn à Qch (to enroll, to take out a subscription for . . . to . . .) VI

aboutir
1. _____ à Qch (to lead to, end at, result in . . .) II
2. _____ dans, en* Qch (to end in . . .) V

aboyer
1. _____ après, à Qn ou Qch (to bark at . . . [*après* often indicates movement] Ex: *un chien qui aboie après le facteur, à la lune*, a dog that barks at the postman, at the moon) V, III

abreuver
1. _____ Qn ou Qch (to water, soak . . .) I
2. s'_____ (of people: to quench one's thirst; of animals: to drink) I
3. s'_____ de Qch (to quench one's thirst for, with . . .) IV
4. _____ Qn de Qch (to overwhelm, shower . . . with . . .) VI

abriter
1. _____ Qn ou Qch (to shelter . . .) I
2. s'_____ (to take cover, shelter) I
3. s'_____ contre Qch (to take cover from . . .) V
4. _____ Qn contre Qch (to shelter . . . from . . .) VI

absenter (s')
1. s'_____ de Qch (to absent oneself from . . .) IV

absorber
1. _____ Qn ou Qch (to absorb . . .) I
2. s'_____ dans Qch (to become engrossed in . . .) V
3. être absorbé dans Qch (to be engrossed in . . .) V

absoudre
1. _____ Qn (to forgive . . .) I
2. _____ Qn de Qch (to forgive . . . for . . .; to absolve . . . of . . .) VI

_____
*See Appendix II: **DANS, EN, À**, p. 298.

abstenir (s')
1. s'_____ de Qch (to abstain, refrain from . . .) IV
2. s'_____ de *Inf.* (to abstain, refrain from ---*ing*) IX-A

abstraire
1. _____ Qch (to abstract . . .) I
2. s'_____ (to withdraw oneself) I
3. s'_____ dans, en* Qch (to become engrossed in . . .) V

abuser
1. _____ Qn (to deceive . . .) I
2. s'_____ (to be mistaken) I
3. _____ de Qch (to abuse, take advantage of . . .) IV

accabler
1. _____ Qn ou Qch (to overwhelm, overburden . . .) I
2. être accablé de Qch (to be overwhelmed, overburdened with
. . . *e.g.*, *de travail*, with work) IV
3. _____ Qn de Qch (to overwhelm, overburden, shower . . .
with . . .) VI

accéder
1. _____ à Qch (to have access to, to comply with . . .) II

accepter
1. _____ Qn ou Qch (to accept . . .) I
2. _____ Qch de Qn (to accept . . . from . . .) VI
3. _____ de *Inf.* (to agree to . . .) IX-A

accoler
1. _____ Qch (to join, place . . . side by side) I
2. s'_____ (of plants: to intertwine) I
3. être accolé à Qch (to be joined to, built onto . . .) II
4. s'_____ à Qch (to be joined to, built onto . . .) III

---

*See Appendix II: **DANS, EN, À**, p. 298.

accomoder
1. _____ Qn ou Qch (to accommodate . . .; to make . . . comfortable; to prepare [food]) I
2. s'_____ (to make oneself comfortable) I
3. s'_____ à Qch (to adapt to . . .) III
4. s'_____ de Qch (to put up with . . .) IV
5. s'_____ avec Qn (to come to an agreement, a compromise with . . .) V
6. _____ Qch à Qch (to fit, adapt . . . to . . .) VI

accompagner
1. _____ Qn ou Qch (to accompany . . .) I
2. s'_____ à Qch (to accompany oneself on . . . *e.g.*, *à la guitare*, on the guitar) III
3. s'_____ de Qch (to be accompanied by, followed by . . .) IV
4. _____ Qn ou Qch à Qch (to accompany . . . on . . . *e.g.*, *au piano*, on the piano) VI

accorder
1. _____ Qn ou Qch (to bring . . . into harmony, accord; to grant, concede . . .; to tune . . . *e.g.*, a musical instrument) I
2. s'_____ (to agree, be in accordance) I
3. s'_____ Qch (to allow oneself . . .) I
4. s'_____ avec Qch (to be in accordance, in keeping with . . .) V
5. s'_____ sur Qch (to agree upon . . .) V
6. _____ Qch à Qn (to grant, concede . . . to . . .) VI
7. _____ Qch avec Qch (to reconcile, bring . . . into accord with . . .) VI

accoter
1. s'_____ à, contre Qch (to lean against . . .) III, V
2. _____ Qch contre, sur Qch (to lean . . . against, on . . .) VI

accoucher
1. _____ de Qn ou Qch (to give birth to . . .) IV

accoutrer
1. s'_____ de Qch (to dress up ridiculously in . . .) IV
2. _____ Qn de Qch (to dress up . . . ridiculously in . . .) VI

accoutumer
1. s'_____ à Qch (to become accustomed to . . .) III
2. _____ Qn à Qch (to accustom . . . to . . .) VI
3. s'_____ à *Inf.* (to become accustomed to ---*ing*) VIII-A
4. _____ Qn à *Inf.* (to accustom . . . to ---*ing*) VIII-B

accréditer
1. _____ Qn ou Qch (to accredit, credit . . .) I
2. _____ Qn auprès de Qn ou Qch (to accredit . . . at, to, with . . .) VI

accrocher
1. _____ Qn ou Qch (to hook, to hang, to grab onto . . .) I
2. s'_____ à Qn ou Qch (to fasten, cling to . . .) III
3. _____ Qch à Qch (to hang, catch . . . on . . .) VI

acculer
1. s'_____ contre, à Qch (to set one's back against . . .) V, III
2. _____ Qn contre, à Qch (to drive . . . back against . . .) VI

accuser
1. _____ Qn (to accuse . . .) I
2. _____ Qch (to own up to . . .; to accentuate . . .) I
3. _____ Qn de Qch (to accuse . . . of . . .) VI
4. _____ Qn de *Inf.* ou *Inf. passé* (to accuse . . . of ---*ing*, of having . . .) IX-B

acharner
1. s'_____ à Qch (to persist in . . .) III
2. s'_____ sur Qn ou Qch (to swoop down on . . .) V
3. s'_____ contre Qn ou Qch (to pursue . . . relentlessly) V

acheminer
1. s'_____ vers, sur Qch (to proceed, make one's way to, towards . . .) V
2. _____ Qn ou Qch vers, sur Qch (to direct, dispatch, put . . . on the road to, towards . . .) VI

acheter
1. _____ Qch (to buy . . .) I
2. _____ Qch à Qn (to buy . . . from . . .) VI
3. _____ Qch à, pour Qn (to buy . . . for . . .) VI

achever
1. _____ Qn ou Qch (to finish, to finish off . . .) I
2. _____ de *Inf.* (to finish ---*ing*) IX-A

acoquiner (s')
1. s'_____ avec Qn (Coll: to take up with . . . [with someone disreputable]) V

acquérir
1. _____ Qch (to acquire . . .) I
2. _____ Qch à Qn (to acquire . . . for . . .) VI

acquiescer
1. _____ à Qch (to agree to, acquiesce to . . .) II

acquitter
1. _____ Qn ou Qch (to acquit . . .) I
2. s'_____ de Qch (to fulfill, carry out . . . Ex: *s'acquitter d'un devoir*, to carry out a duty; *s'acquitter d'une dette*, to pay off a debt) IV
3. s'_____ envers Qn (to repay, to pay off one's debts to . . .) V

adapter
1. s'_____   à Qch (to adapt to . . .) III
2. _____   Qch à Qch (to adapt . . . to . . .) VI

adhérer
1. _____   à Qch (to adhere, stick to . . .) II

adjoindre
1. s'_____   à Qn (to join in with . . .) III
2. _____   Qn ou Qch à Qn ou Qch (to add, join . . . to . . .;
            to unite . . . with . . .) VI

adjuger
1. _____   Qch à Qn (to adjudge, award . . . to . . .) VI

adjurer
1. _____   Qn de *Inf.* (to beseech . . . to . . .) IX-B

admettre
1. _____   Qch (to admit . . .) I
2. _____   Qn à Qch (to let . . . into . . .) VI
3. _____   Qn à *Inf.* (to allow . . . to . . .) VIII-B

administrer
1. _____   Qch à Qn (to administer . . . to . . .) VI

admirer
1. _____   Qn ou Qch (to admire . . .) I
2. _____   Qn de *Inf.* ou *Inf. passé* (to admire . . . for ---*ing*,
            for having . . .) IX-B

adonner (s')
1. s'_____   à Qch (to devote oneself to . . .) III

adorer
1. _____ Qn ou Qch (to adore . . .) I
2. _____ *Inf.* (to adore ---*ing*) VII-A

adosser
1. s'_____ à, contre Qch (to lean back against . . .) III, V
2. _____ Qch à Qch (to lean, to back . . . against . . .) VI

adresser
1. _____ Qch (to address . . .) I
2. s'_____ à Qn ou Qch (to apply to, speak to . . .) III
3. _____ Qn ou Qch à Qn ou Qch (to address, direct . . . to . . .) VI

affairer (s')
1. s'_____ à *Inf.* (to busy oneself, to bustle about ---*ing*) VIII-A
2. être affairé à *Inf.* (to be very busy ---*ing*) VIII-A

affecter
1. _____ Qn (to move, touch . . .) I
2. _____ Qch (to affect, to feign, to assume . . .) I
3. s'_____ de Qch (to be distressed by . . .) IV
4. _____ Qch à Qch (to assign . . . to . . .; to allocate . . . for . . .) VI
5. _____ de *Inf.* (to make a pretense of ---*ing*) IX-A

afficher
1. _____ Qch (to post, display . . .) I
2. s'_____ avec Qn (to be seen everywhere with . . .) V

affilier
1. être affilié à Qn ou Qch (to be affiliated with . . .) II
2. s'_____ à Qch (to affiliate oneself with . . .) III
3. _____ Qn ou Qch à Qch (to affiliate . . . to, with . . .) VI

affliger

1. _____ Qn (to pain, distress . . .) I
2. s'_____ de Qch (to grieve, be distressed over . . .) IV
3. _____ Qn de Qch (to afflict . . . with . . .) VI
4. s'_____ de *Inf.* (to be distressed at ---*ing*) IX-A

affluer

1. _____ à, vers, dans Qch (to flow to, towards, into . . .) II, V
2. _____ à, dans Qch (to flock to . . .) II, V

affoler

1. _____ Qn (to distract, drive . . . crazy; to throw . . . into a panic) I
2. s'_____ de Qn (to fall madly in love with . . .) IV

affranchir

1. s'_____ de Qch (to free oneself of . . .) IV
2. _____ Qn de Qch (to free . . . from . . .) VI

affubler

1. s'_____ de Qch (to dress up in . . . [in something bizarre or ridiculous]) IV
2. _____ Qn de Qch (to dress up . . . in . . .) VI

agir

1. Il s'agit de Qn ou Qch (It concerns, it is a question, a matter of . . .) IV
2. _____ sur Qn ou Qch (to have an influence on . . .) V
3. Il s'agit de *Inf.* (It is a question, a matter of ---*ing*) IX-A

agrafer

1. _____ Qch (to clasp, hook . . .) I
2. s'_____ à Qn ou Qch (to cling to, hang onto . . .) III

agrémenter
1. _____ Qn ou Qch de Qch (to embellish, ornament . . . with . . .) VI

agripper
1. _____ Qch (to clutch, seize, snatch . . .) I
2. s'_____ à Qch (to cling to, clutch at . . .) III

aguerrir
1. s'_____ contre Qch (to become hardened, accustomed to . . .) III, V
2. _____ Qn à Qch (to harden, accustom . . . to . . .) VI

aider
1. _____ Qn (to help . . .) I
2. _____ à Qch (to contribute to, towards . . .) II
3. s'_____ de Qch (to make use of . . .) IV
4. _____ Qn à Inf. (to help . . . to . . .) VIII-B

aimer
1. _____ Qn ou Qch (to like, love . . .) I
2. _____ mieux Qn ou Qch (to prefer . . .) I
3. _____ Inf. (to like to . . .; to like, enjoy ---ing) VII-A
4. _____ mieux Inf. (to prefer ---ing) VII-A
5. _____ à Inf. (Lit: to enjoy, take pleasure in ---ing) VIII-A

ajouter
1. _____ Qch (to add . . .) I
2. _____ Qch à Qch (to add . . . to . . .) VI

ajuster
1. _____ Qch (to adjust, to aim at . . .) I
2. _____ Qn ou Qch avec Qch (to aim at . . . with . . .) VI
3. _____ Qch à Qch (to fit, adjust . . . to . . .) VI

alarmer
1. _____ Qn (to alarm, frighten . . .) I
2. s'_____ de Qch (to be alarmed at, by . . .) IV

aller
1. _____ à Qn (of clothing: to suit, become . . . Used only
in third person, Ex: *Cette robe vous va bien,* that
dress becomes you) II
2. _____ à, dans, en* Qch (to go to, into . . .) II, V
3. Il y va de Qch (to be at stake, Ex: *Il y va de sa vie,* his life
is at stake) IV
4. _____ chez Qn (to go to someone's home, office, estab-
lishment, Ex: *aller chez le dentiste, chez le coif-
feur, chez un ami,* to go to the dentist, to the
hairdresser, to a friend's house) V
5. _____ *Inf.* (to be going to . . . Ex: *Nous allons faire une
promenade cet après-midi,* we're going to take
a walk this afternoon; to go to . . . Ex: *Je suis
allé voir la nouvelle pièce de Ionesco,* I went to
see Ionesco's new play) VII-A

allier
1. _____ Qn ou Qch (to ally, unite . . .) I
2. s'_____ à, avec Qn ou Qch (to form an alliance with . . .)
III, V
3. _____ Qn ou Qch à, avec Qn ou Qch (to ally, unite, combine . . . with . . .) VI

alterner
1. _____ avec Qn ou Qch (to alternate with . . .) V
2. _____ pour *Inf.* (to alternate ---*ing*) X

ambitionner
1. _____ Qch (to be ambitious of, to covet . . .) I
2. _____ de *Inf.* (to aspire to . . .) IX-A

---

*See Appendix I: **PREPOSITIONS OF GEOGRAPHICAL LOCA-
TION** and Appendix II: **DANS, EN, À**, p. 289.

amener
1. _____ Qn (to bring . . .) I
2. _____ à Qch (to lead up to, to bring about . . .) II
3. _____ Qn à Qn ou Qch (to bring . . . to . . . Ex: *amener un enfant à sa mère,* to bring a child to his mother; to bring . . . around to . . . Ex: *amener quelqu'un à une idée,* to bring someone around to an idea) VI
4. _____ Qn *Inf.* (to bring . . . to . . .) VII-B
5. _____ Qn à *Inf.* (to induce, cause . . . to . . . Ex: *Il m'a amené à voir les choses d'une façon plus réaliste,* he made me see things more realistically) VIII-B

amouracher (s')
1. s'_____ de Qn (to be infatuated with . . . [often pejorative]) IV

amuser
1. _____ Qn (to amuse . . .) I
2. s'_____ à Qch (to amuse oneself at, to enjoy . . .) III
3. s'_____ de, aux dépens de Qn (to make fun of . . .) IV, V
4. s'_____ à *Inf.* (to have a good time ---*ing*) VIII-A

annexer
1. _____ Qch (to annex . . .) I
2. _____ Qch à Qch (to attach, annex . . . to . . .) VI

annoncer
1. _____ Qch (to announce, indicate . . . Ex: *Ces nuages annoncent l'orage,* these clouds indicate a storm [is coming]) I
2. _____ Qch à Qn (to announce . . . to . . .) VI

anticiper
1. _____ Qch (to anticipate . . .) I
2. _____ sur Qch (to anticipate . . .; to encroach upon . . .; to pay or spend . . . in advance, Ex: *anticiper sur ses revenues*, to spend one's income in advance) V

apercevoir
1. _____ Qn ou Qch (to catch sight of, catch a glimpse of . . .) I
2. s'_____ de Qch (to notice, realize . . .) IV

apitoyer
1. _____ Qn (to move . . . to pity) I
2. s'_____ sur Qn ou Qch (to be moved to pity over . . .) V

apparaître
1. _____ à Qn (to appear to, before . . .; to become evident, apparent to . . .) II

apparenter
1. être apparenté à Qn (to be related to . . .) II
2. s'_____ à Qn ou Qch (to become related by marriage to . . .; to bear a resemblance to, be of the same nature as . . .) III

appartenir
1. s'_____ (to be one's own boss, to be in control of oneself) I
2. _____ à Qn ou Qch (to belong to . . .) II
3. Il appartient à Qn de *Inf.* (to be one's job, part of one's functions to . . . Ex: *Il appartient au tribunal d'administrer la justice*, it is the job of the court to administer justice) IX-B

appeler
1. _____ Qn ou Qch (to call, call for . . .) I
2. s'_____ Qch (to be named . . .) I
3. en _____ à Qn ou Qch (to appeal to . . .) II
4. _____ Qn à *Inf.* (to call on . . . to . . .) VIII-B

appesantir
1. _____ Qn ou Qch (to weigh down, dull, slow down . . .) I
2. s'_____ sur Qn (to weigh on, become oppressive to . . .) V
3. s'_____ sur Qch (to dwell on . . . *e.g.*, *sur un sujet*, on a subject) V
4. _____ Qch sur Qch (to lean, press down . . . on . . .) VI

applaudir
1. _____ Qn ou Qch (to applaud . . .) I
2. _____ à Qch (to approve of . . . wholeheartedly) II
3. s'_____ de Qch (to pat oneself on the back for . . .) IV
4. s'_____ de *Inf.* ou *Inf. passé* (to pat oneself on the back for ---*ing*, for having . . .) IX-A
5. _____ Qn de *Inf.* ou *Inf. passé* (to commend . . . for ---*ing*, for having . . .) IX-B

appliquer
1. _____ Qch (to affix . . .) I
2. s'_____ à Qch (to work hard at . . .) III
3. s'_____ à Qn ou Qch (to apply to . . . Used only in third person, Ex: *Cette règle s'applique à vous, à votre cas*, this rule applies to you, to your case) III
4. _____ Qch sur Qch (to apply . . . to, on . . .) VI

apporter
1. _____ Qch (to bring . . .) I
2. _____ Qch à Qn (to bring . . . to . . .) VI
3. _____ *du soin à Inf.* (to take care in ---*ing*) VIII-B

apposer
1. ———   Qch (to affix . . .) I
2. ———   Qch à, sur Qch (to affix . . . to, on . . .) VI

appréhender
1. ———   Qn (to seize . . .) I
2. ———   Qn *au corps* (to arrest . . .) I
3. ———   Qch (to fear, be apprehensive about . . .) I
4. ———   de *Inf.* (to dread, fear ---*ing*) IX-A

apprendre
1. ———   Qch (to learn . . .) I
2. ———   Qch à Qn (to teach someone something) VI
3. ———   à *Inf.* (to learn [how] to . . .) VIII-A
4. ———   à Qn à *Inf.* (to teach . . . [how] to . . .) VIII-B

apprêter
1. ———   Qch (to make ready, prepare . . .) I
2. s'———   à Qch (to prepare for . . .) III
3. s'———   à *Inf.* (to prepare to . . .) VIII-A

approcher
1. ———   Qn (to get near, close to . . .) I
2. ———   Qch (to bring . . . near) I
3. ———   de Qn (to approach, come near, close to . . .) IV
4. ———   de Qch (to approach, come near, close to . . . Ex:
Nous approchons de Marseille, we are getting
near Marseille; *approcher du but,* to come near
the mark, the goal; *approcher de la quarantaine,*
to be nearing forty; to resemble, be close to, approximate . . . Ex: *approcher de la vérité,* to be
close to the truth) IV
5. s'———   de Qn ou Qch (to go up to, come near, close to
. . .) IV
6. ———   Qn ou Qch de Qn ou Qch (to bring . . . near to
. . .) VI

approprier
1. s'_____   Qch (to appropriate . . . for oneself) I
2. s'_____   à Qch (to adapt oneself, itself to . . .) III
3. _____   Qch à Qch (to adapt . . . to . . .) VI

approuver
1. _____   Qn ou Qch (to approve, approve of . . .) I
2. _____   Qn de *Inf.* ou *Inf. passé* (to approve of . . . for
     ---*ing*, for having . . .) IX-B

approvisionner
1. _____   Qn ou Qch (to furnish . . . with supplies) I
2. s'_____   [chez un marchand] (to lay in supplies, to get one's
     supplies, one's provisions [at . . .]) I
3. s'_____   en, de Qch (to supply, furnish oneself with . . .)
     V, IV
4. _____   Qn ou Qch de Qch (to supply, furnish . . . with
     . . .) VI

appuyer
1. _____   Qn ou Qch (to support . . .) I
2. _____   sur Qch (to press, press on . . .; to stress, empha-
     size . . .) V
3. s'_____   sur, contre, à Qch (to lean on, against . . .) V, III
4. s'_____   sur Qn (to lean on, rely on . . .) V
5. _____   Qch contre Qch (to lean . . . against . . .) VI
6. _____   Qch sur Qch (to press, rest . . . on . . .) VI

arguer
1. _____   de Qch (to use . . . as an argument, reason, or pre-
     text) IV
2. _____   Qch de Qch (Lit: to conclude, infer, deduce . . .
     from . . .) VI

armer

1. ———— Qn ou Qch (to arm, to strengthen . . .; to load, cock [a gun]) I
2. s'———— de Qch (to arm, equip oneself with . . .) IV
3. s'———— contre Qn ou Qch (to arm oneself against . . .) V
4. ———— Qn ou Qch de Qch (to arm . . . with . . .) VI

arracher

1. ———— Qch (to tear out, up, away . . .) I
2. s'———— de Qch (to tear oneself away from . . . *e.g.*, *d'un livre*, from a book) IV
3. ———— Qch à Qn (to extract, snatch . . . from . . . Ex: *arracher une dent, une promesse à quelqu'un*, to extract a tooth, a promise from someone; *s'arracher les cheveux*, to tear one's hair out) VI
4. ———— Qn à Qch (to save . . . from . . . *e.g.*, *à un danger*, from danger; to pull, draw . . . out of . . . *e.g.*, *au sommeil*, out of sleep) VI
5. ———— Qn ou Qch de Qch (to pull out, drive out . . . from . . .; to snatch . . . from, out of . . . *e.g.*, *des mains de quelqu'un*, out of someone's hands) VI

arranger

1. ———— Qch (to arrange . . .) I
2. ———— Qn (to accommodate . . .) I
3. s'———— (to manage) I
4. s'———— de Qch (to make do with . . .) IV
5. s'———— avec Qn (to come to terms with . . .) V
6. s'———— pour *Inf.* (to make arrangements to . . .) X

arrêter

1. ———— Qn ou Qch (to stop, arrest . . .) I
2. s'———— (to stop, come to a halt) I
3. s'———— sur, à Qch (to dwell on, pay attention to, decide on . . .) V, III
4. ———— ses regards sur Qn (to fix one's glance on . . .) VI
5. ———— de *Inf.* (to stop ---*ing*) IX-A
6. s'———— de *Inf.* (to leave off, give up ---*ing*) IX-A

arriver
1. _____ à Qch (to arrive at . . .) II
2. Il arrive à Qn Qch (to happen to, befall . . . Ex: *Il m'est arrivé une chose terrible*, a terrible thing [has] happened to me) VI
3. _____ à *Inf.* (to manage to . . .; to succeed in ---*ing*) VIII-A
4. en _____ à *Inf.* (to get to the point of, be at the point of ---*ing*) VIII-A
5. Il arrive à Qn de *Inf.* (to happen to . . . to . . . Ex: *Il arrive à tout le monde de se tromper*, everyone makes mistakes) IX-B

arroser
1. _____ Qch (to water, sprinkle . . .) I
2. _____ Qn ou Qch de Qch (to bathe, sprinkle . . . with . . .) VI

asperger
1. _____ Qn ou Qch (to sprinkle . . .) I
2. _____ Qn ou Qch de Qch (to sprinkle . . . with . . .) VI

aspirer
1. _____ à Qch (to aspire to, after . . .) II
2. _____ à *Inf.* (to aspire to . . .) VIII-A

assaillir
1. _____ Qn ou Qch (to assail, assault . . .) I
2. _____ Qn de Qch (to assail, assault . . . with . . .) VI

assaisonner
1. _____ Qch (to season . . .) I
2. _____ Qch de Qch (to season . . . with . . .) VI

assener
1. _____ Qch à Qn (to deal . . . to . . . Ex: *assener un coup à quelqu'un*, to deal someone a blow) VI

asseoir
1. ——— Qn ou Qch (to seat, set . . .) I
2. s'——— (to sit down) I
3. ——— Qn ou Qch sur Qch (to seat . . . on . . .; to base
. . . [*e.g.*, an opinion] on . . .) VI

asservir
1. ——— Qn ou Qch (to enslave . . .) I
2. s'——— à Qch (to submit to . . .) III
3. ——— Qn à Qch (to subject, tie . . . down to . . .) VI

assiéger
1. ——— Qn ou Qch (to besiege . . .) I
2. ——— Qn de Qch (to besiege . . . with . . .) VI

assigner
1. ——— Qn ou Qch (to assign, to allot, to subpoena . . .) I
2. ——— Qch à Qn ou Qch (to assign . . . to . . .) VI

assimiler
1. ——— Qch (to assimilate . . .) I
2. s'——— (to become assimilated) I
3. s'——— à Qn ou Qch (to become assimilated into . . . *e.g.*,
à un groupe, into a group; to compare oneself
with . . .) III

assister
1. ——— Qn (to assist . . .) I
2. ——— à Qch (to attend . . .) II

associer
1. ——— Qn ou Qch (to associate, bring together . . .) I
2. s'——— à, avec Qn (to associate with, go into partnership
with . . .) III ,V
3. s'——— à Qch (to share in, participate in . . .) III
4. ——— Qn ou Qch à Qn ou Qch (to associate . . . with
. . .; to include . . . in . . .) VI

assommer
1. _____ Qn (to stun, kill . . . with a blow; to beat up . . .; Coll: to bore . . .) I
2. _____ Qn de Qch (to strike . . . with . . .; Coll: to tire, bore, pester . . . with . . .) VI

assortir
1. _____ Qn ou Qch (to put together, match . . .) I
2. s'_____ (to match, harmonize) I
3. _____ Qch à Qch (to match . . . with . . .; to suit . . . to . . .) VI

assouvir
1. _____ Qn ou Qch (to sate, assuage . . .) I
2. s'_____ de Qch (to become sated with . . .) IV

assujettir
1. _____ Qn ou Qch (to subjugate . . .; to fasten, secure . . .) I
2. s'_____ à Qch (to subject oneself to, submit to . . .) III
3. _____ Qn ou Qch à Qch (to subject . . . to . . .) VI

assurer
1. _____ Qn ou Qch (to assure, to insure, to secure . . .) I
2. s'_____ de Qch (to make certain of . . .; to secure . . .) IV
3. s'_____ contre Qch (to protect, insure oneself against . . .) V
4. _____ Qn de Qch (to assure . . . of . . .) VI
5. _____ Qch à Qn (to vouch for . . . to . . .) VI

astreindre
1. _____ Qn (to compel . . .) I
2. s'_____ à Qch (to tie oneself down to, subject oneself to . . .) III
3. _____ Qn à Qch (to subject . . . to . . .) VI
4. s'_____ à *Inf.* (to force oneself to . . .) VIII-A
5. _____ Qn à *Inf.* (to compel . . . to . . .) VIII-B

attacher
1. _____ Qch (to attach . . .) I
2. s'_____ à Qn (to be attached to, fond of . . .) III
3. s'_____ à Qch (to be attached to, fasten onto, stick to . . .) III
4. _____ Qn ou Qch à Qn ou Qch (to attach, make . . . attached to . . .) VI
5. s'_____ à *Inf.* (to strive to . . .) VIII-A

attaquer
1. _____ Qn ou Qch (to attack . . .) I
2. s'_____ à Qn ou Qch (to attack, criticize . . .) III
3. s'_____ à Qch (to tackle . . . *e.g.*, a problem) III

attarder
1. _____ Qn (to delay, keep . . . late) I
2. s'_____ (to be late, stay late, lag behind, dally) I
3. s'_____ à *Inf.* (to linger, stay late ---*ing*) VIII-A

atteindre
1. _____ Qn ou Qch (to reach, attain . . .) I
2. _____ à Qch (to reach . . . with difficulty, effort) II
3. _____ Qn de Qch (to hit . . . with . . .) VI

atteler
1. _____ Qch (to harness, yoke . . .) I
2. s'_____ à Qch (to buckle down, settle down to . . . *e.g.*, à *une tâche*, to a task) III
3. _____ Qn ou Qch à Qch (to harness, put . . . to . . .) VI

attendre
1. _____ Qn ou Qch (to wait for . . .) I
2. s'_____ à Qch (to expect . . .) III
3. _____ Qch de Qn (to expect . . . from . . .) VI
4. s'_____ à *Inf.* (to expect to . . .) VIII-A
5. _____ de *Inf.* (to wait to . . .) IX-A

attendrir
1. _____ Qn (to move . . . to pity) I
2. _____ Qch (to tenderize [meat]; to soften . . .) I
3. s'_____ sur Qch (to be moved to pity by . . .) V

attenter
1. _____ à Qch (to make an attempt on, against . . . Ex: *attenter à la vie de quelqu'un*, to make an attempt on someone's life) II

attester
1. _____ Qch (to attest . . .; to testify to . . .) I

attirer
1. _____ Qn ou Qch (to attract, entice . . .) I
2. s'_____ Qch (to bring . . . upon oneself) I
3. _____ Qn à Qn ou Qch (to attract . . . to . . .) VI
4. _____ Qn dans Qch (to lure . . . into . .) VI
5. _____ Qch à, sur Qn (to bring . . . to, on, upon . . .) VI
6. _____ Qch sur Qch (to draw . . . [*e.g.*, one's attention] to . . .) VI

attraper
1. _____ Qn ou Qch (to catch, trap, trick . . .) I
2. _____ Qn à Qch (to catch . . . at . . .) VI
3. _____ Qn à *Inf.* (to catch . . . ---*ing*) VIII-B

attribuer
1. s'_____ Qch (to claim, assume . . .) I
2. _____ Qch à Qn ou Qch (to attribute . . . to . . .; to assign, allot . . . to . . .) VI

augurer
1. _____ Qch de Qch (to augur . . . of . . .; to predict . . . from, for . . .) VI

·

autoriser
1. _____ Qn ou Qch (to authorize . . .) I
2. s'_____ de Qn ou Qch (to cite . . . as an authority; to act on the authority of . . .) IV
3. _____ Qn à *Inf.* (to authorize . . . to . . .) VIII-B

avancer
1. _____ Qn ou Qch (to advance . . .) I
2. s'_____ (to move forward, advance) I
3. _____ de [un certain temps] (to be . . . fast, Ex: *La pendule avance de dix minutes*, the clock is ten minutes fast) IV
4. _____ Qch à Qn (to advance [money] to . . .) VI

aventurer
1. _____ Qch (to venture, risk . . .) I
2. s'_____ (to take a chance) I
3. s'_____ à *Inf.* (to venture to . . .) VIII-A

avertir
1. _____ Qn (to warn, notify . . .) I
2. _____ Qn de Qch (to warn, notify . . . of . . .) VI
3. _____ Qn de *Inf.* (to warn . . . to . . .) IX-B

aveugler
·1. _____ Qn ou Qch (to blind, to plug up, wall up . . .) I
2. s'_____ sur Qch (to shut one's eyes to . . .) V

avilir
1. _____ Qn ou Qch (to debase . . .) I
2. s'_____ (to debase, demean oneself) I
3. s'_____ à *Inf.* (to stoop to . . .; to demean oneself to the point of ---*ing*) VIII-A

aviser

1. _____ Qn (to inform . . .) I
2. _____ à Qch (to see to, to deal with . . .) II
3. s'_____ de Qch (to realize . . .) IV
4. _____ Qn de Qch (to inform . . . of . . .) VI
5. _____ à *Inf.* (to see about, think about ---*ing*) VIII-A
6. s'_____ de *Inf.* (to take it into one's head to . . .) IX-A

avoir

1. _____ Qn ou Qch (to have . . .) I
2. _____ *affaire* à Qn (to have to deal with . . .) III
3. _____ *affaire* avec Qn (to have dealings with . . .) V
4. en _____ à, contre, après Qn (to be angry with . . .) II, V
5. en _____ pour Qch (to take, require . . . Ex: *Elle en a pour trois jours*, it will take her three days) V
6. _____ à *Inf.* (to have to . . .; to have [something] to . . . Ex: *J'ai à travailler*, I have to work, I have work to do) VIII-A
7. _____ Qch à *Inf.* (to have . . . to . . . Ex: *avoir une lettre à écrire*, to have a letter to write) VIII-B

avouer

1. _____ Qch (to acknowledge, confess . . .) I
2. _____ Qn pour Qn ou Qch (to acknowledge, recognize . . . as . . . *e.g., pour fils*, as one's son) VI
3. _____ Qch à Qn (to confess, admit . . . to . . .) VI
4. _____ *Inf. passé* (to admit having . . .) VII-A

B

badiner

1. _____ avec Qch (to trifle, play with . . .) V

baigner
1. ———— Qn ou Qch (to bathe, wash . . .) I
2. être baigné de Qch (to be bathed in . . . *e.g., les yeux baignés de larmes,* eyes bathed in tears) IV
3. ———— dans Qch (to soak in . . .) V
4. ———— Qn ou Qch dans Qch (to immerse, dip . . . in . . .) VI

balancer
1. ———— Qn ou Qch (to balance, to swing, rock . . .) I
2. ———— Qch par Qch (to [counter] balance . . . with . . .) VI

bannir
1. ———— Qn (to banish, exile . . .) I
2. ———— Qn ou Qch de Qch (to banish . . . from . . .) VI

barbouiller
1. ———— Qch (to smear, to daub . . .) I
2. ———— Qn ou Qch de Qch (to smear . . . with . . .) VI

barrer
1. ———— Qch (to bar, block . . . *e.g.,* a door, a road; to cross out . . .) I
2. ———— Qch à, contre Qn (to bar, close off . . . to, against . . .) VI

baser
1. se ——— sur Qch (to be based on, founded on . . .) V
2. ———— Qch sur Qch (to base . . . on . . .) VI

battre
1. _____ Qn ou Qch (to beat . . .) I
2. _____ *des mains* (to clap one's hands)
3. _____ *des pieds* (to stamp one's feet)
4. se _____ avec, contre Qn (to fight with, against . . .) V
5. _____ contre Qch (to beat against . . .) V
6. _____ Qn à Qch (to beat . . . at . . . *e.g.*, *au tennis*, at tennis) VI
7. _____ Qn par Qch (to beat, be ahead of . . . by . . . *e.g.*, *par trois points*, by three points) VI

bénéficier
1. _____ de Qch (to profit by . . .) IV

bercer
1. _____ Qn (to rock . . .) I
2. se _____ de Qch (to delude oneself with . . .) IV
3. _____ Qn de Qch (to beguile . . . with . . .) VI

blâmer
1. _____ Qn ou Qch (to blame . . .) I
2. _____ Qn de Qch (to blame . . . for . . .) VI
3. _____ Qn de *Inf.* ou *Inf. passé* (to blame . . . for ---*ing*, for having . . .) IX-B

blaser
1. _____ Qn ou Qch (to cloy, to blunt . . .) I
2. se _____ de Qch (to become tired of, indifferent to . . .) IV
3. être blasé de, sur Qch (to be tired of, indifferent to . . .) IV, V

blesser
1. _____ Qn ou Qch (to wound, injure, offend . . .) I
2. être blessé à Qch (to be wounded, injured, hurt in . . . *e.g.*, *au bras*, in the arm) II
3. se _____ de Qch (to take offense at . . .) IV
4. se _____ avec Qch (to injure oneself with . . .) V
5. _____ Qn à Qch (to wound, injure . . . in . . . *e.g.*, *au genou*, in the knee, *à la tête*, in the head [exception: *dans le dos*, in the back]) VI
6. _____ Qn de Qch (to wound, injure . . . with . . .) VI

bombarder

1. ———— Qn ou Qch (to bombard . . .) I
2. ———— Qn ou Qch de Qch (to bombard . . . with . . .) VI

bondir

1. ———— de Qch (to leap with . . . *e.g., de joie*, with joy) IV
2. ———— sur Qn ou Qch (to pounce on, leap at . . .) V

border

1. ———— Qn ou Qch (to border . . .; to tuck in . . . Ex: *border quelqu'un dans son lit*, to tuck someone in bed) I
2. ———— Qch de, avec Qch (to border . . . with . . .) VI

borner

1. ———— Qch (to mark out, form the boundary of . . .; to limit . . .) I
2. se ———— à Qch (of people: to restrict oneself to . . .; of things: to be limited to . . . Ex: *Son répertoire se borne à des morceaux classiques*, his repertory is limited to classical pieces) III

bouder

1. ———— Qn ou Qch (to be sulky with, distant toward . . .) I
2. ———— contre Qn (to be sulky with . . .) V

bourrer

1. ———— Qn ou Qch (to stuff, cram . . .) I
2. ———— Qn *de coups* (to pummel, thrash . . .) I
3. se ———— de Qch (to stuff oneself with . . .) IV
4. ———— Qn ou Qch de Qch (to stuff, cram . . . with . . .) VI

braquer

1. ———— Qch (to aim, level, point . . .) I
2. se ———— contre Qn ou Qch (to be stubbornly opposed to, dead set against . . .) V
3. ———— Qn contre Qn ou Qch (to set . . . against . . .) VI
4. ———— *les yeux* sur Qn ou Qch (to fix one's gaze on, to stare at . . . Ex: *Tout le monde avait les yeux*

braqués sur la vedette, everyone was staring at the movie star) VI

briser
1. _____ Qn ou Qch (to break, shatter . . .) I
2. _____ avec Qn (to stop seeing . . .) V

brouiller
1. _____ Qn ou Qch (to mix up, confuse . . .) I
2. se _____ avec Qn (to have a falling out with . . .) V

brûler
1. _____ Qn ou Qch (to burn . . .) I
2. _____ de Qch (to be burning with . . . *e.g.*, *de fièvre*, with fever; *d'amour*, with love) IV
3. _____ de *Inf.* (to be eager to, anxious to . . .) IX-A

buter
1. se _____ à Qn ou Qch (to come up against . . . *e.g.*, a difficulty) III
2. _____ contre Qch (of people: to knock against, stumble over . . .; of things: to butt, strike against . . .) V
3. se _____ contre Qch (to prop oneself up against . . .) V
4. se _____ à *Inf.* (to be dead set on ---*ing*) VIII-A

C

cabrer
1. se _____ (of horses: to rear) I
2. se _____ contre Qch (to balk at, to revolt against . . .) V

cacher
1. _____ Qn ou Qch (to hide . . .) I
2. se _____ à Qn (to hide from . . .) III
3. se _____ de Qn (to keep out of the way of, to hide one's feelings from . . .) IV

4. se _____ de Qch (to make a secret of . . . Usually in the negative, Ex: *Il ne s'en cache pas*, he makes no secret of it) IV

5. _____ Qch à Qn (to hide . . . from . . .) VI

cadrer

1. _____ avec Qch (to agree, tally with . . .) V

calquer

1. _____ Qn ou Qch (to trace, to imitate . . .) I

2. _____ Qch sur Qch (to trace . . . from . . .; to model . . . on . . .) VI

causer

1. _____ Qch (to cause . . .; to talk . . . Ex: *causer politique*, to talk politics) I

2. _____ à Qn (Coll: to talk to . . .) II

3. _____ de Qch (to talk of, about . . .) IV

4. _____ avec Qn (to have a talk with, a chat with . . .) V

céder

1. _____ Qch (to give up . . .) I

2. _____ à Qn ou Qch (to yield to . . .) II

3. ne _____ en rien à Qn (to be someone's equal, Ex: *Elle ne lui cède en rien*, she is his equal in every respect) II

4. _____ Qch à Qn (to give up . . . to . . .; to give in to someone's . . . Ex: *céder à quelqu'un tous ses caprices*, to give in to someone's every whim) VI

ceindre

1. _____ Qn ou Qch (to gird, encircle . . .) I

2. _____ Qch à Qn (to gird . . . on . . .) VI

3. _____ Qn ou Qch de Qch (to gird, encircle . . . with . . .) VI

celer
1. _____ Qch (to hide, conceal . . .) I
2. _____ Qch à Qn (to hide, conceal . . . from . . .) VI

centrer
1. _____ Qch (to center . . .) I
2. _____ Qch sur Qn ou Qch (to center . . . on . . .) VI

certifier
1. _____ Qch (to certify, vouch for . . .) I
2. _____ Qch à Qn (to assure someone of something) VI

cesser
1. _____ Qch (to stop . . .) I
2. _____ de *Inf.* (to stop ---*ing*) IX-A

changer
1. _____ Qn ou Qch (to change, alter . . .) I
2. _____ de Qn ou Qch (to change . . . Ex: *changer d'avis*, to change one's mind; *changer de place*, to change places) IV
3. se _____ en Qn ou Qch (to change into . . .) V
4. _____ Qch contre Qch (to exchange . . . for . . .) VI

charger
1. _____ Qn ou Qch (to load, to transport, to charge . . .) I
2. se _____ de Qch (to take . . . upon oneself) IV
3. _____ Qn de Qch (to charge . . . with . . . *e.g., d'un crime*, with a crime; to entrust . . . with . . . *e.g., d'une mission*, with a mission) VI
4. _____ Qn ou Qch de Qch (to load, overburden . . . with . . .) VI
5. _____ Qn de *Inf.* (to charge, entrust . . . with ---*ing*) IX-B

charmer
1. ———— Qn ou Qch (to charm, bewitch . . .) I
2. être charmé de Qch (to be delighted with . . .) IV
3. être charmé de *Inf.* (to be delighted to . . .) IX-A

chasser
1. ———— Qn ou Qch (to chase, hunt, drive out . . .) I
2. ———— Qn ou Qch de Qch (to drive out . . . from . . .) VI

chausser
1. ———— Qch (to put on . . . on one's feet) I
2. ———— du 38, 40, etc. (to wear size 38, 40, etc. shoe [French sizes]) IV

chercher
1. ———— Qn ou Qch (to look for . . .) I
2. ———— à *Inf.* (to attempt to . . .) VIII-A

chicaner
1. ———— Qn (to quibble with, start a quarrel with . . .) I
2. ———— sur Qch (to quibble over . . .) V
3. ———— Qn sur Qch (to quibble with . . . over . . .) VI
4. ———— Qch à Qn (to quibble over . . . with . . .) VI

chiper
1. ———— Qch (Coll: to swipe . . .) I
2. ———— Qch à Qn (Coll: to swipe . . . from . . .) VI

choisir
1. ———— Qn ou Qch (to choose . . .) I
2. ———— de *Inf.* (to choose to . . .) IX-A

choquer
1. ———— Qn ou Qch (to shock, offend . . .; to clink [glasses]) I
2. se ———— de Qch (to be shocked by, at . . .; to take offense at . . .) IV
3. être choqué de Qch (to be shocked by, at . . .) IV
4. se ———— contre Qch (to collide with . . .) V

circonscrire
1. _____ Qch (to circumscribe . . .) I
2. _____ Qch à Qch (to draw [a circle] around . . . Ex: *circonscrire un cercle à un polygone*, to circumscribe a polygon) VI
3. _____ Qch par Qch (to surround, encircle . . . with . . .) VI

clabauder
1. _____ sur, contre Qn (to speak ill of . . .) V

coiffer
1. _____ Qn (to do someone's hair) I
2. _____ Qch (to cover, cap . . .; to be at the head of, to encompass . . .) I
3. se _____ (to fix, do one's hair) I
4. se _____ de Qch (to put on, wear . . . [on one's head]) IV
5. être coiffé de Qch (to be wearing . . . [on one's head]) IV

coincer
1. _____ Qn (Coll: to corner, catch . . .) I
2. _____ Qch (to wedge, jam . . .) I
3. être coincé dans Qch (Coll: to be caught, stuck in . . .) V

coïncider
1. _____ avec Qch (to coincide with . . .) V

collaborer
1. _____ à Qch (to contribute to . . . *e.g., à une revue*, to a magazine) II
2. _____ avec Qn (to collaborate with . . .) V

coller
1. _____ Qn (Coll: to fail, flunk [a student]) I
2. _____ Qch (to paste, stick, glue . . .) I
3. _____ à Qn ou Qch (to cling, stick, adhere to . . .) II
4. se _____ à, contre Qn ou Qch (to stand close to, cling to . . .) III, V
5. _____ Qch à Qch (to stick, paste, glue . . . to . . .) VI
6. _____ *une gifle* à Qn (Coll: to give . . . a slap, a smack in the face) VI

colleter
1. _____ Qn (to collar . . .) I
2. se _____ avec Qn (to fight, scuffle with . . .) V

colorer
1. _____ Qch (to color . . .) I
2. _____ Qch en Qch (to color something . . . Ex: *colorer une toile en bleu*, to color a canvas blue) VI
3. _____ Qch avec Qch (to color . . . with . . . *e.g., avec un vernis rouge*, with a red glaze) VI
4. _____ Qch de Qch (to embellish, gloss over . . . with . . .) VI

combiner
1. _____ Qch (to combine, to concoct, devise . . .) I
2. se _____ à, avec Qch (in chemistry: to combine with . . .) III, V
3. _____ Qch avec Qch (to combine . . . with . . .) VI

combler
1. _____ Qch (to fill in, fill . . . to the brim) I
2. être comblé de Qn ou Qch (to be filled with . . .; to be showered with . . . *e.g., d'honneurs*, with honors) IV
3. _____ Qn de Qch (to shower, overwhelm . . . with . . .) VI

commander
1. _____ Qch (to command . . .; to order . . . *e.g.*, a book, a dinner) I
2. _____ à Qn (to give orders to, have authority over . . .) II
3. _____ *à ses passions* (to curb one's passions) II
4. _____ Qch à Qn ou Qch (to order . . . from . . .) VI
5. _____ à Qn de *Inf.* (to order . . . to . . .) IX-B

commencer
1. _____ Qch (to begin . . .) I
2. _____ Qn dans Qch (to start, initiate . . . in . . .) VI
3. _____ à ou de *Inf.* (to begin to . . . *À* is more common; *de* is more literary) VIII-A, IX-A
4. _____ par *Inf.* (to begin by ---*ing*) X

commercer
1. _____ avec Qn ou Qch (to trade, deal with . . .) V

commettre
1. _____ Qch (to commit . . . *e.g.*, a crime, an error; to risk . . . *e.g.*, one's reputation) I
2. se ___ (to commit oneself) I
3. se ___ avec Qn (to throw in one's lot with . . . [and thereby compromise oneself]) V

commuer
1. _____ Qch (to commute [a sentence]) I
2. _____ Qch en Qch (to commute . . . to . . .) VI

communiquer
1. _____ Qch (to communicate, convey, impart . . .) I
2. se ___ à Qch (to spread to . . .) III
3. _____ avec Qn (to be in communication with, in touch with . . .) V
4. _____ avec Qch (to lead into . . . Ex: *une porte qui communique avec le salon*, a door which leads into the living room) V
5. _____ Qch à Qn ou Qch (to communicate, convey, transmit . . . to . . .) VI

comparer
1. _____ Qn ou Qch à Qn ou Qch (to compare . . . [in a general way] to, with . . .) VI
2. _____ Qn ou Qch avec Qn ou Qch (to compare . . . [methodically] with . . .) VI

compatir

1. _____ à Qch (to sympathize with, feel for . . . Ex: *Nous compatissons à leur douleur*, we feel for them in their sorrow) II

complaire

1. _____ à Qn (Lit: to please . . .) II
2. se _____ dans, en* Qch (to take pleasure in . . .) V
3. se _____ à *Inf.* (to take pleasure in ---*ing*) VIII-A

complimenter

1. _____ Qn (to compliment, congratulate . . .) I
2. _____ Qn pour Qch (to compliment, congratulate . . . for . . .) VI
3. _____ Qn sur, de Qch (to compliment, congratulate . . . on . . .) VI

comploter

1. _____ Qch (to plot, scheme . . .) I
2. _____ de *Inf.* (to plot to . . .) IX-A

composer

1. _____ Qch (to compose, make up . . .) I
2. se _____ de Qn ou Qch (to be composed of, consist of . . .) IV
3. _____ avec Qn ou Qch (to come to terms with . . .) V

comprendre

1. _____ Qn ou Qch (to understand ... .) I
2. ne _____ *rien* à Qch (to know nothing about, to not understand anything in . . . Ex: *Je ne comprends rien à la géométrie*, I don't know the first thing about geometry) II

---

*See Appendix II: **DANS, EN, À**, p. 298.

compromettre
1. _____ Qn ou Qch (to compromise . . .) I
2. se _____ (to compromise oneself) I
3. se _____ avec Qn (to compromise oneself with . . .) V
4. être compromis dans Qch (to be implicated in . . .) V

compter
1. _____ Qn ou Qch (to count . . .) I
2. _____ avec Qn ou Qch (to reckon with . . .) V
3. _____ sur Qn ou Qch (to count on, rely on . . .) V
4. _____ Qch à Qn [pour Qch] (to pay someone . . . [for
   . . .] Ex: *compter mille francs à quelqu'un*, to
   pay someone a thousand francs) VI

concéder
1. _____ Qch (to concede, grant . . .) I
2. _____ Qch à Qn (to grant . . . to . . .) VI

concentrer
1. _____ Qch (to concentrate, focus . . .) I
2. se _____ [sur Qch] (to concentrate [on . . .] Ex: *Laissez-moi
   tranquille, j'essaye de me concentrer*, leave me
   alone, I'm trying to concentrate) V

concerter
1. _____ Qch (to concert, arrange . . .) I
2. se _____ avec Qn (to act in concert with, to connive with
   . . .) V

concilier
1. _____ Qn ou Qch (to conciliate, reconcile . . .) I
2. se _____ Qch (to win over, gain . . . Ex: *se concilier l'es-
   time de tout le monde*, to gain the esteem of
   everyone) I
3. se _____ avec Qn ou Qch (to agree with, jibe with . . .) V
4. _____ Qn ou Qch avec Qn ou Qch (to reconcile, harmonize . . . with . . .) VI

concorder

1. _____ avec Qch (to agree, tally with . . .) V

concourir

1. _____ à Qch (to contribute toward, be directed toward . . .) II
2. _____ avec Qn (to cooperate with . . .) V
3. _____ pour Qch (to compete for . . .) V
4. _____ à *Inf.* (to combine, unite, conspire to . . . Ex: *Tout concourt à prouver son innocence*, everything tends to prove his innocence) VIII-A

condamner

1. _____ Qn (to condemn, sentence . . .) I
2. _____ Qn à Qch (to condemn, sentence . . . to . . .) VI
3. _____ Qn à *Inf.* (to condemn . . . to . . .) VIII-B

condenser

1. _____ Qch (to condense . . .) I
2. _____ Qch en Qch (to condense . . . into . . .) VI

condescendre

1. _____ à Qch (to condescend to, agree [with disdain] to . . .) II
2. _____ à *Inf.* (to condescend to, deign to . . .) VIII-A

conduire

1. _____ Qn ou Qch (to conduct, lead, drive . . .) I
2. _____ Qn ou Qch à Qch (to lead, take . . . to . . .) VI
3. _____ Qn à *Inf.* (to lead, induce . . . to . . .) VIII-B

confédérer

1. _____ avec Qn ou Qch (to unite with . . .) V

conférer
1. _____ de Qch (to talk over, confer about . . .) IV
2. _____ avec Qn (to confer with . . .) V
3. _____ Qch à Qn (to confer . . . on . . .) VI
4. _____ de Qch avec Qn (to confer about . . . with . . .) IV

confesser
1. _____ Qch (to confess . . .) I
2. _____ Qn (to receive the confession of . . . Ex: *Le prêtre confessa le pénitent*, the priest confessed the penitent) I
3. se _____ (to confess one's sins) I
4. se _____ à Qn (to confess one's sins to . . .) III
5. se _____ de Qch (to confess having done . . .) IV
6. _____ Qch à Qn (to confess . . . to . . .) VI

confier
1. se _____ à, en Qn ou Qch (to put one's trust in, to confide in . . .) III, V
2. _____ Qch à Qn (to entrust someone with something; to tell someone something in confidence) VI

confiner
1. _____ Qn ou Qch (to confine, imprison, shut up . . .) I
2. _____ à Qch (to border on . . . *e.g.*, a country; to verge on . . . *e.g.*, madness) II
3. se _____ dans Qch (to limit oneself to, specialize in . . .) V
4. _____ Qn dans Qch (to shut up . . . in . . .) VI

confisquer
1. _____ Qch (to confiscate . . .) I
2. _____ Qch à Qn (to confiscate . . . from . . .) VI

confondre

1. —— Qn ou Qch (to confuse, mix up, confound . . .) I
2. se —— (to become bewildered, confused; to intermingle, be indistinguishable) I
3. être confondu de Qch (to be dumbfounded at . . .) IV
4. se —— en Qch (to blend into . . .; to be profuse in . . . Ex: *se confondre en excuses*, to apologize profusely) V
5. se —— avec Qch (to be confused with, indistinguishable from . . .) V
6. —— Qn ou Qch avec Qn ou Qch (to mistake . . . for . . .) VI

conformer

1. —— Qch (to form, shape . . .) I
2. se —— à Qch (to conform to, comply with . . .) III
3. —— Qch à Qch (to make . . . conform to . . .) VI

confronter

1. —— Qn ou Qch (to confront, compare . . .) I
2. —— Qn ou Qch avec Qn ou Qch (to confront, compare . . . with . . .) VI

conjurer

1. —— Qch (to conjure up or away, to ward off . . .) I
2. se —— contre Qn (to plot together, conspire against . . .) V
3. se —— à *Inf.* (to unite, conspire to . . .) VIII-A
4. —— Qn de *Inf.* (to beseech . . . to . . .) IX-B

connaître

1. —— Qn ou Qch (to know, be acquainted with . . .) I
2. se —— en Qch (to know a lot about, to be a good judge of . . .) V

consacrer
1. _____ Qn ou Qch (to consecrate . . .) I
2. se _____ à Qch (to devote oneself to . . .) III
3. _____ Qch à Qn ou Qch (to dedicate, devote . . . to . . .) VI

conseiller
1. _____ Qn ou Qch (to advise, counsel . . .) I
2. _____ Qch à Qn (to recommend . . . to . . .) VI
3. _____ à Qn de *Inf.* (to advise . . . to . . .) IX-B

consentir
1. _____ à Qch (to consent to . . .) II
2. _____ à *Inf.* (to consent to, be willing to . . .) VIII-A

consister
1. _____ dans* Qch (to consist of, to lie in . . . Ex: *La valeur de l'or consiste dans sa rareté,* the value of gold lies in its scarcity) V
2. _____ en* Qch (to consist of, be composed of . . . Ex: *Ce travail consiste en recherches minutieuses,* this job consists of very detailed research; *le problème consiste en ceci,* the problem is this) V
3. _____ à *Inf.* (to consist of, to lie in ---*ing*) VIII-A

consoler
1. _____ Qn (to console, comfort . . .) I
2. se _____ de Qch (to get over . . .) IV
3. _____ Qn de Qch (to console . . . for . . .) VI

conspirer
1. _____ contre Qn ou Qch (to plot against . . .) V
2. _____ à *Inf.* (to conspire to . . .) VIII-A

---

*See Appendix II: **DANS, EN, À,** p. 298.

constituer

1. _____ Qn ou Qch (to constitute, form, make up . . .) I
2. se _____ en Qch (to form, set oneself up as . . . Ex: *Ils se constituèrent en gouvernement révolutionnaire,* they formed a revolutionary government; *ils se constituèrent en arbitre du bon goût,* they set themselves up as the arbiter of good taste) V
3. _____ Qch à Qn (to settle . . . on . . . Ex: *constituer une annuité à quelqu'un,* to settle an annuity on someone) VI

consulter

1. _____ Qn ou Qch (to consult . . .) I
2. _____ avec Qn (to consult with, confer with . . .) V
3. _____ Qn sur Qch (to consult . . . on, about . . .) VI

contenter

1. _____ Qn ou Qch (to satisfy, gratify . . .) I
2. se _____ de Qch (to be content, satisfied with . . .) IV
3. se _____ de *Inf.* (to be content, satisfied with ---*ing*) IX-A

contester

1. _____ Qch (to contest, dispute . . .) I
2. _____ sur Qch (to wrangle, argue over . . .) V

continuer

1. _____ Qch (to continue . . .) I
2. _____ à ou de *Inf.* (to continue to . . .; to keep on ---*ing*) VIII-A, IX-A

contraindre

1. _____ Qn ou Qch (to constrain, restrain . . .) I
2. se _____ à ou de *Inf.* (to stop oneself from ---*ing*) VIII-A, IX-A
3. _____ Qn à *Inf.* (to compel, force . . . to . . .) VIII-B
4. être contraint de *Inf.* (to be obliged to . . .) IX-A

contrarier
1. _____ Qn ou Qch (to thwart, oppose, vex . . .) I
2. être contrarié de Qch (to be annoyed, vexed by, at . . .) IV

contraster
1. _____ Qch (to contrast, set . . . in contrast) I
2. _____ avec Qch (to stand in contrast to, form a contrast with . . .) V

contrevenir
1. _____ à Qch (to contravene, violate . . .) II

contribuer
1. _____ Qch (to contribute . . .) I
2. _____ à Qch (to contribute to, play a part in . . .) II
3. _____ Qch à Qch (to contribute . . . to . . .) VI

convaincre
1. _____ Qn (to convince . . .) I
2. se _____ de Qch (to convince oneself of . . .) IV
3. _____ Qn de Qch (to convince . . . of . . .; to prove . . . guilty of . . .) VI

convenir
1. _____ à Qn ou Qch (to suit, be suited to, for . . .; to be agreeable to . . .) II
2. _____ de Qch (to agree on . . .; to acknowledge, admit . . .) IV
3. _____ de *Inf.* (to agree to . . .) IX-A
4. Il convient de *Inf.* (It is fitting, advisable to . . .) IX-A

converger
1. _____ sur, vers Qn ou Qch (to coverge on, towards . . .) V

converser
1. _____ avec Qn (to converse with . . .) V

convertir
1. _____ Qn ou Qch (to convert . . .) I
2. se _____ à Qch (to convert to . . . Ex: *se convertir au christianisme*, to convert to Christianity) III
3. _____ Qn à Qch (to convert . . . to . . .) VI
4. _____ Qch en Qch (to convert . . . to, into . . .) VI

convier
1. _____ Qn (to invite . . .) I
2. _____ Qn à Qch (to invite . . . to . . .) VI
3. _____ Qn à *Inf.* (to invite, urge . . . to . . .) VIII-B

coopérer
1. _____ à Qch (to cooperate on, in . . .) II
2. _____ avec Qn (to cooperate with . . .) V

coordonner
1. _____ Qch (to coordinate . . .) I
2. _____ Qch à, avec Qch (to coordinate . . . with . . .) VI

copier
1. _____ Qn ou Qch (to copy, imitate . . .) I
2. _____ sur Qn ou Qch (to copy from . . .) V
3. _____ Qch sur Qn ou Qch (to copy . . . from . . .) VI

correspondre
1. _____ à Qch (to tally, agree with, correspond to . . .) II
2. _____ avec Qn (to correspond with . . .) V

corriger
1. _____ Qn ou Qch (to correct . . .) I
2. se _____ de Qch (to break oneself of . . . *e.g., d'une mauvaise habitude*, of a bad habit) IV
3. _____ Qn de Qch (to cure, break . . . of . . .) VI

costumer
1. _____ Qn (to dress . . . up) I
2. se _____ en Qch (to dress up as . . .) V
3. _____ Qn en Qch (to dress . . . up as . . .) VI

coucher
1. _____ Qn ou Qch (to put . . . to bed; to put down, lay down, flatten . . .) I
2. se _____ (to go to bed) I
3. _____ Qch dans Qch (to write down, enter . . . in . . .) VI
4. _____ Qn *sur son testament*, to mention someone in one's will) VI

coudre
1. _____ Qch (to sew . . .) I
2. _____ Qch à Qch (to sew . . . on, to . . .) VI

courir
1. _____ Qch (to run . . . *e.g.*, a risk; to pursue, to roam, to frequent . . .) I
2. _____ à Qch (to race to, flock to . . .) II
3. _____ après Qn ou Qch (to run after, pursue . . .) V
4. _____ *Inf.* (to run to . . . Ex: *J'ai couru lui dire les nouvelles*, I ran to tell him the news) VII-A

couronner
1. _____ Qn (to crown . . .) I
2. _____ Qn de Qch (to crown . . . with . . .) VI

coûter
1. _____ Qch (to cost . . .) I
2. _____ Qch à Qn (to cost, cause someone something, Ex: *Cela lui a coûté la vie*, that cost him his life; *cela lui a coûté une fortune*, that cost him a fortune) VI
3. Il en coûte à Qn de *Inf.* (It is painful, difficult for . . . to . . .) IX-B

couvrir

1. _____ (to cover . . .) I
2. se _____ de Qch (to become covered with . . .) IV
3. être couvert de Qch (to be covered with . . .) IV
4. _____ Qn ou Qch de Qch (to cover . . . with . . .) VI

craindre

1. _____ Qn ou Qch (to fear . . .) I
2. _____ pour Qn ou Qch (to fear for . . .) V
3. _____ de *Inf.* (to fear, be afraid of ---*ing*) IX-A

cramponner

1. _____ Qn (Coll: to pester . . .) I
2. _____ Qch (to clamp . . . together) I
3. se _____ à Qn (Coll: to cling to, hang on to . . .) III
4. se _____ à Qch (to cling to, hold fast to, hang on to . . .) III

créditer

1. _____ Qch de Qch (to credit . . . with . . . Ex: *créditer un compte de vingt dollars*, to credit an account with twenty dollars) VI

crever

1. _____ Qn (to exhaust, work . . . to death) I
2. _____ Qch (to burst, split . . .; to puncture [a tire]) I
3. _____ de Qch (Coll: to be bursting with . . . Ex: *crever de rire*, to split one's sides laughing; Coll: to be dying of . . . *e.g.*, *de faim*, of hunger; *d'ennui*, of boredom) IV

cribler

1. _____ Qch (to sift, riddle . . .) I
2. _____ Qn ou Qch de Qch (to riddle . . . with . . .) VI

crier

1. _____ Qch (to cry, cry out, shout . . .) I
2. _____ *au feu* (to cry out "fire") II
3. _____ *au secours* (to cry out for help) II
4. _____ de Qch (to cry out with . . . *e.g., de douleur,* with pain) IV
5. _____ contre Qn (to cry out against, rail against . . .) V
6. _____ après Qn (to carp at, bawl out . . .) V
7. _____ Qch à Qn (to shout, cry out . . . at, to . . .) VI
8. _____ à Qn de *Inf.* (to shout to . . . to . . .) IX-B

croire

1. _____ Qn ou Qch (to believe . . .) I
2. se _____ Qch (to think oneself . . . Ex: *Il se croit un génie*, he thinks he's a genius) I
3. _____ à Qch (to believe in: to have faith in the reality, veracity, truth, or likelihood of . . . Ex: *Le médecin croit à une tuberculose*, the doctor thinks that it's tuberculosis; *croire aux promesses de quelqu'un*, to believe someone's promises; *croire aux revenants*, to believe in ghosts; *croire à la possibilité d'une guerre*, to believe that war is possible) II
4. _____ en Qn (to believe in, have confidence in . . . Ex: *croire en ses amis*, to trust one's friends; *croire en Dieu*, to believe in God) V
5. _____ *Inf.* (to think, believe that . . . Ex: *Il croit entendre des voix*, he thinks he hears voices) VII-A

croiser

1. _____ Qn ou Qch (to cross, thwart, meet, pass . . .) I
2. se _____ (to cross, Ex: *Nos lettres se sont croisées*, our letters crossed [in the mail]) I
3. se _____ avec Qn ou Qch (to meet, pass . . .; of letters: to cross with . . .) V

croître

1. _____ en Qch (to grow, increase in . . . *e.g., en nombre*, in number) V

croupir
1. ———— dans Qch (to wallow in . . .) V

cuirasser
1. ———— Qn (to armor . . .) I
2. se ———— (to put on armor) I
3. se ———— contre Qn ou Qch (to steel oneself, protect oneself against . . .) V

cuire
1. ———— Qch (to cook . . .) I
2. ———— [Qch] à Qch (to cook [. . .] in, on . . . Ex: *cuire
au four,* to bake, roast; *cuire à l'eau,* to boil;
cuire à la broche, to cook on a spit) VI

D

daigner
1. ———— *Inf.* (to deign to, condescend to . . .) VII-A

danser
1. ———— Qch (to dance . . . *e.g.,* the polka) I
2. ———— avec Qn (to dance with . . .) V

dater
1. ———— Qch (to date . . .) I
2. ———— de Qch (to date from . . .; to be dated . . .) IV

débarrasser
1. ———— Qch (to disencumber . . .; to clear . . . *e.g.,* the
table) I
2. se ———— de Qn ou Qch (to get rid of . . .; to extricate oneself from . . .) IV
3. ———— Qn de Qn ou Qch (to rid, relieve . . . of . . .; to
help . . . off with . . .) VI

débattre

1. _____ Qch (to debate, discuss . . .) I
2. se _____ avec Qch (to struggle with . . . *e.g., avec un problème*, with a problem) V
3. se _____ contre Qch (to struggle against . . .) V

débiter

1. _____ Qn ou Qch de Qch (to debit . . . with . . . *e.g., d'une somme*, with an amount) VI
2. _____ Qch à Qn ou Qch (to debit . . . to . . .) VI

déblatérer

1. _____ Qch (to bluster, hurl . . . *e.g.*, insults, threats) I
2. _____ contre Qn (to shout abuse, rail at . . .) V
3. _____ Qch contre Qn (to hurl . . . [*e.g.*, abuse] at . . .) VI

déborder

1. _____ de Qch (to overflow with . . . *e.g., d'enthousiasme*, with enthusiasm) IV
2. être débordé de Qch (to be overwhelmed, snowed under with . . . *e.g., de travail*, with work) IV

déboucher

1. _____ Qch (to clear, unstop, uncork . . .) I
2. _____ dans Qch (to empty into . . .) V
3. _____ sur Qch (to open onto . . .) V

débrouiller

1. _____ Qch (to unravel, disentangle, make out . . .) I
2. se _____ (to extricate oneself [from a difficult situation]; Coll: to get along, manage) I
3. se _____ avec Qch (Coll: to get by on, manage with . . . Ex: *se débrouiller avec $90 par semaine*, to get by on $90 a week) V

débuter

1. ———— dans Qch (to start in, make one's debut in . . .) V
2. ———— par *Inf.* (to begin by ---*ing*) X

décerner

1. ———— Qch à Qn (to bestow . . . on . . .; to award . . .
to . . .) VI
2. ———— *un mandat d'arrêt* contre Qn (to issue a warrant
for someone's arrest) VI

décevoir

1. ———— Qn (to disappoint . . .) I
2. être déçu par Qn ou Qch (to be disappointed by, in . . .) V

déchaîner

1. ———— Qn ou Qch (to unleash, let loose . . .) I
2. se ——— (to be unleashed; of a storm: to break out) I
3. se ——— contre Qn ou Qch (to fly into a rage against . . .)
V
4. ———— Qn ou Qch contre Qn ou Qch (to let loose, trigger
. . . against . . .) VI

décharger

1. ———— Qn ou Qch (to unburden, unload . . .) I
2. se ——— de Qn ou Qch (to get rid of, free oneself of . . .)
IV
3. se ——— de Qch sur Qn (to shift the responsibility for . . .
onto . . .) IV
4. se ——— dans Qch (to flow, empty into . . .) V
5. ———— Qn de Qch (to relieve, discharge, acquit . . . of
. . .) VI
6. ———— Qch sur Qn (to vent . . . [*e.g.*, one's anger] on . . .)
VI
7. ———— Qch sur, contre Qn ou Qch (to fire [a gun] at . . .)
VI

décider
1. _____ Qch (to decide, settle . . .) I
2. _____ de Qch (to determine, to determine the outcome of . . .) IV
3. se _____ pour, contre Qch (to decide in favor of, against . . .; to decide on, against . . . Ex: *Je me suis décidé pour une Renault,* I've decided on [decided to buy] a Renault) V
4. se _____ à *Inf.* (to make up one's mind, resolve to . . .) VIII-A
5. être décidé à *Inf.* (to be determined, resolved to . . .) VIII-A
6. _____ Qn à *Inf.* (to persuade . . . to . . .) VIII-B
7. _____ de *Inf.* (to decide to . . .) IX-A

déclamer
1. _____ Qch (to declaim . . .) I
2. _____ contre Qn ou Qch (to inveigh against . . .) V

déclarer
1. _____ Qn ou Qch (to declare . . .) I
2. se _____ pour, contre Qn ou Qch (to come out in favor of, against . . .) V
3. _____ Qch à Qn (to make . . . known to . . .; to declare [war] on . . .) VI

déconseiller
1. _____ Qch à Qn (to advise someone against something) VI
2. _____ à Qn de *Inf.* (to advise . . . not to . . .) IX-B

décorer
1. _____ Qn ou Qch (to decorate . . .) I
2. _____ Qn ou Qch de Qch (to decorate . . . with . . .) VI

découler
1. _____ de Qch (to derive, follow, issue from . . .) IV

découper
1. ———— Qch (to cut out, carve . . .) I
2. se ———— sur Qch (to stand out against . . .) V

décourager
1. ———— Qn ou Qch (to discourage, dishearten . . .) I
2. se ———— (to become discouraged) I
3. ———— Qn de Qch (to discourage . . . from . . .) VI
4. ———— Qn de *Inf.* (to discourage . . . from ---*ing*) IX-B

découvrir
1. ———— Qn ou Qch (to uncover, discover . . .; to discern
       . . . [in the distance]) I
2. se ———— (to take off one's hat; to lower one's guard; to
       come into sight, come to light; of the sky: to
       clear up) I
3. se ———— à Qn (to confide in . . .) III
4. ———— Qch à Qn (to divulge, expose . . . to . . .) VI

dédaigner
1. ———— Qn ou Qch (to scorn, disdain . . .) I
2. ———— de *Inf.* (to not deign to . . .) IX-A

dédier
1. ———— Qch à Qn (to dedicate . . . to . . .) VI

dédire (se)
1. se ———— de Qch (to take back, retract, go back on . . .) IV

dédommager
1. ———— Qn (to compensate, indemnify . . .) I
2. se ———— de Qch (to recoup oneself for . . .) IV
3. ———— Qn de Qch (to compensate, indemnify . . . for
       . . .) VI

déduire
1. ———— Qch (to deduce, infer, deduct . . .) I
2. ———— Qch de Qch (to deduce, infer, deduct . . . from
       . . .) VI

défaire
1. _____ Qn ou Qch (to undo, destroy . . .) I
2. se _____ de Qn (to get rid of . . .) IV
3. se _____ de Qch (to rid oneself of . . .; to break oneself of . . . *e.g.*, *d'une mauvaise habitude*, of a bad habit) IV

défendre
1. _____ Qn ou Qch (to defend, protect . . .) I
2. se _____ (to defend oneself; Coll: to get along, to hold one's own) I
3. se _____ de, contre Qch (to protect, shield oneself from, against . . .) IV, V
4. _____ Qch à Qn (to forbid someone something) VI
5. _____ Qn ou Qch contre Qn ou Qch (to defend, protect . . . from, against . . .) VI
6. se _____ de *Inf.* ou *Inf. passé* (to deny ---ing, having . . .) IX-A
7. se _____ de *Inf.* (Lit: to refrain from, keep from --- ing; often in the negative, Ex: *Je ne pus me défendre de rire*, I couldn't keep from laughing) IX-A
8. Il est défendu de *Inf.* (It is forbidden to . . . Ex: *Il est défendu de fumer*, "smoking is prohibited") IX-A
9. _____ à Qn de *Inf.* (to forbid . . . to . . .) IX-B

déférer
1. _____ à Qn (to defer to . . .) II
2. _____ à Qch (to comply with, accede to . . .) II

défier
1. _____ Qch (to defy, brave . . .) I
2. se _____ de Qn ou Qch (to mistrust . . .) IV
3. _____ Qn à Qch (to challenge . . . to . . .) VI
4. _____ Qn de *Inf.* (to defy, dare . . . to . . .) IX-B

dégager
1. _____ Qn ou Qch (to disengage, to redeem . . .) I
2. se _____ (to emerge, to become apparent) I
3. se _____ de Qch (to free oneself of, extricate oneself from
. . .; of vapors, odors: to be given off by, to
emanate, escape from . . .) IV
4. _____ Qn ou Qch de Qch (to extricate, release, separate
. . . from . . .) VI

dégarnir
1. _____ Qch (to clear, empty, strip . . .) I
2. se _____ (to thin out, empty out) I
3. _____ Qch de Qch (to clear, empty, strip . . . of . . .) VI

dégénérer
1. _____ de Qch (to degenerate from . . .) IV
2. _____ en Qch (to degenerate into . . .) V

dégorger
1. _____ Qch (to disgorge, unstop . . .) I
2. _____ dans Qch (to overflow, discharge into . . .) V

dégoûter
1. _____ Qn (to disgust . . .) I
2. se _____ de Qn ou Qch (to take a dislike to, become fed
up with . . .) IV
3. être dégoûté de Qch (to be tired of, sick of . . .) IV
4. _____ Qn de Qch (to make someone dislike . . .; to disgust . . . with . . .) VI

dégoutter
1. _____ de Qch (to drip, trickle from . . .; to be dripping
with . . .) IV

déguiser
1. _____ Qn ou Qch (to disguise . . .) I
2. se _____ en Qch (to disguise oneself as . . .) V
3. _____ Qn en Qch (to disguise . . . as . . .) VI

déjeuner

1. _____ de Qch (to breakfast, lunch on . . .; to have a breakfast, lunch of . . .) IV

délayer

1. _____ Qch (to thin, add water to . . .) I
2. _____ Qch dans Qch (to thin . . . with . . .; to mix . . . with . . . [something liquid]) VI

délecter

1. se _____ à, de Qch (to delight in, take pleasure in . . .) III, IV
2. se _____ à *Inf.* (to delight in, take pleasure in ---*ing*) VIII-A

déléguer

1. _____ Qn ou Qch (to delegate . . .) I
2. _____ Qn à Qch (to delegate, appoint . . . to . . .) VI
3. _____ Qch à Qn (to delegate, hand over . . . to . . .) VI
4. _____ Qn pour *Inf.* (to delegate . . . to . . .) X

délibérer

1. _____ Qch (to deliberate over, discuss . . .) I
2. _____ de Qch (to deliberate . . .; to decide . . . [by debate or deliberation]) IV
3. _____ avec Qn (to deliberate with . . .) V
4. _____ sur Qch (to deliberate on . . .) V

délier

1. _____ Qch (to untie, undo . . .) I
2. _____ Qn de Qch (to release . . . from . . . *e.g., d'une promesse*, from a promise) VI

délivrer

1. _____ Qn (to rescue, free . . .) I
2. se _____ de Qn ou Qch (to free oneself, rid oneself of . . .) IV
3. _____ Qn de Qch (to free . . . of . . .; to rescue, deliver . . . from . . .) VI

déloger

1. —— de Qch (to move out of . . . *e.g., d'une maison,* out of a house) IV
2. —— Qn ou Qch de Qch (to oust, evict . . . from . . .; to drive . . . out of . . .) VI

demander

1. —— Qn ou Qch (to ask, ask for . . .) I
2. se —— Qch (to wonder . . .) I
3. —— Qch à Qn (to ask someone [for] something) VI
4. —— à *Inf.* (to ask to . . .) VIII-A
5. —— à Qn de *Inf.* (to ask . . . to . . .) IX-B

démarrer

1. —— de Qch (to cast off from, get out of . . .) IV

démettre

1. —— Qch (to dislocate . . . *e.g.,* a shoulder) I
2. —— Qn (to dismiss . . . [from a job]) I
3. se —— de Qch (to resign from . . . *e.g., de ses fonctions,* from office) IV
4. —— Qn de Qch (to dismiss . . . from . . .) VI

démontrer

1. —— Qch (to demonstrate, prove . . .) I
2. —— Qch à Qn (to demonstrate, prove . . . to . . .) VI

démordre

1. —— de Qch (to let go of, abandon . . . Usually in the negative, Ex: *Il ne démordra pas de sa résolution,* he won't give up his resolution) IV

démunir

1. —— Qch (to strip, deplete . . .) I
2. se —— de Qch (to allow oneself to run short of, to part with . . .) IV
3. être démuni de Qch (to be out of, short of . . .) IV
4. —— Qch de Qch (to strip, empty . . . of . . .) VI

dénier
1. _____ Qch (to deny, disclaim . . .) I
2. _____ Qch à Qn (to deny someone something) VI

dénoncer
1. _____ Qch (to denounce, expose, reveal . . .) I
2. _____ Qn (to denounce, inform against . . .) I
3. se _____ à Qn (to give oneself up to . . . *e.g.*, *à la police*, to the police) III
4. _____ Qn à Qn (to denounce . . . to . . .) VI

dénuer
1. se _____ de Qch (Lit: to part with, deprive oneself of . . .) IV
2. être dénué de Qch (to be devoid of, without . . . Ex: *être dénué de tout intérêt*, to be totally lacking in interest) IV

départir
1. _____ Qch (Lit: to divide, dispense, distribute . . .) I
2. se _____ de Qch (to give up, abandon, depart from . . . Ex: *Il ne se départait pas de son calme*, he kept his composure) IV

dépêcher
1. _____ Qn ou Qch (to dispatch . . .) I
2. se _____ (to hurry) I
3. se _____ de *Inf.* (to hurry to . . .) IX-A

dépendre
1. _____ de Qn ou Qch (to depend on . . . Ex: *Le succès de ce projet dépend de vous*, the success of this project depends on you) IV
2. Il dépend de Qn de *Inf.* (It is up to, it rests with . . . to . . .) IX-B

dépenser
1. ———— Qch (to spend, consume . . . *e.g.,* money, energy) I
2. se ———— pour Qn (to exert oneself, to go to a lot of trouble for . . .) V

dépêtrer
1. se ———— de Qch (to extricate oneself from . . .) IV
2. ———— Qn de Qch (to extricate . . . from . . .; to get . . . out of . . .) VI

dépiter
1. ———— Qn (to vex . . .) I
2. se ———— (to take offense) I
3. se ———— de *Inf.* (to be vexed, annoyed to . . .; at ---*ing*) IX-A

déplaire
1. ———— à Qn (to displease, offend . . .) II
2. N'en déplaise à Qn (Ex: *Ne vous en déplaise,* [ironic] with your permission, if you have no objection) II
3. Il déplaît à Qn de *Inf.* (It displeases . . . to . . . Ex: *Il me déplaît de les voir souffrir,* I don't like to see them suffer) IX-B

déplorer
1. ———— Qch (to deplore, grieve over . . .) I
2. ———— de *Inf.* ou *Inf. passé* (to regret very much ---*ing,* having . . .) IX-A

déposséder
1. ———— Qn (to dispossess . . .) I
2. ———— Qn de Qch (to dispossess, deprive . . . of . . .; to oust . . . from . . .) VI

dépouiller
1. ———— Qn ou Qch (to skim, strip, despoil . . .) I
2. se ———— de Qch (to strip oneself, divest oneself of . . .) IV
3. ———— Qn de Qch (to deprive, strip . . . of . . .) VI

dépourvoir
1. être dépourvu de Qch (to be devoid of, lacking in . . .) IV

députer
1. ———— Qn (to deputize . . .) I
2. ———— Qn à Qch (to appoint . . . to . . .) VI

déranger
1. ———— Qn ou Qch (to disturb, trouble . . .; to put . . . out of order) I
2. se ———— pour Qn ou Qch (to go out of one's way for . . .) V
3. se ———— pour *Inf.* (to go out of one's way to . . .) X

dériver
1. ———— Qch (to divert . . . *e.g.,* a stream) I
2. ———— de Qch (to arise from, be derived from . . .; of streams, rivers: to be diverted from . . . *e.g.,* from a course) IV
3. ———— Qch de Qch (to divert . . . from . . .) VI

dérober
1. ———— Qn ou Qch (Lit: to steal . . .; to hide . . .) I
2. se ———— (to give way, Ex: *Le sol se déroba sous leurs pas,* the ground gave way under their feet) I
3. se ———— à Qch (to escape, evade . . . *e.g., à ses obligations,* one's obligations) III
4. ———— Qch à Qn (Lit: to steal . . . from . . . Ex: *On m'a dérobé mes bijoux,* someone has taken my jewels) VI

déroger
1. ———— à Qch (to depart from . . . *e.g., à l'usage,* from custom; to derogate from . . .) II

désabonner
1. se ———— à Qch (to cancel one's subscription to . . .) III
2. ———— Qn à Qch (to cancel someone's subscription to . . .) VI

désabuser

1. _____ Qn (to disabuse, enlighten . . .) I
2. se _____ de Qch (to have one's eyes opened, lose one's illusions about . . .) IV
3. _____ Qn de Qch (to disabuse . . . of . . .) VI

désaccoutumer

1. se _____ de Qch (to get out of the habit of . . .) IV
2. se _____ de *Inf.* (to get out of the habit of, become unused to ---*ing*) IX-A
3. _____ Qn de *Inf.* (to break . . . of the habit of, to get . . . out of the habit of ---*ing*) IX-B

descendre

1. _____ Qn ou Qch (Coll: to knock . . . down) I
2. _____ Qch (to go down . . . *e.g.*, a street, the stairs; to bring down, lower . . .) I
3. _____ à Qch (to get off [*e.g.*, the train, bus] at . . .) II
4. _____ de Qn ou Qch (to be descended from . . .) IV
5. _____ de Qch (to get off, to come down from . . .) IV
6. _____ *Inf.* (to go down[stairs] to . . .; to stop off to . . .) VII-A

désenchanter

1. _____ Qn (to disenchant, disillusion . . .) I
2. être désenchanté de Qch (to be disenchanted, disillusioned with . . .) IV
3. _____ Qn de Qch (to disenchant, disillusion . . . with . . .) VI

désencombrer

1. _____ Qch (to disencumber, clear . . . *e.g.*, a road) I
2. _____ Qch de Qch (to clear, free . . . of . . .) VI

désennuyer

1. _____ Qn (to divert, cheer up [someone who is bored]) I
2. se _____ à *Inf.* (to relieve one's boredom [by] ---*ing*) VIII-A

désespérer
1. ———— Qn (to discourage, dishearten . . .) I
2. ———— de Qn ou Qch (to despair of . . .; to lose hope in . . .) IV
3. ———— de *Inf.* (to despair of ---*ing*) IX-A

déshabituer
1. se ———— de Qch (to break oneself of the habit of . . .; to become unaccustomed to . . .) IV
2. ———— Qn de Qch (to break . . . of the habit, to make . . . lose the habit of . . .) VI
3. se ———— de *Inf.* (to break oneself of the habit of, to lose the habit of ---*ing*) IX-A
4. ———— Qn de *Inf.* (to break . . . of the habit of ---*ing*; to disaccustom . . . to ---*ing*) IX-B

désigner
1. ———— Qn ou Qch (to designate, point out, appoint . . .) I
2. ———— Qn à, pour Qch (to appoint . . . to . . .; to nominate . . . for . . .; to recommend . . . for . . .) VI
3. ———— Qch à Qn (to point out . . . to . . .) VI
4. ———— Qn pour *Inf.* (to appoint, designate, qualify . . . to . . .) X

désintéresser
1. ———— Qn (to buy out . . .; to pay off [a creditor]) I
2. se ———— de Qn ou Qch (to lose interest, to take no further interest in . . .) IV

désirer
1. ———— Qn ou Qch (to desire, want . . .) I
2. ———— *Inf.* (to want to, wish to . . .) VII-A

désister (se)
1. se ———— de Qch (to desist from . . .; to waive . . . *e.g.*, a claim) IV

désobéir
1. ———— à Qn ou Qch (to disobey . . .; to break . . . *e.g.*, a rule, a law) II

désoler
1. ———— Qn (to distress, grieve . . .) I
2. se ——— de *Inf.* (to be distressed to . . .; at ---*ing*) IX-A
3. être désolé de *Inf.* ou *Inf. passé* (to be sorry to . . ., to have . . .) IX-A

désolidariser (se)
1. se ——— de, d'avec Qn ou Qch (to break one's ties with, separate oneself from . . .) IV, V

dessaisir
1. se ——— de Qch (to relinquish, give up . . .) IV
2. ———— Qn de Qch (to dispossess . . . of . . .) VI

destiner
1. se ——— à Qch (to intend to take up . . . *e.g.*, a profession) III
2. ———— Qn ou Qch à Qch (to intend, mean . . . for . . .; to destine . . . to . . .; to plan a career for . . . in . . .) VI
3. être destiné à *Inf.* (to be destined, doomed to . . .) VIII-A

destituer
1. ———— Qn (to dismiss, remove . . . from office) I
2. être destitué de Qch (to be deprived of, lacking in, without . . .) IV
3. ———— Qn de Qch (to dismiss . . . from . . .; to deprive . . . of . . .) VI

détacher
1. se ——— de Qn ou Qch (to separate, break away from . . .) IV
2. se ——— sur Qch (to stand out against . . .) V
3. ———— Qn ou Qch de Qn ou Qch (to separate, detach . . . from . . .) VI

déteindre
1. _____ Qch (to take the color out of . . .) I
2. _____ sur Qn (to influence, make its mark on . . .) V
3. _____ sur Qch (of colors: to fade, bleed, run on . . .) V

déterminer
1. _____ Qch (to determine, settle, cause . . .) I
2. se _____ à *Inf.* (to make up one's mind to . . .) VIII-A
3. _____ Qn à *Inf.* (to induce, decide . . . to . . .) VIII-B
4. _____ de *Inf.* (to resolve, decide to . . .) IX-A

détester
1. _____ Qn ou Qch (to detest, hate . . .) I
2. _____ *Inf.* (to hate to . . .; to detest ---*ing*) VII-A

détourner
1. _____ Qch (to divert, turn aside . . .) I
2. se _____ de Qn ou Qch (to turn away, turn aside from . . .) IV
3. _____ Qn ou Qch de Qn ou Qch (to divert, turn . . . aside from . . .; to entice . . . away from . . .) VI

déverser
1. _____ Qch (to pour, pour out, dump . . .) I
2. se _____ dans Qch (to flow, pour into . . .) V
3. _____ Qch sur Qch (to pour, dump . . . on . . .) VI

dévêtir
1. _____ Qn (to undress . . .) I
2. se _____ (to disrobe) I
3. se _____ de Qch (to divest oneself of . . .) IV

devoir
1. _____ Qch (to owe . . . *e.g.*, money) I
2. se _____ à Qn ou Qch (to have a duty, an obligation to . . . *e.g.*, *à sa patrie*, to one's country; *à ses enfants*, to one's children) III

3. _____ Qch à Qn (to owe someone something) VI
4. _____ *Inf.* (to have to, be supposed to, must . . . Ex: *Je dois partir tout de suite*, I have to leave immediately; *Elle doit être malade*, she must be sick) VII-A
5. se _____ de *Inf.* (to be one's duty to . . .) IX-A
6. _____ à Qn de *Inf.* (to owe it to . . . to . . .) IX-B

dévouer
1. être dévoué à Qn (to be devoted to . . .) II
2. se _____ pour Qn (to sacrifice oneself for . . .) V
3. se _____ pour *Inf.* (to sacrifice oneself [in order] to . . .) X

dicter
1. _____ Qch (to dictate, impose . . .) I
2. _____ Qch à Qn (to dictate, prescribe . . . to . . .) VI

différencier
1. se _____ de Qn ou Qch (to distinguish oneself from, be different from . . .) IV
2. _____ entre Qch et Qch (to distinguish between . . . and . . .) V
3. _____ Qn ou Qch de Qn ou Qch (to differentiate . . . from . . .) VI

différer
1. _____ Qch (to defer, put off, postpone . . .) I
2. _____ de Qch (to differ in . . . *e.g.*, *d'opinion*, in opinion; to be different in . . .) IV
3. _____ de Qn ou Qch (to differ from . . .) IV
4. _____ sur Qch (to differ on . . .) V
5. _____ de, à *Inf.* (Lit: to put off, postpone ---*ing*) IX-A, VIII-A

diminuer
1. _____ Qch (to reduce . . .) I
2. _____ de Qch (to diminish in . . .) IV

dîner
1. _____ de Qch (to dine on . . .) IV

dire
1. _____ Qch (to say, tell . . .) I
2. _____ Qch à Qn (to tell, say . . . to . . .) VI
3. _____ Qch de Qn ou Qch (to say . . . about . . .) VI
4. _____ à Qn de *Inf.* (to tell, order . . . to . . .) IX-B

diriger
1. _____ Qch (to direct, manage, guide . . .) I
2. se _____ vers Qn ou Qch (to head for, go up to . . .) V
3. _____ Qch contre Qn (to aim, level . . . [*e.g.*, an accusation] at . . .) VI
4. _____ Qch sur, vers Qn ou Qch (to direct, aim, point . . . at, towards . . .) VI

disconvenir
1. _____ de Qch (to disagree with . . .; usually in negative: to admit, not deny . . . Ex: *Je n'en disconviens pas*, I don't deny it) IV

discourir
1. _____ sur Qch (to discourse, hold forth on . . .) V

discréditer
1. _____ Qn ou Qch (to discredit, disparage . . .) I
2. se _____ auprès de Qn (to fall into discredit with, lose the esteem of . . .) V

disculper
1. se _____ de Qch (to exculpate oneself from, clear oneself of . . .) IV
2. _____ Qn de Qch (to clear . . . of . . .; to exonerate . . . from . . .) VI

discuter
1. _____ Qch (to discuss, debate, question . . .) I
2. _____ de Qch [avec Qn] (to discuss, talk over . . . [with . . .]) IV
3. _____ sur Qch [avec Qn] (to discuss, to quibble about . . . [with . . .]) V

disparaître
1. _____ de Qch (to disappear from . . .) IV

dispenser
1. se _____ de Qch (to excuse oneself from, to get out of . . .) IV
2. _____ Qch à Qn (to dispense, distribute . . . to . .) VI
3. _____ Qn de Qch (to exempt, excuse . . . from . . .) VI
4. se _____ de *Inf.* (to excuse oneself from, to get out of ---*ing*) IX-A
5. _____ Qn de *Inf.* (to excuse, exempt . . . from ---*ing*) IX-B

disposer
1. _____ Qch (to arrange, set out . . .) I
2. _____ de Qn ou Qch (to dispose of . . .; to have . . . at one's disposal) IV
3. _____ Qn à Qch (to dispose . . . to . . .; to prepare . . . [psychologically] for . . .) VI
4. se _____ à *Inf.* (to get ready to . . .) VIII-A
5. _____ Qn à *Inf.* (to dispose, incline, prepare . . . to . . .) VIII-B

disputer
1. _____ Qch (to dispute, contest . . .) I
2. se _____ avec Qn (to quarrel with . . .) V
3. se _____ pour Qch (to quarrel, wrangle over, about . . .) V
4. _____ Qch à Qn (to contend with someone for something) VI

disserter
1. _____ sur Qch (to hold forth on [a subject]) V

dissimuler
1. _____ Qch (to hide, cover up . . .) I
2. _____ Qch à Qn (to hide, keep . . . from . . .) VI

dissuader
1. _____ Qn de Qch (to dissuade . . . from . . .) VI
2. _____ Qn de *Inf.* (to dissuade . . . from ---*ing*) IX-B

distinguer
1. _____ Qn ou Qch (to distinguish . . .) I
2. se _____ de Qn ou Qch (to distinguish oneself from, stand out from . . .) IV
3. se _____ [de Qn ou Qch] par Qch (of people: to distinguish oneself by . . .; of things: to be remarkable for . . .) V
4. _____ entre deux choses (to distinguish between . . .) V
5. _____ Qn ou Qch de, d'avec Qn ou Qch (to distinguish . . . from . . .) VI

distraire
1. _____ Qn ou Qch (to divert, distract, entertain . . .) I
2. _____ Qn de Qch (to divert, distract . . . from . . .; to take someone's mind off . . .) VI

distribuer
1. _____ Qch (to distribute, give out, arrange . . .) I
2. _____ Qch à Qn (to distribute, give out . . . to . . .) VI

diverger
1. _____ de Qch (to diverge from . . .) IV

divertir

1. _____ Qn ou Qch (to divert, amuse . . .) I
2. se _____ (to amuse oneself) I
3. se _____ de Qn ou Qch (to be amused by . . .) IV
4. se _____ à *Inf.* (to amuse oneself [by] ---*ing*) VIII-A

diviser

1. _____ Qch (to divide . . .) I
2. se _____ en Qch (to divide, be divided into . . .) V
3. _____ Qch entre Qn (to divide . . . among . . .) VI
4. _____ Qch en Qch (to divide . . . into . . .) VI

divorcer

1. _____ d'avec, avec Qn (to divorce . . .) V

documenter

1. _____ Qch (to document . . .) I
2. se _____ sur Qch (to collect material, gather documentary evidence on . . .) V
3. _____ Qn sur Qch (to furnish someone with information, documents on, about . . .) VI

dominer

1. _____ Qn ou Qch (to dominate, to tower above . . .) I
2. se _____ (to be in control of oneself) I
3. _____ sur Qn ou Qch (to prevail, have dominion over . . .) V

donner

1. _____ Qch (to give . . .) I
2. se _____ à Qn ou Qch (to give oneself up to, to devote oneself to . . .) III
3. _____ dans Qch (to fall into . . . *e.g., dans un piège,* into a trap; to fall into, go in for . . . Ex: *Il donne dans le fanatisme,* he is becoming a fanatic) V
4. se _____ pour Qn ou Qch (to claim to be, to present oneself as . . .) V
5. _____ sur Qch (to look out on, to face . . . *e.g.,* the garden, the street) V

6. _____ Qn ou Qch à Qn (to give . . . to . . .) VI
7. _____ Qch pour, contre Qch (to exchange . . . for . . .) VI
8. _____ à *Inf.* à Qn (to give someone something to . . . Ex: *donner à boire à quelqu'un*, to give someone something to drink) VIII-B
9. _____ à Qn de *Inf.* (to permit, enable . . . to . . .) IX-B
10. Il est donné à Qn de *Inf.* (It is possible for . . . to . . .) IX-B

doter
1. _____ Qn (to give a dowry to . . .) I
2. _____ Qch (to endow, equip . . .) I
3. _____ Qn ou Qch de Qch (to endow, equip . . . with . . .; Lit: [figurative sense] to endow . . . with . . .) VI

doubler
1. _____ Qn (to pass . . . *e.g.*, on a road; to replace [an actor]) I
2. _____ Qch (to double . . .; to fold . . . in half; to line . . . *e.g.*, a coat; to dub . . . *e.g.*, a film; to pass . . . *e.g.*, on a highway) I
3. _____ Qch de Qch (to line, dub . . . with . . .) VI

douer
1. être doué pour Qch (to have a gift for . . .) V
2. _____ Qn de Qch (to endow . . . with . . .) VI

douter
1. _____ de Qn (to doubt, mistrust . . .) IV
2. _____ de Qch (to doubt . . .) IV
3. se _____ de Qch (to suspect, surmise . . .) IV
4. _____ de *Inf.* ou *Inf. passé* (to doubt that one will, has . . . Ex: *Je doute d'arriver à l'heure*, I doubt that I will arrive on time; *je doute de lui avoir dit cela*, I doubt that I told him that) IX-A

draper
1. _____ Qch (to drape, cover . . .) I
2. se _____ dans, de Qch (to drape oneself in . . .; to make a show of . . . Ex: *se draper dans sa vertu*, to make a show of one's virtue) V, IV

dresser
1. _____ Qn (to train . . .) I
2. _____ Qch (to raise, erect, prepare, draw up . . .) I
3. se _____ contre Qn ou Qch (to rise up against . . .) V
4. _____ Qn à *Inf.* (to train . . . to . . .) VIII-B

E

ébahir
1. _____ Qn (to astound, flabbergast . . .) I
2. s'_____ de Qch (to be amazed, dumbfounded at, by . . .) IV
3. s'_____ de *Inf.* (to be amazed, dumbfounded at ---*ing*) IX-A

éblouir
1. _____ Qn (to dazzle . . .) I
2. être ébloui de Qch (to be dazzled by . . .) IV

écarter
1. _____ Qn ou Qch (to separate . . .; to divert, move . . . aside) I
2. s'_____ de Qch (to deviate, stray from . . .) IV
3. _____ Qn ou Qch de Qch (to separate . . . from . . .; to move, lead . . . away from . . .) VI

échanger
1. _____ Qch (to exchange . . .) I
2. _____ Qch contre, pour Qch (to exchange, barter . . . for . . .) VI

échapper
1. _____ à Qn ou Qch (to escape, escape from . . . Ex: *Son nom m'échappe*, his name escapes me; *Il alla au Mexique pour échapper à la police*, he went to Mexico to escape from the police; to slip out of, away from . . . Ex: *La tasse m'a échappé des mains*, the cup slipped out of my hands; *Une remarque indiscrète m'a échappé*, I let slip an indiscreet remark) II
2. s'_____ de Qch (to escape from . . .) IV

échoir
1. _____ à Qn (to fall to, befall . . .) II

éclaircir
1. _____ Qch (to clear up, lighten, explain, clarify . . .) I
2. _____ Qn sur Qch (to enlighten . . . on . . .) VI

éclater
1. _____ en Qch (to burst into . . . *e.g.*, *en applaudissements*, into applause; *en sanglots*, into sobs) V
2. _____ *de rire* (to burst out laughing)

écouter
1. _____ Qn ou Qch (to listen to . . .) I
2. _____ *Inf.* Qn ou Qch (to listen to someone or something . . .) VII-B

écraser
1. _____ Qn ou Qch (to crush, run over . . .) I
2. être écrasé de Qch (to be overburdened, overwhelmed with . . .) IV
3. être écrasé par Qch (to be crushed, run over by . . .) V
4. _____ Qn de Qch (to overwhelm, overburden . . . with . . .) VI

écrire
1. _____ Qch (to write . . .) I
2. _____ à Qn (to write to . . .) II
3. _____ Qch à Qn (to write . . . to . . .) VI

effacer
1. _____ Qch (to erase, obliterate . . .) I
2. s'_____ devant Qn ou Qch (to yield, accede to . . .) V
3. _____ Qch de Qch (to erase . . . from . . .) VI

effarer
1. _____ Qn (to scare, bewilder . . .) I
2. s'_____ de Qn ou Qch (to be scared, frightened by, at . . .) IV

effaroucher
1. _____ Qn (to scare away, startle . . .) I
2. s'_____ de Qn ou Qch (to be scared, startled by . . .) IV

efforcer (s')
1. s'_____ de *Inf.* (to strive, try hard to . . .) IX-A

effrayer
1. _____ Qn (to frighten . . .) I
2. s'_____ de Qch (to be frightened at, by . . .) IV

élancer
1. _____ à Qn (to cause pain to . . . by a throbbing, twinging sensation, Ex: *Le doigt m'élance,* my finger is throbbing) II
2. s'_____ *sur un cheval, sur une moto, sur une bicyclette,* to leap onto, astride a horse, a motorcycle, a bicycle) V

élever
1. _____ Qn ou Qch (to bring up . . . *e.g.,* a child; to raise, erect . . .) I
2. s'_____ à Qch (to rise to . . .; to amount to . . . Ex: *L'addition s'élève à 20 francs,* the bill comes to 20 francs) III
3. s'_____ au-dessus de Qch (to rise above . . .) V
4. s'_____ contre Qn ou Qch (to protest against . . .) V

éliminer
1. _____ Qn ou Qch (to eliminate . . .) I
2. _____ Qn ou Qch de Qch (to eliminate . . . from . . .) VI

éloigner
1. _____ Qn ou Qch (to remove, distance, send away . . .) I
2. s'_____ de Qn ou Qch (to stray, digress, move away from, become estranged from . . .) IV
3. _____ Qn ou Qch de Qch (to move, remove, send . . . away from . . .) VI
4. _____ Qn de Qn (to alienate, separate . . . from . . .) VI

émailler
1. _____ Qch (to enamel, glaze . . .) I
2. _____ Qch de Qch (to sprinkle . . . with . . . Ex: *émailler un texte de citations*, to sprinkle a text with quotations) VI

émanciper
1. _____ Qn ou Qch (to emancipate . . .) I
2. s'_____ de Qch (to free oneself from . . .) IV
3. _____ Qn de Qch (to free . . . from . . .) VI

émaner
1. _____ de Qn ou Qch (to emanate from . . .) IV

emballer
1. _____ Qn (Coll: to excite, thrill . . .) I
2. _____ Qch (to wrap up, pack . . .; to race [a motor]) I
3. s'_____ (of horses: to run away; of people [Coll.]: to get carried away) I
4. s'_____ de Qn ou Qch (Coll: to be crazy about, to have a sudden passion for . . .) IV
5. être emballé par Qch (to be crazy about, to have a sudden passion for . . .) V

embarquer
1. ────── Qn ou Qch (to embark, to ship, to load . . .) I
2. s'────── dans Qch (to embark in, get into . . . [especially a risky affair]) V
3. ────── Qn dans Qch (to draw . . . into . . . [especially something risky]) VI
4. ────── Qch dans Qch (to load . . . in . . .) VI

embarrasser
1. ────── Qn ou Qch (to encumber, hamper, obstruct . . .) I
2. s'────── de Qch (to burden, trouble oneself with . . .) IV
3. ────── Qn de Qch (to encumber . . . with . . .) VI

embrancher
1. ────── Qch (to join up . . . *e.g.*, roads, pipes) I
2. s'────── sur Qch (to branch off from . . .) V

émerger
1. ────── de Qch (to emerge from . . .) IV

émerveiller
1. ────── Qn (to amaze, astonish . . .) I
2. s'────── de Qch (to marvel at, be astonished at, by . . .) IV

emmitoufler
1. ────── Qn (to bundle up . . .) I
2. s'────── dans, de Qch (to bundle up in . . .) V, IV
3. ────── Qn dans, de Qch (to bundle up . . . in . . .) VI

émouvoir
1. ────── Qn (to stir up, affect, move . . .) I
2. s'────── (to be moved, anxious, upset) I
3. s'────── de Qch (to be moved, upset by . . .) IV
4. être ému par Qch (to be moved, upset by . . .) V

empaqueter
1. ────── Qch (to wrap up . . .) I
2. ────── Qch dans. Qch (to wrap up . . . in . . .) VI

emparer (s')
1. s'────── de Qn ou Qch (to seize, take hold of . . .) IV

empêcher
1. _____ Qch (to prevent, hinder . . .) I
2. s'_____ de *Inf.* (to refrain from ---*ing*; Especially in the negative: Ex: *Elle ne pouvait s'empêcher de rire*, she couldn't help laughing) IX-A
3. _____ Qn ou Qch de *Inf.* (to prevent . . . from ---*ing*) IX-B

empêtrer
1. _____ Qn ou Qch (to entangle, involve, hamper . . .) I
2. s'_____ de Qn ou Qch (to become entangled, involved with . . .; to hamper, burden oneself with . . .) IV
3. s'_____ dans Qch (to become entangled in . . .) V
4. _____ Qn dans Qch (to involve, entangle . . . in . . .) VI

empiéter
1. _____ sur Qn ou Qch (to encroach upon . . .) V

empiffrer
1. s'_____ de Qch (Coll: to stuff oneself with . . . *e.g.*, *de bonbons*, with candy) IV
2. _____ Qn de Qch (Coll: to stuff . . . with . . .) VI

employer
1. _____ Qn ou Qch (to use, employ . . .) I
2. s'_____ (to be used, Ex: *Cette expression ne s'emploie plus*, that expression is no longer used) I
3. s'_____ à Qch (to apply oneself, devote oneself to . . .) III
4. _____ Qn à Qch (to employ . . . at, in . . .; to occupy . . . with . . .) VI
5. _____ Qn comme Qch (to employ . . . as . . . *e.g.*, *comme secrétaire*, as a secretary) VI
6. s'_____ à *Inf.* (to spend one's time ---*ing*; to work hard at ---*ing*) VIII-A
7. _____ [son temps, son argent] à *Inf.* (to use . . . to, for . . . Ex: *J'ai employé mon après-midi de congé à faire des courses en ville*, I used my afternoon off to do errands downtown) VIII-B

emporter
1. ———— Qn ou Qch (to carry away, take away . . .) I
2. s'———— (to lose one's temper) I
3. s'———— contre Qn ou Qch (to flare up at, inveigh against . . .) V
4. l' ———— sur Qn ou Qch (to prevail over, get the better of, overcome . . .) V

empreindre
1. ———— Qch (to imprint, stamp . . .) I
2. ———— Qch de Qch (to imprint, stamp . . . with . . .) VI

empresser (s')
1. s'———— auprès de Qn (to be attentive to, to make a fuss over . . .) V
2. s'———— à *Inf.* (to be eager to . . .) VIII-A
3. s'———— de *Inf.* (to hurry, hasten to . . .) IX-A

emprunter
1. ———— Qch (to borrow . . .) I
2. ———— Qch à Qn ou Qch (to borrow . . . from . . .) VI

enamourer (s')
1. s'———— de Qn (Lit: to become enamored of . . .) IV
2. être enamouré de Qn (Lit: to be enamored of . . .) IV

encadrer
1. ———— Qch (to frame . . .) I
2. ———— Qch de Qch (to frame . . . with . . .) VI

enchanter
1. ———— Qn ou Qch (to bewitch, charm, delight . . .) I
2. être enchanté de Qch (to be delighted with . . .) IV
3. être enchanté de *Inf.* (to be delighted to . . .) IX-A

enchasser
1. _____ Qch (to enshrine, set [a stone], insert . . .) I
2. _____ Qch dans Qch (to enshrine, set, insert . . . in . . .) VI

enchérir
1. _____ sur Qn (to outbid . . . *e.g.*, in an auction; to outdo . . .) V
2. _____ sur Qch (to surpass, go beyond . . .) V

enchevêtrer
1. _____ Qch (to mix up, confuse, tangle up . . .) I
2. s'_____ dans Qch (to become confused, mixed up, tangled up in . . .) V

enclaver
1. _____ Qch (to enclose, wedge in, dovetail . . .) I
2. _____ Qch dans Qch (to enclose, wedge . . . in . . .) VI

encombrer
1. _____ Qn ou Qch (to encumber, congest, load down . . .) I
2. s'_____ de Qch (to burden oneself, saddle oneself with . . .) IV

encourager
1. _____ Qn ou Qch (to encourage . . .) I
2. _____ Qn à *Inf.* (to encourage . . . to . . .) VIII-B

enduire
1. _____ Qch (to coat, smear, plaster . . .) I
2. _____ Qch de Qch (to coat, smear, plaster . . . with . . .) VI

endurcir
1. _____ Qn ou Qch (to harden, toughen . . .) I
2. s'_____ à Qch (to become inured, hardened to . . .) III
3. _____ Qn à Qch (to inure . . . to . . .) VI

enfermer
1. _____ Qn ou Qch (to shut, lock . . . up; to enclose . . .) I
2. _____ Qn ou Qch dans Qch (to enclose, shut . . . up in
 . . .) VI

enfuir (s')
1. s'_____ (to run away, escape, flee) I
2. s'_____ de Qch (to run away, escape, flee from . . .) IV

engager
1. _____ Qn ou Qch (to pledge, engage, begin, involve, enlist . . .) I
2. s'_____ chez Qn (to enter the service of . . .) V
3. s'_____ dans Qch (to enter, venture into . . .) V
4. s'_____ à *Inf.* (to undertake to . . .; to pledge one's word
 to . . .) VIII-A
5. _____ Qn à *Inf.* (to advise, urge . . . to . . .) VIII-B

englober
1. _____ Qch (to include, embrace . . .) I
2. _____ Qch dans Qch (to include . . . in . . .; to join,
 annex . . . to . . .) VI

engouer (s')
1. s'_____ de Qn (to become infatuated with . . .) IV

engraisser
1. _____ Qn (to fatten [animals]) I
2. _____ Qch (to fertilize [land]) I
3. s'_____ de Qch (to thrive on, grow fat, rich on . . .) IV

enhardir
1. _____ Qn (to embolden . . .) I
2. s'_____ à, jusqu'à *Inf.* (to venture to, to be so bold as to
 . . .) VIII-A
3. _____ Qn à *Inf.* (to encourage . . . to . . .) VIII-B

enivrer
1. _____ Qn (to intoxicate, inebriate . . .) I
2. s'_____ de Qch (to become intoxicated, inebriated with
. . .) IV

enjamber
1. _____ Qch (to step over, stride over, span . . .) I
2. _____ sur Qch (to project over . . .; to encroach on
. . .) V

enjoindre
1. _____ Qch (to enjoin . . .) I
2. _____ à Qn de *Inf.* (to enjoin, direct . . . to . . .) IX-B

enlever
1. _____ Qn ou Qch (to remove, take away, take up, lift
up, carry away . . .) I
2. _____ Qn ou Qch à Qn (to take . . . from, away from
. . .) VI
3. _____ Qch de Qch (to remove . . . from . . .) VI

ennuyer
1. _____ Qn (to bore, annoy, bother . . .) I
2. s'_____ (to be bored) I
3. s'_____ de Qn (to miss . . .) IV
4. s'_____ à *Inf.* (to be bored [with] ---*ing*) VIII-A
5. s'_____ à *mourir* à *Inf.* (to be bored to death ---*ing*)
VIII-A

enorgueillir
1. _____ Qn (to make . . . proud, puffed up) I
2. s'_____ de Qch (to pride oneself on, to boast of . . .) IV
3. s'_____ de *Inf. passé* (to pride oneself on, to boast of having . . .) IX-A

enquérir (s')
1. s'_____ de Qn ou Qch (to ask, inquire about . . .) IV

enrager
1. faire *enrager* Qn (to drive . . . crazy) I
2. ———— de Qch (to be furious about . . .) IV
3. être enragé contre Qn (to be furious at . . .) V
4. ———— de *Inf.* ou *Inf. passé* (to be furious at ---*ing*, at having . . . Ex: *Il enrageait d'avoir agi si bêtement*, he was furious at having acted so stupidly) IX-A

enrichir
1. ———— Qn ou Qch (to enrich, make . . . wealthy) I
2. s'———— de Qch (to grow rich on, grow richer in . . .) IV
3. s'———— en Qch (to grow rich, richer in . . .) V
4. ———— Qch de Qch (to enrich . . . with . . .) VI

enrober
1. ———— Qch (to coat, cover, wrap . . .) I
2. ———— Qch de Qch (to coat, cover . . . with . . .) VI
3. ———— Qch dans Qch (to wrap . . . in . . .) VI

enrôler
1. ———— Qn (to enroll, recruit, enlist . . .) I
2. s'———— dans Qch (to enroll, enlist in . . .) V
3. ———— Qn dans Qch (to enroll, enlist . . . in . . .) VI

enrouler
1. ———— Qch (to roll up, wind, wrap up . . .) I
2. s'———— autour de Qch (to wind, coil around . . .) V
3. ———— Qch dans Qch (to wrap up . . . in . . .) VI

enseigner
1. ———— Qch (to teach . . .) I
2. ———— Qch à Qn (to teach . . . to . . .) VI
3. ———— à Qn à *Inf.* (to teach . . . to, how to . . .) VIII-B

entendre
1. _____ Qn ou Qch (to hear, understand, intend, mean . . .) I
2. s'_____ (to understand one another, to get along) I
3. ne _____ rien à Qch (to know nothing about . . . Ex: *Je n'entends rien aux mathématiques*, I don't know the first thing about mathematics) II
4. _____ *parler* de Qn ou Qch (to hear of, about . . .) IV
5. s'_____ avec Qn (to get along with . . .) V
6. _____ *Inf.* (to intend, mean to . . .) VII-A
7. _____ *Inf.* Qn ou Qch (to hear someone or something . . . Ex: *J'entends chanter les oiseaux*, I hear the birds singing) VII-B
8. s'_____ à *Inf.* (to understand, know how to . . .) VIII-A

enter
1. _____ Qch (to graft . . .) I
2. _____ Qch sur Qch (to graft . . . on, onto . . .) VI

entêter
1. _____ Qn (to give . . . a headache; to make . . . giddy; to go to someone's head) I
2. s'_____ dans Qch (to persist [obstinately] in . . .) V
3. s'_____ à *Inf.* (to be bent on ---*ing*; to persist in ---*ing*) VIII-A

enthousiasmer
1. _____ Qn (to fill . . . with enthusiasm) I
2. s'_____ pour Qn ou Qch (to be enthusiastic, go into raptures over . . .) V

enticher
1. s'_____ de Qn ou Qch (to be infatuated with, crazy about . . .) IV
2. être entiché de Qn ou Qch (to be infatuated with, crazy about . . .) IV

entortiller

1. _____ Qn (to get the better of, outwit . . .) I
2. _____ Qch (to twist, complicate . . .) I
3. s'_____ autour de Qch (to twist, wind around . . .) V
4. s'_____ dans Qch (to get entangled in . . .) V
5. _____ Qch autour de Qch (to wind, twist . . . around . . .) VI
6. _____ Qch dans Qch (to wrap up . . . in . . .) VI

entourer

1. _____ Qn ou Qch (to surround . . .) I
2. s'_____ de Qn ou Qch (to surround oneself with . . .) IV
3. _____ Qn ou Qch de Qn ou Qch (to surround . . . with . . .) VI

entraîner

1. _____ Qn ou Qch (to carry along or away, to entail, to lead to . . .; to train . . . *e.g.*, an athlete) I
2. _____ Qn à Qch (to train, coach . . . in . . .) VI
3. _____ Qn dans Qch (to lead . . . into . . ., involve . . . in . . . Ex: *entraîner quelqu'un dans le vice, dans une aventure*, to lead someone into vice, into an adventure) VI
4. s'_____ à *Inf.* (to train, accustom oneself to . . .) VIII-A
5. _____ Qn à *Inf.* (to lead, cause . . . to . . .) VIII-B

entrecouper

1. _____ Qch (to interrupt, intersect . . .) I
2. _____ Qch de Qch (to interrupt, intersperse . . . with . . .) VI

entrelarder

1. _____ Qch (to lard . . .) I
2. _____ Qch de Qch (to lard, interlard . . . with . . .) VI

entremêler
1. _____ Qch (to blend, mix . . .) I
2. s'_____ (to intermingle) I
3. s'_____ dans Qch (to interfere in . . .) V
4. _____ Qch de, parmi Qch (to intermingle, intersperse
. . . with, among . . .) VI

entremettre (s')
1. s'_____ dans Qch (to intervene in . . .) V
2. s'_____ pour Qn dans Qch (to intercede, act as a go-
between for . . . in . . .) V
3. s'_____ pour Qn auprès de Qn (to intercede for, on behalf
of . . . with . . .) V

entreprendre
1. _____ Qch (to undertake . . .) I
2. _____ Qn (to start a discussion with . . .; to attempt to
convince, seduce . . .) I
3. _____ de *Inf.* (to undertake to . . .) IX-A

entrer
1. _____ dans, en, à* Qch (to enter, go into, come into, be
included in, play a part in . . .; *entrer dans une
colère terrible*, to fly into a rage) V, II
2. _____ *en ménage* (to set up housekeeping) V
3. _____ *en religion* (to enter a religious order) V

entretenir
1. _____ Qn ou Qch (to maintain, support, keep up . . .) I
2. s'_____ avec Qn (to converse, chat with . . .) V
3. s'_____ de Qch (to converse, talk about . . .) IV
4. _____ Qn de Qch (to talk to . . . about . . .) VI

envier
1. _____ Qn ou Qch (to be envious of . . .) I
2. _____ Qch à Qn (to envy someone something) VI

---

*See Appendix II: **DANS, EN, À**, p. 298.

environner
1. ———— Qn ou Qch (to surround . . .) I
2. s'———— de Qn ou Qch (to surround oneself with . . .) IV
3. être environné de Qch (to be surrounded with, by . . .) IV

envoyer
1. ———— Qn ou Qch (to send . . .) I
2. ———— *chercher* Qn ou Qch (to send for . . .) I
3. ———— Qn ou Qch à Qn ou Qch (to send . . . to . . .) VI
4. ———— Qn *Inf.* (to send . . . to . . .) VII-B

épargner
1. ———— Qn ou Qch (to save, spare, be sparing with . . .) I
2. ———— Qch à Qn (to spare someone something, Ex: *Epargnez-moi les détails,* spare me the details) VI

épiloguer
1. ———— sur Qch (to split hairs, go on endlessly about . . .) V

époumoner (s')
1. s'———— à *Inf.* (to talk, shout oneself hoarse, out of breath ---*ing*) VIII-A

épouvanter
1. ———— Qn (to terrify . . .) I
2. être épouvanté de Qch (to be astounded, appalled by . . . Ex: *être épouvanté de la montée des prix,* to be astounded by the rise in prices) IV
3. être épouvanté par Qch (to be terrified by . . .) V

éprendre (s')
1. s'———— de Qn (to become infatuated with, to fall in love with . . .) IV
2. s'———— de Qch (to take a fancy to, develop a passion for . . .) IV

épuiser
1. _____ Qn ou Qch (to exhaust, use up, wear out . . .) I
2. s'_____ en Qch (to exhaust oneself in . . . Ex: *s'épuiser en efforts inutiles*, to exhaust oneself in useless endeavors) V
3. s'_____ à *Inf.* (to exhaust oneself ---*ing*) VIII-A

équivaloir
1. _____ à Qch (to be equivalent to . . .) II
2. _____ à *Inf.* (to be equivalent to, tantamount to ---*ing*) VIII-A

éreinter
1. _____ Qn ou Qch (to break the back of . . . *e.g.*, of a horse; to criticize . . . unmercifully, Ex: *Ce film a été éreinté par les critiques*, this film was panned by the critics) I
2. s'_____ à Qch (to wear oneself out at . . .) III
3. s'_____ à *Inf.* (to wear oneself out ---*ing*) VIII-A

ergoter
1. _____ sur Qch (to split hairs, quibble about . . .) V

ériger
1. _____ Qch (to erect, establish . . .) I
2. s'_____ en Qch (to set oneself up as, to pose as . . . Ex: *Il s'érige en expert*, he sets himself up as an expert) V
3. _____ Qn ou Qch en Qch (to set . . . up as . . .; to elevate . . . to . . .) VI

escrimer (s')
1. s'_____ à *Inf.* (to try hard to . . .; to peg away at ---*ing*) VIII-A

escroquer
1. _____ Qn (to swindle . . .) I
2. _____ Qch à Qn (to rob, cheat someone out of something) VI

espérer
1. _____ Qch (to hope for . . .) I
2. _____ en Qn ou Qch (to trust in, put one's trust in . . . *e.g., en Dieu,* in God) V
3. _____ Qch de Qn ou Qch (to expect . . . from . . .) VI
4. _____ *Inf.* (to hope to . . .) VII-A

esquinter
1. _____ Qn ou Qch (Coll: to exhaust, ruin, smash, criticize severely . . .) I
2. s'_____ Qch (Coll: to ruin, "wreck" one's . . . Ex: *s'esquinter les yeux,* to ruin one's eyes; *s'esquinter le tempérament,* to worry too much) I
3. s'_____ à *Inf.* (Coll: to exhaust oneself, "kill" oneself ---*ing*) VIII-A
4. s'_____ Qch à *Inf.* (Coll: to ruin one's . . . ---*ing,* Ex: *s'esquinter les yeux à lire sans lumière,* to ruin one's eyes reading without light) VIII-B

essayer
1. _____ Qch (to try, try on, try out . . .) I
2. s'_____ à Qch (to try one's hand, one's skill at . . .) III
3. _____ de Qch (to try . . . *e.g.,* wine, food, a restaurant) IV
4. s'_____ à *Inf.* (to try one's hand, one's skill at ---*ing*) VIII-A
5. _____ de *Inf.* (to try to . . .) IX-A

étayer
1. _____ Qch (to prop up, stay, support . . .) I
2. s'_____ contre Qch (to steady oneself against . . .) V
3. _____ Qch de Qch (to prop up, support . . . with . . .) VI

étendre

1. _____ Qch (to spread, stretch out, extend, dilute . . .) I
2. s'_____ sur Qch (to stretch out on . . . *e.g., sur l'herbe*, on the grass; to expatiate on . . . *e.g., sur un sujet*, on a subject) V
3. _____ Qch de Qch (to dilute, stretch . . . with . . .) VI

étonner

1. _____ Qn (to surprise, astonish . . .) I
2. s'_____ de Qch (to be surprised, astonished at, by . . .) IV

être

1. _____ à, dans, en* Qch (to be at, in . . . Ex: *Elle est à San Francisco*, she is in San Francisco) II, V
2. en _____ à Qch (to have reached, to be at . . . Ex: *J'en suis au deuxième chapitre*, I'm on the second chapter)
3. _____ *tout* à Qch (to be involved in, devoting one's time to . . . Ex: *Elle est tout à son travail*, she is involved in her work)
4. _____ à Qn (to belong to . . . Ex: *Ce livre est à moi*, this is my book; to be at someone's disposal, Ex: *Je suis à vous dans un instant*, I'll be with you in a moment) III
5. _____ de Qn (to be by, be created by . . . Ex: *Ce tableau est d'Ingres*, this painting is by Ingres) IV
6. _____ de* Qch (to be from . . . *e.g.*, from Chicago; to be a member of, to participate in . . . Ex: *Il est de la famille*, he is one of the family) IV
7. _____ en Qch (to be dressed in . . . Ex: *Ils étaient en tenue de soirée*, they were wearing evening clothes) V
8. en _____ pour Qch (to have spent, expended . . . to no avail; to have nothing for . . . Ex: *Il en est pour ses frais*, he has nothing for his trouble, for what he spent) V

---

*See Appendix I: **PREPOSITIONS OF GEOGRAPHICAL LOCATION**, p. 289.

9. ———— *pour quelque chose, pour beaucoup*; *n'être pour rien* dans Qch (to have something, a lot; to have nothing to do with . . . Ex: *Nous n'avons été pour rien dans cette affaire*, we had no part in this business) V

10. ———— Qch pour Qn (to be, to mean . . . to . . . Ex: *Il n'est rien pour moi*, he means nothing to me) VI

11. ———— à *Inf.* (of people: to be occupied, in the midst of ---*ing*; of things: *Ce jambon est à cuire*, this ham is to be cooked, isn't cooked; *cette maison est à vendre*, this house is for sale) VIII-A

12. C'est à Qn de *Inf.* (to be one's duty, one's turn to . . . Ex: *C'est à vous de le faire*, it's up to you to do it) IX-B

évader (s')
1. s'———— de Qch (to escape from . . .) IV

évanouir (s')
1. s'———— (to vanish, disappear; to faint, swoon) I
2. s'———— de Qch (to faint from . . . *e.g.*, *de peur*, from fear) IV

évertuer (s')
1. s'———— à, pour *Inf.* (to strive to . . .) VIII-A, X

évincer
1, ———— Qn (to evict, oust . . .) I
2. ———— Qn de Qch (to evict, eject . . . from . . .) VI

éviter
1. ———— Qn ou Qch (to avoid . . .) I
2. ———— Qch à Qn (to spare someone something, *e.g.*, trouble) VI
3. ———— de *Inf.* (to avoid ---*ing*) IX-A

exceller
1. _____ dans, en* Qch (to excel in, at . . .) V
2. _____ à *Inf.* (to excel at ---*ing*) VIII-A

excepter
1. _____ Qn ou Qch de Qch (to except, exclude . . . from . . .) VI

exciter
1. _____ Qn ou Qch (to excite, arouse, stir up, provoke . . .) I
2. s'_____ (to get excited, worked up) I
3. _____ Qn à Qch (to exhort, incite . . . to . . .) VI
4. _____ Qn contre Qn (to set . . . against . . .) VI

exclure
1. _____ Qn ou Qch (to exclude, preclude . . .) I
2. _____ Qn ou Qch de Qch (to exclude . . . from . . .) VI

excuser
1. _____ Qn ou Qch (to excuse, pardon . . .) I
2. s'_____ de Qch (to apologize for . . .) IV
3. s'_____ auprès de Qn (to make apologies to . . .) V
4. s'_____ de *Inf.* ou *Inf. passé* (to apologize for ---*ing*, for having . . .) IX-A
5. _____ Qn de *Inf.* ou *Inf. passé* (to excuse . . . for ---*ing*, for having . . .; to excuse, exempt . . . from ---*ing*) IX-B

exempter
1. _____ Qn de Qch (to exempt, excuse . . . from . . .) VI
2. s'_____ de *Inf.* (to abstain from, get out of ---*ing*) IX-A
3. _____ Qn de *Inf.* (to exempt . . . from ---*ing*) IX-B

---

*See Appendix II: **DANS, EN, À**, p. 298.

exercer

1. _____ Qn ou Qch (to train, exert, exercise, practice . . .) I

2. s'_____ à Qch (to practice . . .) III

3. s'_____ à *Inf.* (to practice ---*ing*) VIII-A

4. _____ Qn à *Inf.* (to train . . . to . . .) VIII-B

exhorter

1. _____ Qn à Qch (to exhort . . . to . . .) VI

2. _____ Qn à *Inf.* (to exhort, urge . . . to . . .) VIII-B

exiger

1. _____ Qch (to demand, require . . .) I

2. _____ Qch de Qn (to demand, require, exact . . . from . . .) VI

exonérer

1. _____ Qn ou Qch (to exonerate, exempt . . .) I

2. _____ Qn ou Qch de Qch (to exonerate, exempt, free . . . from . . .) VI

expliquer

1. _____ Qch (to explain . . .) I

2. s'_____ avec Qn (to justify oneself to . . .; to have it out with . . .) V

3. s'_____ sur Qch (to explain one's views on, one's conduct in . . .) V

4. _____ Qch à Qn (to explain . . . to . . .) VI

exposer

1. _____ Qn ou Qch (to expose, exhibit, set forth . . .) I

2. s'_____ à Qch (to expose oneself to . . . *e.g., à un danger*, to danger; to lay oneself open to . . . *e.g., à des critiques*, to criticism) III

3. _____ Qn ou Qch à Qch (to expose . . . to . . .) VI

exprimer

1. _____ Qch (to express, to squeeze out . . .) I

2. _____ Qch à Qn (to express . . . to . . .) VI

3. _____ Qch de Qch (to squeeze out . . . from . . . *e.g.,* juice from an orange) VI

expulser
1. ———— Qn ou Qch (to expel, eject . . .) I
2. ———— Qn ou Qch de Qch (to expel, eject . . . from . . .)
        VI

extasier (s')
1. s'———— sur Qch (to go into raptures over . . .) V

exténuer
1. ———— Qn (to exhaust, tire out . . .) I
2. s'———— à *Inf.* (to exhaust oneself ---*ing*) VIII-A

extorquer
1. ———— Qch (to extort . . .) I
2. ———— Qch à Qn (to extort . . . from . . .) VI

extraire
1. ———— Qch (to extract, take out, excerpt . . .) I
2. s'———— de Qch (to extricate oneself from . . .) IV
3. ———— Qn ou Qch de Qch (to extract, excerpt . . . from
        . . .) VI

F

fâcher
1. ———— Qn (to anger . . .) I
2. se ———— (to get angry) I
3. se ———— de Qch (to be angered by . . .) IV
4. être fâché de Qch (to be angry at, sorry for . . .) IV
5. se ———— avec Qn (to have a falling out with . . .) V
6. se ———— contre Qn (to get angry with . . .) V
7. être fâché contre Qn (to be angry with, sore at . . .) V
8. être fâché de *Inf.* ou *Inf. passé* (to be vexed, angry, sorry to
        . . ., to have . . .) IX-A

faciliter

1. ———— Qch (to facilitate, make . . . easier) I
2. ———— Qch à Qn (to facilitate, make . . . easier for . . .) VI

façonner

1. ———— Qn ou Qch (to work, shape, form . . .) I
2. se ———— à Qch (to accustom oneself to . . .) III

faillir

1. ———— *Inf.* (to almost . . . Ex: *J'ai failli manquer le train*, I almost missed the train) VII-A

faire

1. ———— Qch (to make, do . . .) I
2. se ———— à Qn ou Qch (to get accustomed to . . .) III
3. ———— *attention* à Qn ou Qch (to pay attention to . . .) III
4. être fait pour Qn ou Qch (to be made for, cut out for . . .) V
5. ———— Qch à Qn (to make, do . . . for, to . . .) VI
6. ———— Qn ou Qch de Qn ou Qch (to make . . . from, out of . . .) VI
7. ne ———— que *Inf.* (to only, to do nothing but . . . Ex: *Elle ne fait que travailler*, she does nothing but work) VII-A
8. se ———— *Inf.* (to have oneself, get oneself . . . Ex: *Il s'est fait nommer à un poste important*, he got himself appointed to an important position) VII-A
9. ———— *Inf.* Qn ou Qch (to have, make someone or something . . . Ex: *Il fait attendre ses clients*, he makes his clients wait) VII-B
10. ———— *Inf.* Qch à Qn (to have something done by someone, to someone, or for someone, Ex: *J'ai fait lire la lettre à mon frère*, I had my brother read the letter OR I had the letter read to my brother: to avoid ambiguity, use *par* for the first meaning in place of *à*. *J'ai fait faire une robe à ma mère*, I had a dress made for my mother OR I had my mother make a dress: to avoid ambiguity, use *pour* for the first meaning in place of *à*.) VII-B

11. ne _____ que de *Inf.* (to have just, to have only just . . .
Ex: *Il ne fait que d'arriver*, he has [only] just
arrived) IX-A
12. être fait pour *Inf.* (to be made to . . ., for ---*ing*) X

falloir
[Impersonal verb]
1. Il faut Qch à Qn (to be lacking, necessary to . . . Must be
used with an indirect object pronoun, Ex: *Il me
faut un nouveau parapluie*, I need a new um-
brella) VI
2. Il faut *Inf.* (to be necessary to . . . Ex: *Il faut travailler pour
réussir*, one must work in order to succeed; *Il
faut partir*, [I] [you] [we] [they] must leave) VII-
A
3. Il faut à Qn *Inf.* (to need to, to have to . . . Must be used
with an indirect object pronoun, Ex: *Il lui faut
rentrer tout de suite*, he has to go home immediately) VII-B

familiariser
1. se _____ avec Qch (to familiarize oneself with, to get to
know . . .) V
2. _____ Qn avec Qch (to familiarize . . . with . . .; to accustom . . . to . . .) VI

farcir
1. _____ Qch (to stuff . . .) I
2. _____ Qch de Qch (to stuff . . . with . . .) VI

farfouiller
1. _____ dans Qch (Coll: to rummage [about] in . . .) V

fatiguer
1. _____ Qn ou Qch (to fatigue, tire, tire out . . .) I
2. être fatigué de Qn ou Qch (to be tired of . . .) IV
3. se _____ à *Inf.* (to get tired ---*ing*) VIII-A
4. _____ Qn ou Qch à *Inf.* (to tire someone or something
---*ing*) VIII-B

feindre
1. _____ Qch (to feign . . .) I
2. _____ de *Inf.* (to pretend to . . .) IX-A

féliciter
1. se _____ de Qch (to be pleased with . . .; to pat oneself on the back for . . .) IV
2. _____ Qn de, pour ou sur Qch (to congratulate, compliment . . . for, on . . .) VI
3. _____ Qn de *Inf. passé* (to congratulate, compliment . . . for, on having . . .) IX-B

fendre
1. _____ Qch (to cleave, split . . .; to break [one's heart]) I
2. se _____ (to split, crack) I
3. se _____ de Qch (Coll: to fork out, to offer to pay . . .) IV

fermer
1. _____ Qch (to close, shut . . .) I
2. _____ Qch à Qn (to close . . . to, on . . . Ex: *fermer la porte à quelqu'un*, to close the door on someone) VI

ferrer
1. _____ Qn ou Qch (to fit, mount . . . with iron; to shoe a [horse]) I
2. être ferré en Qch (Coll: to be skilled in, good in . . . Ex: *Il n'est pas très ferré en français*, he is not very good in French) V
3. être ferré sur Qch (Coll: to know all about . . .) V

fiancer
1. se _____ avec, à Qn (to become engaged to . . .) V, III

ficher
1. se _____ de Qn ou Qch (Coll: to not care about, to make fun of . . .) IV

fier (se)
1. se _____ à Qn ou Qch (to trust, rely on, confide in . . .) III

figurer
1. _____ Qn ou Qch (to represent . . .) I
2. se _____ Qch (to imagine, fancy . . .) I
3. _____ dans Qch (to figure in, appear in, play a role in . . .) V
4. _____ sur Qch (to appear on . . .) V

finir
1. _____ Qch (to finish, end . . .) I
2. en _____ avec Qn ou Qch (to have done with, be done with . . .) V
3. _____ de *Inf.* (to finish ---*ing*) IX-A
4. _____ par *Inf.* (to finish, end, end up by ---*ing*) X

fixer
1. _____ Qn (to stare at . . .) I
2. _____ Qch (to fix, fasten, determine . . .) I
3. se _____ à Qch (to stick to, hold fast to . . . *e.g., à une opinion*, to an opinion; to be fastened to . . .) III
4. se _____ à, dans, en* Qch (to settle in . . . *e.g., à Paris,* in Paris) III, V
5. se _____ sur Qch (to be set on, fixed on . . .) V
6. être fixé sur Qn ou Qch (to have no further doubts about . . .) V
7. _____ Qn sur Qch (to give . . . definite information about . . .) VI
8. _____ Qch sur Qn ou Qch (to fix, fasten . . . on . . . Ex: *fixer les yeux sur quelqu'un,* to gaze at, fix one's eyes on someone) VI

---

*See Appendix I: **PREPOSITIONS OF GEOGRAPHICAL LOCATION**, p. 289.

flatter

1. _____ Qn (to flatter . . .; to stroke [an animal]) I
2. se _____ de Qch (to give oneself credit for . . .) IV
3. être flatté de Qch (to feel flattered by . . .) IV
4. _____ Qn de Qch (to delude, lead . . . on with . . .) VI
5. se _____ de *Inf.* (to flatter oneself, feel sure that one will . . . Ex: *Il se flatte de réussir*, he is quite confident that he will succeed) IX-A
6. se _____ de *Inf. passé* (to give oneself credit for having . . .) IX-A

flirter

1. _____ avec Qn ou Qch (to flirt with . . .) V

foisonner

1. _____ de Qch (to be swarming with . . .) IV
2. _____ en Qch (to abound in . . .) V

foncer

1. _____ Qch (to darken . . .; to dig a [well]; to fit a bottom to [a cask]) I
2. _____ sur Qn (to rush, charge [at] . . .) V

fonder

1. _____ Qch (to found, start, set up . . .) I
2. se _____ sur Qch (to put one's reliance on, to be based on . . .) V
3. _____ Qch sur Qch (to ground, base . . . on . . .) VI
4. être fondé à *Inf.* (to be entitled to . . .; to be justified in ---*ing*) VIII-A

fondre

1. _____ Qch (to melt, dissolve . . .) I
2. _____ sur Qn (to swoop down on, pounce on . . .) V
3. _____ en Qch (to melt, dissolve into . . . Ex: *fondre en larmes*, to dissolve into tears) V

forcer
1. ———— Qn ou Qch (to force, compel, break open, break through . . .) I
2. se ———— à *Inf.* (to force oneself to . . .) VIII-A
3. ———— Qn à ou de *Inf.* (to force, compel . . . to . . . *À* is more common; *de* is more literary) VIII-B, IX-B
4. être forcé de *Inf.* (to be forced to . . .) IX-A

forfaire
1. ———— à Qch (Lit: to forfeit . . . *e.g.*, *à l'honneur*, one's honor; to fail in . . . Ex: *forfaire à ses engagements*, to fail to uphold one's commitments) II

formaliser (se)
1. se ———— de Qch (to take offense at . . .) IV

former
1. ———— Qn ou Qch (to form, shape, train . . .) I
2. ———— Qn à Qch (to train, school . . . in . . .) VI

fortifier
1. ———— Qn ou Qch (to strengthen, fortify, confirm . . .) I
2. se ———— dans Qch (to strengthen one's . . . Ex: *se fortifier dans sa résolution*, to strengthen one's resolve) V
3. ———— Qn dans Qch (to encourage, strengthen . . . in . . .) VI

fouiller
1. ———— dans Qch (to search, rummage in . . .) V

fourmiller
1. ———— de Qn ou Qch (to be swarming with, full of . . .) IV

fournir

1. _____ à Qch (to provide for, supply, defray . . . Ex: *fournir à l'entretien de quelqu'un*, to provide for someone's needs) II

2. _____ Qn en Qch (to supply, provide . . . with . . . Ex: *Je peux vous fournir en livres*, I can provide you with books) VI

3. _____ Qch à Qn (to supply, provide . . . to, for . . . Ex: *Cette pâtisserie me fournit mes gâteaux*, I buy cakes at this pastry shop) VI

fourrer

1. se _____ dans Qch (Coll: to get entangled in . . . *e.g., dans une mauvaise affaire*, in a bad affair) V

2. _____ Qch dans Qch (Coll: to stuff, cram, bury, poke . . . in, into . . .) VI

frapper

1. _____ Qn ou Qch (to strike, hit . . .) I

2. être frappé de Qch (to be stricken with . . . *e.g., d'une maladie*, with a disease; to be struck, surprised by . . .) IV

3. _____ à la porte (to knock at, on the door) II

4. être frappé de *Inf.* (to be surprised to . . .) IX-A

fraterniser

1. _____ avec Qn (to fraternize with . . .) V

frayer

1. _____ Qch (to clear, open up . . . *e.g.*, a road) I

2. _____ avec Qn (to associate, consort with . . .) V

3. _____ Qch à Qn (to clear, open up . . . for . . . Ex: *frayer un passage à quelqu'un*, to clear a path for someone) VI

frémir

1. _____ de Qch (to shudder, quiver with . . . *e.g., de peur*, with fear) IV

froisser

1. _____   Qn (to offend . . .; to hurt someone's feelings) I
2. _____   Qch (to rumple, crumple, bruise . . .) I
3. se _____ (to take offense) I
4. se _____ de Qch (to take offense at . . .) IV

frotter

1. _____   Qn ou Qch (to rub, polish . . .) I
2. se _____ à Qn ou Qch (to provoke, to meddle with . . .; to rub shoulders with . . .) III
3. se _____ contre Qn ou Qch (person or animal as subject: to rub against . . .) V
4. _____   contre Qch (thing as subject [*e.g.*, a piece of a mechanism]: to rub, grind against . . .) V

frustrer

1. _____   Qn (to frustrate, disappoint, defraud . . .) I
2. _____   Qn de Qch (to defraud . . . of . . .) VI

fulminer

1. _____   contre Qn ou Qch (to inveigh against . . .) V

G

gagner

1. _____   Qn ou Qch (to earn, win, reach . . .) I
2. se _____ (of diseases: to be catching) I
3. _____   à Qch (to win at, in . . . Ex: *gagner aux échecs*, to win at chess; *gagner à la loterie*, to win [in] the lottery; to profit, gain by . . .) II
4. _____   en Qch (to gain, increase in . . . *e.g.*, *en prestige*, in prestige) V

5. être gagné par Qch (to be overcome by, with . . . *e.g., par l'émotion*, by, with emotion) V
6. _____ Qn à Qch (to win . . . over to . . . *e.g., à une cause*, to a cause) VI
7. _____ Qch à Qch (to win . . . at, in . . . Ex: *gagner de l'argent au jeu*, to win money gambling) VI
8. _____ à *Inf.* (to gain, profit by ---*ing*, Ex: *Elle gagne à être connue*, the better you know her, the more you like her) VIII-A
9. _____ de *Inf.* (to obtain the result, the advantage of ---*ing*) IX-A

garantir
1. _____ Qch (to guarantee, vouch for . . .) I
2. _____ Qch à Qn (to guarantee someone something) VI
3. _____ Qn ou Qch de Qch (to protect, shelter . . . from . . .) VI
4. _____ Qn ou Qch contre Qch (to protect, insure . . . against . . .) VI

garder
1. _____ Qn ou Qch (to keep, guard, protect . . .; to stay in . . . Ex: *garder le lit*, to stay in bed) I
2. se _____ de Qn ou Qch (to beware of . . .) IV
3. _____ Qn ou Qch de Qch (to protect . . . from . . .) VI
4. se _____ de *Inf.* (to take care not to . . .) IX-A

garer
1. _____ Qch (to park, garage . . .) I
2. se _____ (to get out of the way; to park one's car) I
3. se _____ de Qch (to get out of the way of . . .) IV

garnir
1. _____ Qch (to furnish, trim, garnish, decorate . . .) I
2. _____ Qch de Qch (to furnish, trim, garnish, decorate . . . with . . . Ex: *garnir un balcon de fleurs*, to decorate a balcony with flowers) VI

gausser (se)
1. se ___ de Qn ou Qch (Lit: to poke fun at . . .) IV

gaver
1. ___ Qn (to cram [poultry]; to feed . . . forcibly) I
2. se ___ (to eat excessively) I
3. se ___ de Qch (to gorge oneself on . . .) IV
4. être gavé de Qch (Coll: to be showered with . . . *e.g.*, *d'honneurs*, with honors) IV

gémir
1. ___ de Qch (to groan, moan with . . . *e.g.*, *de douleur*, with pain) IV
2. ___ sur Qch (to bemoan . . . Ex: *gémir sur son sort*, to bemoan one's fate) V

gendarmer (se)
1. se ___ contre Qn ou Qch (to fly off the handle at . . .; to be up in arms against . . .) V

glisser
1. ___ de Qch (to slip out of . . . Ex: *Le verre m'a glissé des mains*, the glass slipped out of my hands) IV
2. se ___ dans Qch (to slip, steal into . . .) V
3. ___ sur Qch (to slip, slide, glide over, on . . .) V
4. ___ sur Qn (to make little or no impression on . . .) V
5. ___ Qch à Qn (to slip . . . to . . .) VI
6. ___ Qch dans Qch (to slip . . . into . . .) VI
7. ___ Qch sous Qch (to slip . . . under . . .) VI

glorifier
1. ___ Qn ou Qch (to glorify, praise, celebrate . . .) I
2. se ___ de Qch (to boast of . . .) IV
3. se ___ de *Inf.* ou *Inf. passé* (to boast of ---*ing*, of having . . .) IX-A

gloser
1. ———— Qch (to gloss [a text]) I
2. ———— sur Qch (to discuss . . . exhaustively and often futilely) V

gonfler
1. ———— Qn ou Qch (to inflate, swell . . .) I
2. se —— (to become inflated, distended) I
3. se —— de Qch (to swell up with . . . *e.g.*, *d'orgueil*, with pride) IV
4. ———— Qn ou Qch de Qch (to fill, inflate . . . with . . .) VI

gorger
1. ———— Qn (to cram [poultry]) I
2. ———— Qch (to glut, saturate . . .) I
3. se —— (to stuff, gorge oneself) I
4. être gorgé de Qch (to be stuffed, filled, glutted, saturated with . . . Ex: *La terre était gorgée d'eau*, the ground was saturated with water) IV

goûter
1. ———— (to taste, enjoy . . .) I
2. ———— à Qch (to sample, take a little of . . .; to taste . . . critically) II
3. ———— de Qch (to try out, try . . . for the first time, *e.g.*, a food, a trade) IV

grandir
1. ———— Qch (to enlarge, increase . . .) I
2. ———— en Qch (to grow, increase in . . . *e.g.*, *en sagesse*, in wisdom) V

gratifier
1. ———— Qn de Qch (to bestow, confer something on someone) VI

gratter
1. ———— Qn ou Qch (to scratch . . .) I
2. ———— *de la guitare, du violon* (to play the guitar, the violin mediocrely) IV

graver
1. _____ Qch (to engrave, carve . . .; to cut [a record]) I
2. _____ Qch dans Qch (to engrave, carve, imprint . . . in . . .) VI
3. _____ Qch sur Qch (to engrave, carve . . . on . . .) VI

greffer
1. se _____ sur Qch (to be added to . . .) V
2. _____ Qch sur Qch (to graft . . . on, onto . . .; to add . . . to . . .) VI

grever
1. _____ Qch (to burden . . . financially; to encumber, entail [an estate]; to mortgage, assess [property]) I
2. être grevé de Qch (to be burdened with, saddled with . . . Ex: *un homme grevé de dettes*, a man burdened with debts) IV
3. _____ Qn ou Qch de Qch (to burden, saddle . . . with . . .) VI

griller
1. _____ Qch (to grill, broil, toast . . .) I
2. _____ de *Inf.* (to be anxious, itching to . . .) IX-A

grimper
1. _____ Qch (to climb . . .) I
2. _____ à Qch (to climb, climb up, climb to . . .) II
3. _____ sur Qch (to climb up on . . .) V

griser
1. _____ Qn (to intoxicate . . .; to go to someone's head, Ex: *Les succès l'ont grisé*, success has gone to his head) I
2. se _____ (to get tipsy) I
3. se _____ de Qch (to become intoxicated with, to revel in . . .) IV
4. _____ Qn de Qch (to intoxicate, turn someone's head with . . .) VI

gronder
1. _____ Qn (to scold . . .) I
2. _____ Qn de *Inf. passé* (to scold . . . for having . . .) IX-B

grouiller
1. _____ de Qch (to swarm, teem with, be crawling with . . .) IV

guérir
1. _____ Qn ou Qch (to cure, heal . . .) I
2. se _____ (to recover, to cure oneself) I
3. _____ de Qch (to recover from, get over . . .) IV
4. se _____ de Qch (to cure, rid oneself of . . .) IV
5. _____ Qn de Qch (to cure . . . of . . .) VI

guerroyer
1. _____ contre Qn ou Qch (to wage war against . . .) V

guider
1. _____ Qn ou Qch (to guide . . .) I
2. se _____ sur Qch (to follow, to use . . . as a point of reference) V

H

habiliter
1. _____ Qn à *Inf.* (to enable, entitle . . . to . . .) VIII-B

habiller
1. _____ Qn ou Qch (to dress . . .) I
2. s'_____ de Qch (to dress in . . . *e.g., d'une vieille robe de chambre*, in an old bathrobe) IV
3. s'_____ en Qn (to dress as . . . *e.g., en Pierrot*, as a clown) V
4. s'_____ en [une couleur] (to dress in . . . *e.g., en bleu*, in blue) V
5. _____ Qn ou Qch de Qch (to dress . . . in . . .) VI
6. _____ Qn ou Qch en Qn (to dress . . . as . . .) VI
7. _____ Qn ou Qch en [une couleur] (to dress . . . in . . .) VI

habiter

1. _____ [un endroit] (to reside, live in . . . Ex: *habiter un palais, la campagne, Paris,* to live in a palace, in the country, in Paris) I

2. _____ à [un endroit] (to have one's home in, at . . . Ex: *habiter à la campagne, à Paris,* to live in the country, in Paris) II

3. _____ chez Qn (to live at the home of . . .) V

4. _____ dans* *une rue, une avenue* (to live on a street, an avenue) V

5. _____ sur* *une route, un boulevard* (to live on a highway, a boulevard) V

habituer

1. s'_____ à Qn ou Qch (to get used to . . .) III

2. _____ Qn à Qn ou Qch (to accustom . . . to . . .) VI

3. s'_____ à *Inf.* (to get used to ---*ing*) VIII-A

4. _____ Qn à *Inf.* (to accustom . . . to ---*ing*) VIII-B

haler

1. _____ Qch (to haul, tow . . .) I

2. _____ sur Qch (to haul, pull on . . .) V

harceler

1. _____ Qn (to harass, pester . . .) I

2. _____ Qn de Qch (to pester . . . with . . .) VI

harmoniser

1. _____ Qch (to harmonize, match, blend . . .) I

2. s'_____ avec Qn ou Qch (to harmonize, to be in keeping with . . .) V

hasarder

1. _____ Qch (to risk . . .) I

2. se _____ à *Inf.* (to venture to, dare to . . .) VIII-A

hâter

1. _____ Qn ou Qch (to hasten, hurry . . .) I

2. se _____ de *Inf.* (to hasten, hurry to . . .) IX-A

---

*See Appendix I: **PREPOSITIONS OF GEOGRAPHICAL LOCATION**, p. 289.

hérisser
1. _____ Qch (to bristle, stiffen, ruffle . . .) I
2. se _____ *de peur* (to bristle, stiffen with fear)
3. être hérissé de Qch (to be spiked, studded with . . .) IV
4. _____ Qch de Qch (to spike, stud . . . with . . .) VI

hériter
1. _____ de Qn (to be the heir of . . .) IV
2. _____ de Qch (to inherit . . .) IV
3. _____ Qch de Qn (to inherit . . . from . . .) VI

hésiter
1. _____ à *Inf.* (to hesitate to . . .) VIII-A

heurter
1. _____ Qn ou Qch (to run into, collide with . . .) I
2. se _____ à Qch (to come up against, run into . . . Ex: *se heurter à un obstacle*, to run into a problem) III
3. _____ contre Qch (to beat against . . .) V
4. se _____ contre Qn (to encounter, bump into . . .) V
5. _____ sur Qch (to beat on . . .) V
6. _____ Qch contre Qch (to knock . . . against . . . Ex: *heurter son pied contre la porte*, to stub one's foot against the door) VI

hocher
1. _____ (de) *la tête* (to nod, shake one's head)

honorer
1. _____ Qn ou Qch (to honor . . .) I
2. s'_____ de Qch (to feel honored by . . .; to pride oneself on . . .) IV
3. _____ Qn ou Qch de Qch (to honor . . . by, with . . .) VI
4. s'_____ de *Inf.* ou *Inf. passé* (to be honored, proud to . . ., to have . . .) IX-A

humilier
1. _____ Qn (to humiliate . . .) I
2. s'_____ de *Inf.* ou *Inf. passé* (to be humiliated by, at
---*ing*, by, at having . . .) IX-A

hypnotiser
1. _____ Qn (to hypnotize . . .) I
2. s'_____ sur Qch (to be fascinated by . . .) V
3. être hypnotisé par Qn ou Qch (to be hypnotized, enthralled
by . . .) V

I

identifier
1. _____ Qn ou Qch (to identify . . .) I
2. s'_____ avec, à Qn ou Qch (to identify with . . .) V, III
3. _____ Qn ou Qch avec Qn ou Qch (to identify . . . with
. . .) VI

ignorer
1. _____ Qn ou Qch (to be unaware of . . .) I

illuminer
1. _____ Qn ou Qch (to illuminate . . .) I
2. s'_____ de Qch (to light up with . . . *e.g.*, *de joie*, with
joy) IV

illustrer
1. _____ Qch (to illustrate . . .) I
2. s'_____ dans Qch (to become famous in . . .) V
3. s'_____ par Qch (to become famous for, through . . .) V

imaginer

1. _____ Qch (to imagine, suppose . . .) I
2. s'_____ être Qn ou Qch (to fancy oneself . . . Ex: *Il s'imagine être un homme galant*, he thinks he's a ladies' man) VII-A
3. s'_____ *Inf.* (to imagine, believe that . . . Ex: *Il s'imagine chanter comme Caruso*, he thinks he sings like Caruso) VII-A
4. _____ de *Inf.* (to have the idea to . . .) IX-A

imbiber

1. _____ Qch (to absorb . . .) I
2. s'_____ de Qch (to become saturated with . . .) IV
3. _____ Qn ou Qch de Qch (to saturate, imbue . . . with . . .) VI

imiter

1. _____ Qn ou Qch (to imitate . . .) I
2. être imité de Qn (to be imitated by . . .) IV

immiscer

1. s'_____ dans Qch (to interfere in, with . . .) V
2. _____ Qn dans Qch (to involve . . . in . . .) VI

immoler

1. _____ Qn ou Qch (to immolate, sacrifice . . .) I
2. _____ Qn ou Qch à Qn ou Qch (to sacrifice . . . to . . .) VI

immuniser

1. _____ Qn (to immunize . . .) I
2. _____ Qn contre Qch (to immunize . . . against . . .) VI

impatienter

1. _____ Qn (to make . . . impatient) I
2. s'_____ (to lose patience) I
3. s'_____ de Qch (to get tired of . . .) IV
4. s'_____ contre Qn (to lose patience with . . .) V
5. s'_____ de *Inf.* (to grow annoyed with, tired of ---*ing*) IX-A

implanter
1. _____ Qch (to implant . . .) I
2. s'_____ dans Qch (to take root in . . .) V
3. _____ Qch dans Qch (to implant . . . in . . .) VI

impliquer
1. _____ Qn (to implicate, involve . . .) I
2. _____ Qch (to imply, indicate . . .) I
3. _____ Qn dans Qch (to implicate, involve . . . in . . .) VI

importer
[Only in third person]
1. _____ à Qn ou Qch (to be important, to matter to . . .
Ex: *Les notes importent aux étudiants*, grades
are important to students) II
2. *Il importe de Inf.* (it is important, essential to . . .) IX-A
3. *Il importe à Qn de Inf.* (it is important, essential to . . . to
. . . Ex: *Il importe à Pierre de terminer son
projet*, Pierre is very anxious to finish his project)
IX-B

importuner
1. _____ Qn (to importune, bother . . .) I
2. _____ Qn de Qch (to bother, annoy . . . with . . .) VI

imposer
1. _____ Qch (to impose . . . Ex: *imposer un impôt*, to impose a tax) I
2. en _____ (to inspire respect, admiration)
3. en _____ à Qn (to impose on, deceive . . .) II
4. s'_____ à, chez Qn (to force oneself on . . .) III, V
5. _____ Qch à Qn (to impose, force . . . on . . .) VI

imprégner
1. _____ Qn ou Qch (to impregnate . . .) I
2. s'_____ de Qch (to imbue oneself with . . .) IV
3. _____ Qn ou Qch de Qch (to impregnate . . . with . . .)
VI

impressionner
1. _____ Qn (to impress . . .) I
2. s'_____ de Qch (to be impressed with . . .) IV
3. être impressionné par Qn ou Qch (to be impressed by . . .) V

imputer
1. _____ Qch à Qn ou Qch (to attribute [something negative] to . . .; to accuse someone of something) VI
2. _____ Qch à, sur Qch (to deduct . . . from . . .; to charge . . . to . . . Ex: *imputer une somme à un compte*, to deduct a sum from an account) VI
3. _____ à Qn de *Inf.* (to accuse . . . of ---*ing*) IX-B

inciter
1. _____ Qch (to urge, incite to . . .) I
2. _____ Qn à Qch (to incite . . . to . . .) VI
3. _____ Qn à *Inf.* (to incite . . . to . . .) VIII-B

incliner
1. _____ Qch (to slant, lower . . .) I
2. s'_____ (to bow) I
3. _____ à Qch (to favor, lean towards . . .) II
4. s'_____ devant Qch (to yield to . . .) V
5. s'_____ devant Qn ou Qch (to bow to . . .) V
6. s'_____ sur Qn ou Qch (to bend over . . .) V
7. _____ à *Inf.* (to be disposed to . . .) VIII-A
8. _____ Qn à *Inf.* (to predispose . . . to . . .) VIII-B

incomber
[Only in third person]
1. _____ à Qn (to be incumbent on, Ex: *Les affaires d'état incombent au souverain*, duties of state are incumbent on the ruler) II
2. *Il incombe à Qn de Inf.* (it behoves one to . . .) IX-B

incorporer

1. _____ Qn ou Qch (to incorporate, draft . . .) I
2. s'_____ avec Qn ou Qch (to become one with . . .) V
3. s'_____ dans, à Qch (to incorporate oneself in . . .) V, III
4. _____ Qn ou Qch dans, à Qch (to incorporate, blend . . . into . . .; to draft . . . into . . .) VI

incriminer

1. _____ Qn ou Qch (to incriminate, indict . . .) I
2. _____ Qn dans Qch (to incriminate . . . in . . .) VI

incruster

1. _____ Qch (to encrust, inlay . . .) I
2. s'_____ dans Qch (to get stuck in . . .) V
3. _____ Qch de Qch (to inlay . . . with . . .) VI
4. _____ Qn ou Qch dans Qch (to embed . . . in . . .) VI

inculper

1. _____ Qn de Qch (to charge . . . with . . . *e.g.*, *de meurtre*, with murder) VI

inculquer

1. _____ Qch (to instill, inculcate . . .) I
2. _____ Qch à Qn (to instill . . . in . . .) VI

indemniser

1. _____ Qn (to compensate . . .) I
2. _____ Qn de Qch (to compensate . . . for . . .) VI

indigner

1. _____ Qn (to make someone indignant) I
2. s'_____ (to become indignant) I
3. s'_____ de Qch (to become indignant at, about . . .) IV
4. s'_____ contre Qn (to become indignant at, with . . .) V

indiquer
1. _____ Qn ou Qch (to indicate, point out . . .) I
2. _____ Qn ou Qch à Qn (to indicate, point out . . . to . . .) VI

indisposer
1. _____ Qn (to make someone ill; to disagree with . . .) I
2. _____ Qn contre Qn ou Qch (to set . . . against . . .) VI

induire
1. _____ Qn *en erreur, en tentation* (to lead . . . into error, into temptation) I

infecter
1. _____ Qn ou Qch (to infect, contaminate . . .) I
2. _____ Qn ou Qch de Qch (to infect, contaminate . . . with . . .) VI

inféoder
1. s'_____ à Qn ou Qch (to swear allegiance to . . .) III

inférer
1. _____ Qch (to infer . . .) I
2. _____ Qch de Qch (to infer . . . from . . .) VI

infester
1. _____ Qch (to infest . . .) I
2. être infesté de Qch (to be infested with . . .) IV
3. _____ Qch de Qch (to infest . . . with . . .) VI

infiltrer (s')
1. s'_____ dans Qch (to seep into . . .) V
2. s'_____ à travers Qch (to seep through . . .) V

infliger
1. _____ Qch (to inflict, impose . . .) I
2. _____ Qch à Qn ou Qch (to inflict, impose . . . on . . .) VI

influer
1. _____ sur Qn ou Qch (to have an effect on . . .; to influence . . .) V

informer
1. _____ Qn (to inform . . .) I
2. s'_____ de Qn ou Qch (to find out about . . .) IV
3. _____ contre Qn (to inform, testify against . . .) V
4. _____ sur Qn ou Qch (to investigate . . .) V
5. _____ Qn de Qch (to inform . . . of . . .) VI

infuser
1. _____ Qch (to infuse, steep . . .) I
2. _____ Qch à Qn (to instill . . . in . . .; to inspire someone with something) VI
3. _____ Qch dans Qch (to steep, infuse . . . in . . .) VI

ingénier
1. s'_____ à *Inf.* (to figure out how to . . .; to be clever enough to . . .) VIII-A

ingérer
1. _____ Qch (to ingest . . .) I
2. s'_____ dans Qch (to meddle in . . .) V

initier
1. _____ Qn ou Qch (to initiate . . .) I
2. s'_____ à Qch (to become familiar with . . .) III
3. _____ Qn à Qch (to familiarize . . . with . . .; to reveal something to someone) VI

innocenter
1. _____ Qn (to clear, justify . . .) I
2. s'_____ de Qch (to clear oneself of . . .) IV
3. _____ Qn de Qch (to clear . . . of . . .; to declare . . . not guilty of . . .) VI

inoculer

1. ———— Qch à Qn (to infect someone with something) VI
2. ———— Qn contre Qch (to vaccinate . . . against . . .) VI

inonder

1. ———— Qn ou Qch (to inundate, flood . . .) I
2. être inondé de Qch (to be deluged with, *e.g.*, *de travail*, with work) IV
3. ———— Qn ou Qch de Qch (to deluge, inundate . . . with . . .) VI

inquiéter

1. ———— Qn (to trouble . . .; to make . . . uneasy) I
2. s'———— de Qn ou Qch (to worry about . . .) IV

inscrire

1. ———— Qn (to enroll, register . . .) I
2. ———— Qch (to inscribe . . .) I
3. s'———— à Qch (to enroll oneself at . . . *e.g.*, *à l'université*, at college) III
4. s'———— dans, sur Qch (to put one's name down in, on . . . *e.g.*, *dans le registre*, in the register; *sur la liste*, on the list) V
5. s'———— pour Qch (to sign up for . . .) V
6. ———— Qn à Qch (to enroll, register . . . in . . . *e.g.*, *inscrire un enfant à l'école*, to régister a child in school) VI
7. ———— Qch dans, sur Qch (to inscribe . . . in, on . . . *e.g.*, *inscrire son nom sur la liste*, to write one's name on the list) VI

insérer

1. ———— Qch (to insert . . .) I
2. ———— Qch dans, sous Qch (to insert . . . in, under . . .) VI

insinuer

1. _____ Qch (to insinuate . . .) I
2. s'_____ dans Qch (to insinuate oneself into . . .; to worm one's way into . . .) V
3. s'_____ entre Qch (to work one's way between . . .) V
4. _____ Qch à Qn (to insinuate . . . to . . .) VI

insister

1. _____ sur Qch (to insist on, emphasize . . .) V
2. _____ pour, à *Inf.* (to insist on ---*ing*) X, VIII-A

inspirer

1. _____ Qn ou Qch (to inspire . . .) I
2. s'_____ de Qn ou Qch (to take one's inspiration from . . .; to base one's work on . . .) IV
3. être inspiré par Qn ou Qch (to be inspired by . . .) V
4. _____ Qch à Qn (to inspire, fill someone with something, Ex: *Il a inspiré son enthousiasme aux autres*, he filled the others with his enthusiasm) VI

instruire

1. _____ Qn (to instruct . . .) I
2. s'_____ de Qch (to inform oneself, to find out about . . .) IV
3. s'_____ dans, en* Qch (to learn, learn how to do . . .) V
4. être instruit par Qch (to learn by . . . e.g., *par l'expérience*, by experience) V
5. _____ Qn de Qch (to inform . . . of . . .) VI
6. _____ Qn dans, en* Qch (to teach someone . . .; to teach someone how to do . . .) VI
7. _____ Qn à *Inf.* (to instruct . . . to . . .) VIII-B

instrumenter

1. _____ Qch (to score, orchestrate . . .) I
2. _____ contre Qn (to order legal proceedings against . . .) V

---

*See Appendix II: **DANS, EN, À**, p. 298.

insulter
1. ———— Qn (to insult . . .) I
2. ———— à Qch (to lack respect for . . . Ex: *insulter aux dieux*, to lack respect for the gods) II

insurger
1. ———— contre Qn ou Qch (to revolt against . . .) V

intégrer
1. ———— Qch (to integrate . . .) I
2. s'———— dans Qch (to combine with . . .; to become assimilated into . . .) V

intenter
1. ———— Qch à, contre Qn (to bring . . . against . . . Ex: *intenter un procès contre quelqu'un*, to bring a suit against someone, to sue someone) VI

intercaler
1. ———— Qch (to intercalate . . .) I
2. ———— Qch dans Qch (to intercalate, insert . . . in . . .) VI

intercéder
1. ———— pour Qn ou Qch auprès de Qn (to intercede for . . . with . . .) V

interdire
1. ———— Qch (to forbid, prohibit . . .) I
2. s'———— Qch (to refuse oneself something) I
3. ———— Qch à Qn (to forbid someone something; to not allow someone something) VI
4. ———— Qn de Qch (to suspend . . . from . . . *e.g., de ses fonctions*, from his or her duties) VI
5. ———— à Qn de *Inf.* (to forbid . . . to . . .) IX-B

intéresser
1. ———— Qn ou Qch (to interest, concern . . .) I
2. s'———— à Qn ou Qch (to be interested in . . .) III
3. s'———— dans Qch (to have a financial, vested interest in . . .) V
4. ———— Qn à Qch (to interest . . . in . . .) VI
5. ———— Qn dans Qch (to involve, give . . . a financial interest in . . .) VI

interner
1. ———— Qn (to intern, imprison . . .) I
2. ———— Qn dans Qch (to intern, imprison . . . in . . .) VI

interpeller
1. ———— Qn (to question, call out to, heckle . . .) I
2. ———— Qn sur Qch (to question . . . about . . .) VI

interposer
1. s'———— (to intervene) I
2. s'———— dans Qch (to intervene in . . .) V
3. s'———— entre Qn ou Qch (to come between . . .) V
4. ———— Qn ou Qch entre Qn ou Qch (to place . . . between . . .) VI

interroger
1. ———— Qn (to interrogate, question . . .) I
2. ———— Qn sur Qn ou Qch (to interrogate . . . about . . .) VI

intervenir
1. ———— dans Qch (to intervene in . . .) V

intimer
1. ———— Qch (to indicate, signify . . .; to intimate . . .) I
2. ———— Qch à Qn (to indicate, signify, intimate . . . to . . .) VI

introduire
1. _____ Qn ou Qch (to insert, bring in, present . . .) I
2. s'_____ dans Qch (to penetrate, to slip into . . .) V
3. _____ Qn ou Qch dans Qch (to insert . . . in . . .; to usher . . . into . . .) VI

invectiver
1. _____ Qn ou Qch (to abuse . . .; to call . . . names) I
2. _____ contre Qn ou Qch (to inveigh against . . .) V

inventer
1. _____ Qch (to invent, make up . . .) I
2. _____ de *Inf.* (to have the idea to . . .) IX-A

investir
1. _____ Qch (to invest . . .; to besiege . . .) I
2. _____ Qn de Qch (to invest, entrust . . . with . . . Ex: *investir quelqu'un de pleins pouvoirs*, to grant full powers to someone) VI

inviter
1. _____ Qn (to invite . . .) I
2. _____ Qn à Qch (to invite, ask . . . to . . .) VI
3. _____ Qn à *Inf.* (to invite, ask . . . to . . .) VIII-B

irriter
1. _____ Qn ou Qch (to irritate . . .) I
2. s'_____ de Qch (to grow angry about . . .) IV
3. s'_____ contre Qn (to grow angry with . . .) V
4. s'_____ à *Inf.* (to get irritated at ---*ing*) VIII-A

isoler
1. _____ Qn ou Qch (to isolate . . .) I
2. s'_____ de Qn ou Qch (to isolate oneself from . . .) IV
3. _____ Qn de, d'avec Qn ou Qch (to isolate . . . from . . .) VI

J

jaillir

1. _____ de Qch (to spurt from . . .) IV

jalonner

1. _____ Qch (to stake, mark out . . .) I
2. _____ Qch à Qn (to stake out, mark . . . for . . .) VI

jalouser

1. _____ Qn ou Qch (to envy, be jealous of . . .) I

jaser

1. _____ de Qn ou Qch (to chatter about . . .) IV

jeter

1. _____ Qn ou Qch (to throw . . .) I
2. se _____ à Qch (to throw oneself at, in . . . *e.g., aux pieds de quelqu'un*, at someone's feet; *à l'eau*, in the water) III
3. se _____ dans, en* Qch (to throw oneself into, in . . .; to flow, empty into . . . Ex: *La Seine se jette dans l'Atlantique*, the Seine empties into the Atlantic Ocean) V
4. se _____ contre, par, sur Qn ou Qch (to throw oneself against, through, on . . .) V
5. _____ Qch à Qn (to throw . . . to . . .) VI
6. _____ Qn ou Qch contre, dans, en*, par, sur Qn ou Qch (to throw . . . against, in, through, on . . .) VI

joindre

1. _____ Qn ou Qch (to join, clasp . . .) I
2. se _____ à Qn ou Qch [pour *Inf.*] (to join with . . . [in order to . . .]) III
3. _____ Qn ou Qch à Qn ou Qch (to join . . . to . . .; to combine . . . with . . .) VI

---

*See Appendix II: **DANS, EN, À**, p. 298.

joncher
1. _____ Qch de Qch (to strew, scatter . . . with . . .) VI

jongler
1. _____ avec Qch (to juggle . . .) V

jouer
1. _____ Qch (to play, *e.g.*, music; to bet, *e.g.*, money; to risk, *e.g.*, one's reputation) I
2. _____ Qn (to trick . . .) I
3. _____ à Qn (to play at being . . . Ex: *jouer à la paysanne*, to play at being a peasant. Note: the pronoun *Y* is used in substitutions. *Elle joue à la paysanne, elle y joue*; she plays at being a peasant, she plays at it) II
4. _____ à Qch (to play at . . . *e.g.*, *à l'amour*, at love; to play a game, Ex: *jouer aux cartes*, to play cards) II
5. _____ de Qch (to play an instrument, *e.g.*, *du piano*, the piano; *de la guitare*, the guitar) IV
6. se _____ de Qn ou Qch (to make fun of . . .; to take . . . lightly) IV
7. _____ avec Qn ou Qch (to play with . . .) V
8. _____ sur Qch (to speculate on . . .; to play on [words]) V
9. _____ *un tour* à Qn (to play a trick on . . .) VI
10. _____ à *Inf.* (to play at ---*ing*) VIII-A

jouir
1. _____ de Qn ou Qch (to enjoy . . .; to take pleasure in . . .) IV

juger
1. _____ Qn ou Qch (to judge . . .) I
2. _____ de Qch (to imagine . . . Ex: *Jugez de ma surprise*, imagine my surprise) IV
3. *À en juger par Qch* (judging by . . . Ex: *Il n'est pas très doué, à en juger par ses réponses*, he's not very smart, judging by his answers)

4. _____ sur Qch (to judge by, on . . . *e.g., sur les apparences*, on appearances) V

5. _____ Qn ou Qch sur Qch (to judge . . . by, on . . .) VI

jurer

1. _____ Qch (to swear . . .) I

2. _____ avec Qch (to clash with . . .) V

3. _____ sur Qch (to swear on, by . . .) V

4. _____ Qch à Qn (to swear . . . to . . .) VI

5. _____ de *Inf.* ou *Inf. passé* (to swear to . . ., to have . . .) IX-A

justifier

1. _____ Qn ou Qch (to justify . . .) I

2. _____ de Qch (to prove, give an account of . . .) IV

3. se _____ de Qch (to prove one's innocence of . . .) IV

4. _____ Qn de Qch (to prove . . . innocent of . . .) VI

L

lâcher

1. _____ Qn ou Qch (to release, let go of . . .; Coll: to drop . . . [*e.g.*, a friend]) I

2. _____ Qch à Qn (to let loose, throw . . . at . . .) VI

laisser

1. _____ Qn ou Qch (to leave, allow . . .) I

2. _____ Qch à Qn (to leave . . . to . . .; to bequeath . . . to . . .) VI

3. _____ Qn ou Qch à Qn (to leave . . . to . . .; to rely on someone for . . . Ex: *laisser les tâches ingrates à quelqu'un*, to leave the dirty work to someone) VI

4. _____ Qn à Qn ou Qch (to leave, abandon . . . to . . .) VI

5. _____   *Inf.* Qn ou Qch (to allow . . . to . . .) VII-B
6. ne _____   pas de *Inf.* (to continue to . . .; to not fail to . . .
     Ex: *La situation politique ne laisse pas de m'in-*
     quiéter, the political situation continues to wor-
     ry me, is a source of worry to me) IX-A

lambrisser
   1. _____   Qch (to panel . . .) I
   2. _____   Qch de Qch (to panel . . . with . . .) VI

lamenter
   1. se _____   sur Qn ou Qch (to lament . . .; to cry over . . .) V
   2. se _____   de *Inf. passé* (to lament, bewail having . . .) IX-A

lancer
   1. _____   Qn ou Qch (to throw, hurl, launch . . .) I
   2. se _____   dans Qch (to take up . . .; to get involved in . . .
     e.g., dans les affaires, in business) V
   3. _____   Qch à Qn (to throw . . . at . . .) VI
   4. _____   Qn ou Qch contre Qn ou Qch (to throw, hurl . . .
     against . . .) VI
   5. _____   Qn ou Qch dans Qch (to throw, launch . . . in,
     into . . .) VI

languir
   1. _____   de Qch (to languish with . . . *e.g., d'amour*, with
     love) IV
   2. _____   pour Qn (to long for . . .) V
   3. _____   après Qch (to long for . . .) V

larder
   1. _____   Qch (to lard . . .) I
   2. _____   Qn ou Qch de Qch (to lard . . . with . . .; to rid-
     dle . . . with . . .) VI

lasser
   1. _____   Qn ou Qch (to tire . . .) I
   2. se _____   de Qn ou Qch (to grow tired of . . .) IV
   3. se _____   à *Inf.* (to tire oneself by ---*ing*) VIII-A

4. _____ Qn à *Inf.* (to tire . . . ---*ing*) VIII-B
5. se _____ de *Inf.* (to grow bored with ---*ing*) IX-A

laver
1. _____ Qn ou Qch (to wash . . .) I
2. se _____ Qch (to wash one's . . . Ex: *se laver les mains*, to wash one's hands) I
3. se _____ de Qch (to cleanse oneself of . . .) IV
4. _____ Qn ou Qch de Qch (to cleanse . . . of . . .) VI
5. _____ Qch à Qn (to wash someone's . . . *e.g.*, face; *laver la tête à quelqu'un*, to chew someone out) VI

légiférer
1. _____ sur Qn ou Qch (to legislate on . . .) V

léguer
1. _____ Qch (to bequeath . . .) I
2. _____ Qch à Qn (to leave, bequeath . . . to . . .) VI

lésiner
1. _____ sur Qch (to be stingy with . . .) V

leurrer
1. _____ Qn ou Qch (to lure, entice . . .; to lead . . . on) I
2. se _____ (to deceive oneself) I
3. _____ Qn par Qch (to lead . . . on with . . . *e.g.*, *par de fausses promesses*, with false promises) VI

lever
1. _____ Qn ou Qch (to raise, lift . . .) I
2. se _____ (to get up) I
3. se _____ de Qch (to get up from . . .) IV

libérer
1. _____ Qn ou Qch (to liberate, free . . .) I
2. _____ Qn ou Qch de Qn ou Qch (to liberate, free . . . from . . .) VI

lier

1. ———— Qn ou Qch (to tie, bind . . .) I
2. se ———— avec Qn (to become friendly, intimate with . . .) V
3. ———— Qn ou Qch à Qch (to tie, bind . . . to . . .) VI

liguer

1. ———— Qn ou Qch (to associate . . . in a league) I
2. ———— avec, contre Qn ou Qch (to conspire with, against . . .) V

limiter

1. ———— Qch (to limit . . .) I
2. se ———— à Qch (to limit, restrict oneself to . . .) III
3. se ———— à *Inf.* (to limit oneself to ---*ing*) VIII-A

lire

1. ———— Qch (to read . . .) I
2. ———— Qch *à haute voix, à voix basse* (to read . . . aloud, softly) I
3. ———— dans Qch (to read in, from . . .) V
4. ———— Qch à Qn (to read . . . to . . .) VI

lisérer

1. ———— Qch (to border, edge . . .) I
2. ———— Qch de Qch (to edge . . . with . . .) VI

livrer

1. ———— Qn ou Qch (to deliver, betray, surrender . . .) I
2. se ———— à Qn ou Qch (to surrender to . . .; to turn oneself in to . . .) III
3. ———— Qn ou Qch à Qn ou Qch (to deliver, hand over . . . to . . .) VI
4. ———— *passage à Qn ou Qch* (to make way for . . .) VI

localiser

1. ———— Qn ou Qch (to locate, localize . . .) I
2. se ———— dans Qch (to become localized in . . .) V
3. ———— Qn ou Qch dans Qch (to center, localize . . . in . . .) VI

loger

1. _____ Qn ou Qch (to lodge, give lodging to . . .; to accommodate, place, fit . . .) I
2. _____ à, dans [un endroit] (to lodge, reside in, on . . . e.g., *à un hôtel,* in a hotel; *dans un vieux quartier,* in an old neighborhood; *au 1ᵉʳ étage,* on the second floor) II, V
3. se _____ dans Qch (to become lodged, stuck in . . .) V
4. _____ Qn à Qch (to put . . . on, in . . . Ex: *On l'avait logé au troisième étage,* they had put him on the fourth floor) VI
5. _____ Qch dans Qch (to lodge, stick . . . in . . .) VI

lorgner

1. _____ Qn ou Qch (to peer at . . .; to have an eye on . . .) I

lotir

1. _____ Qch (to divide, parcel out . . .) I
2. _____ Qn de Qch (to allot something to someone) VI

loucher

1. _____ de Qch (to squint, be cross-eyed in . . . Ex: *loucher de l'oeil gauche,* to have a crossed left eye)
2. _____ vers, sur Qn ou Qch (Coll: to covet . . .; to eye . . . longingly) V

louer

1. _____ Qn ou Qch (to praise . . .) I
2. se _____ de Qn ou Qch (to be pleased, satisfied with . . .) IV
3. _____ Qn ou Qch de Qch (to praise . . . for . . .) VI
4. se _____ de *Inf. passé* (to congratulate oneself for having . . .) IX-A
5. _____ Qn de *Inf. passé* (to congratulate . . . for having . . .) IX-B

louer
1. ———— Qch (to rent . . .) I
2. ———— Qch à Qn (to rent . . . from, to . . .) VI

lutter
1. ———— avec, contre Qn ou Qch (to fight with, against . . .) V

M

macérer
1. ———— Qch (to macerate . . .) I
2. ———— Qch dans Qch (to macerate . . . in . . .) VI

mâcher
1. ———— Qch (to chew, champ at . . .) I
2. ———— Qch à Qn (to make . . . easy for . . .; *mâcher la besogne à quelqu'un*, to make someone's work easier for them; *mâcher les mots à quelqu'un*, to mince words with someone) VI

maigrir
1. ———— Qn (to make someone look thinner, Ex: *Cette robe la maigrit*, that dress makes her look thinner) I
2. ———— de Qch (to lose [weight], Ex: *Elle a maigri de cinq kilos*, she has lost five kilos) IV

maintenir
1. ———— Qch (to maintain . . .) I
2. se ———— contre Qch (to hold out against . . .) V
3. se ———— dans, en* Qch (to remain in . . . e.g., *dans ses fonctions*, in office; *en bonne santé*, in good health) V

---

*See Appendix II: **DANS, EN, À**, p. 298.

4. ———— Qn dans, en* Qch (to maintain, keep . . . in . . . *e.g., dans la pénurie*, in poverty; *en servitude*, in servitude) VI

majorer
1. ———— Qch (to overestimate [a bill, a charge]) I
2. ———— Qch de Qch (to raise the price of . . . by . . .) VI

manger
1. ———— Qn ou Qch (to eat . . .) I
2. ———— Qn ou Qch de Qch (to eat up . . . with . . . *e.g., de caresses*, with kisses; *des yeux*, with one's eyes) VI

manifester
1. ———— Qch (to demonstrate, show, reveal . . .) I
2. se ———— à Qn (to show, reveal oneself to . . .) III
3. ———— Qch à Qn (to demonstrate, reveal, show . . . to . . .) VI

manquer
1. ———— Qn ou Qch (to miss, *e.g.*, a train; to fumble, *e.g.*, a shot) I
2. ———— à Qn ou Qch (to be lacking to . . . Ex: *Le temps lui manque*, he, she is pressed for time; to be missed emotionally by . . . Ex: *Les enfants manquent aux parents*, the parents miss the children) II
3. ———— à Qch (to break, *e.g., à sa parole*, one's word) II
4. ———— de Qch (to lack, be deficient in . . . Ex: *manquer de talent*, to lack talent) IV
5. ne ———— pas de *Inf.* (to be sure to, not fail to . . . Ex: *Il ne manquera pas de venir*, he will not fail to come) IX-A
6. ———— [de] *Inf.* (to nearly . . . Ex: *Il a manqué* [de] *mourir*, he nearly died) IX-A, VII-A

marbrer
1. ———— Qch (to marble . . .) I
2. ———— Qch de Qch (to marble . . . with . . .) VI

---

*See Appendix II: **DANS, EN, À**, p. 298.

marchander
1. ———— Qn (to haggle with . . .) I
2. ———— Qch (to haggle over . . .) I
3. ———— Qch avec Qn (to haggle over . . . with . . .) VI

marier
1. ———— Qn ou Qch (to give . . . in marriage; to perform a marriage for . . .; to blend, *e.g.,* colors) I
2. se ——— avec, à Qn (to marry . . .) V, III
3. ———— Qn ou Qch avec, à Qn ou Qch (to marry . . . to . . .; to join . . . with . . .) VI

mariner
1. ———— Qch (to marinate . . .) I
2. ———— Qch dans Qch (to marinate . . . in . . .) VI

marquer
1. ———— Qn ou Qch (to mark, indicate . . .; to score [points]) I
2. être marqué de Qch (to be marked, disfigured with, by . . .) IV
3. ———— Qch à Qch (to mark . . . with, in . . . *e.g., au crayon,* in pencil) VI
4. ———— Qn ou Qch de Qch (to mark, disfigure . . . with . . . *e.g., de taches,* with splotches) VI

marteler
1. ———— Qch (to hammer . . .) I
2. ———— *le cerveau à Qn* (to worry . . .) VI

masquer
1. ———— Qn ou Qch (to mask, conceal . . .) I
2. ———— Qch à Qn (to conceal . . . from . . .) VI

matcher
1. ———— Qn contre Qn (to match . . . against . . . [in a sports event]) VI

maugréer
1. _____ contre Qn ou Qch (to grumble at . . .) V

médire
1. _____ de Qn ou Qch (to speak ill of . . .) IV

méditer
1. _____ Qch (to ponder . . .; to have . . . in mind) I
2. _____ sur Qch (to reflect on . . .) V

méfier (se)
1. se ____ de Qn ou Qch (to be wary of . . .; to mistrust . . .) IV

méjuger
1. _____ de Qn ou Qch (to misjudge . . .) IV

mélanger
1. _____ Qch (to mix . . .) I
2. _____ Qch avec Qch (to mix . . . with . . .) VI

mêler
1. _____ Qch (to mix, mingle . . .) I
2. se ____ à, dans Qch (to mingle, participate in . . .) III, V
3. se ____ de Qch (to interfere in . . .; to get involved in . . .) IV
4. _____ Qch à, avec Qch (to mix . . . with . . .) VI
5. _____ Qn à, dans Qch (to implicate, involve . . . in . . .) VI

menacer
1. _____ Qn ou Qch (to menace . . .) I
2. _____ Qn de Qch (to threaten . . . with . . .) VI
3. _____ de *Inf.* (to threaten to . . .) IX-A

ménager

1. _____ Qch (to take care of . . .; to use . . . sparingly) I
2. se _____ (to take it easy) I
3. _____ Qch à Qn (to dole out . . . to . . .) VI

mener

1. _____ Qn ou Qch (to lead . . .) I
2. _____ à Qn ou Qch (to lead to . . .) III
3. _____ Qn *Inf.* (to take . . . to . . . Ex: *mener un prison-*
nier voir son avocat, to take a prisoner to see
his lawyer) VII-B

mentionner

1. _____ Qch (to mention . . .) I
2. _____ Qch à Qn (to mention . . . to . . .) VI

mentir

1. _____ à Qn (to lie to . . .) II
2. _____ sur Qch (to lie about . . .) V

méprendre (se)

1. se _____ sur Qn ou Qch (to be mistaken about . . .) V
2. se _____ quant à Qn ou Qch (to be mistaken regarding
. . .) V

mépriser

1. _____ Qn ou Qch (to scorn . . .) I
2. _____ Qn de *Inf.* ou *Inf. passé* (to scorn . . . for ---*ing*,
for having . . .) IX-B

mériter

1. _____ Qn ou Qch (to merit, deserve . . .) I
2. _____ de *Inf.* (to deserve to . . .) IX-A

mesurer
1. _____ Qn ou Qch (to measure . . .) I
2. se _____ avec, à Qn (to match oneself against . . .) V, III
3. _____ Qn ou Qch à Qn ou Qch (to measure . . . to,
against . . .; to proportion . . . to . . .) VI

mésuser
1. _____ de Qch (to misuse . . .) IV

métamorphoser
1. _____ Qn ou Qch (to metamorphose, transform . . .) I
2. se _____ en Qn ou Qch (to turn, change into . . .) V
3. _____ Qn ou Qch en Qn ou Qch (to turn, change . . .
into . . .) VI

mettre
1. _____ Qch (to put, place . . .; to put . . . down; to put
on [clothes]) I
2. se _____ à Qch (to start, begin . . . Ex: *se mettre au travail*, to start work; *se mettre à table*, to sit down
at the table; *se mettre au lit*, to get into bed) III
3. _____ Qn à Qch (to put . . . to . . . Ex: *mettre un pri-
sonnier à mort*, to put a prisoner to death) VI
4. se _____ à *Inf.* (to begin to . . .) VIII-A
5. _____ Qch à *Inf.* (to set, put . . . out to . . . Ex: *mettre
le linge à sécher*, to put the laundry out to dry)
VIII-B

meubler
1. _____ Qch (to furnish . . .) I
2. _____ Qch de Qch (to furnish . . . with, in . . .) VI

meurtrir
1. _____ Qn ou Qch (to bruise . . .) I
2. _____ Qn *de coups* (to beat . . . black and blue) I

militer

1. _____ pour, contre, en faveur de Qn ou Qch (to militate for, against, in favor of . . .) V

miser

1. _____ Qch (to bet, wager . . .) I
2. _____ sur Qn ou Qch (to bet on . . .) V
3. _____ Qch sur Qn ou Qch (to bet . . . on . . .) VI

modeler

1. _____ Qn ou Qch (to model, mould, shape . . .) I
2. se _____ sur Qn ou Qch (to model oneself on, after . . .) V
3. _____ Qn ou Qch sur Qn ou Qch (to model . . . on, after . . .) VI

monter

1. _____ Qch (to take up . . . *e.g.*, a suitcase; to go up . . . *e.g.*, a staircase; to stage . . . *e.g.*, a play) I
2. se _____ [*la tête*] (to get excited) I
3. _____ à* Qch (to ride . . . *e.g.*, *à bicyclette*, a bicycle; *à cheval*, horseback; to climb . . . Ex: *monter à une échelle*, to climb a ladder) II
4. se _____ à Qch (to amount to . . . Ex: *L'addition se monte à vingt dollars*, the bill adds up to twenty dollars) III
5. _____ dans, en* Qch (to board, get on . . . Ex: *monter en voiture*; *dans le bus*, to get in the car, on the bus) V
6. _____ *sur la scène, sur les planches* (to go on the stage) V
7. se _____ en Qch (to outfit oneself in . . .; to stock up on . . .) V
8. _____ *la tête* à Qn [contre Qn] (to get someone upset [with someone]) VI
9. _____ *le coup* à Qn (Coll: to deceive someone) VI
10. _____ Inf. (to go upstairs in order to . . .) VII-A

*See Appendix II: **DANS, EN, À**, p. 298.

montrer
1. _____ Qn ou Qch (to show . . .) I
2. se _____ [+ adjectif] (to show oneself to be . . . *e.g.*, brave) I
3. _____ Qn ou Qch *du doigt* (to point out . . .) I
4. _____ Qn ou Qch à Qn (to show . . . to . . .) VI
5. _____ à Qn à *Inf.* (to show . . . how to . . .) VIII-B

moquer (se)
1. se _____ de Qn ou Qch (to make fun of . . .; to not care about . . .) IV
2. se _____ de *Inf.* (to not care about ---*ing*) IX-A

mordre
1. _____ Qn ou Qch (to bite . . .) I
2. se _____ Qch (to bite one's . . . Ex: *se mordre la langue,* to bite one's tongue) I
3. _____ à Qch (to take a bite of . . .) II
4. _____ dans Qch (to sink one's teeth into . . .) V
5. _____ sur Qch (to encroach on . . .) V

morigéner
1. _____ Qn (to lecture, scold . . .) I
2. _____ Qn de *Inf.* ou *Inf. passé* (to scold . . . for ---*ing*, for having . . .) IX-B

mouiller
1. _____ Qn ou Qch (to moisten, wet . . .) I
2. _____ Qn ou Qch de Qch (to moisten, wet . . . with . . .) VI

mouler
1. _____ Qch (to cast, mould . . .; to outline . . .) I
2. se _____ sur Qn ou Qch (to model oneself on, after . . .) V
3. _____ Qn ou Qch sur Qn ou Qch (to model . . . on, after . . .; to fashion . . . after . . .) VI

mourir

1. _____ de Qch (to die, be dying of . . . *e.g., de pneu-monie*, of pneumonia; *de peur*, of fright) IV
2. _____ [d'envie] de *Inf.* (to be dying to . . .) IX-A

munir

1. se _____ de Qch (to provide oneself with . . .) IV
2. _____ Qn ou Qch de Qch (to provide, furnish . . . with . . .) VI

murer

1. _____ Qch (to wall up, wall in . . .) I
2. se _____ (to isolate oneself) I
3. _____ Qch de Qch (to wall up . . . with . . .) VI

murmurer

1. _____ Qch (to murmer . . .) I
2. _____ contre Qn ou Qch (to complain about, protest against . . .) V
3. _____ Qch à Qn (to murmur . . . to . . .) VI
4. _____ Qch contre Qn ou Qch (to mutter . . . against . . .) VI

mutiner (se)

1. se _____ contre Qn ou Qch (to mutiny, rebel against . . .) V

N

nager

1. _____ dans Qch (to swim in . . . *e.g., dans le lac*, in the lake; Lit: to be swimming in . . . *e.g., dans le sang*, in blood; Coll: to be swimming in [one's clothes]) V

naître
1. _____ à Qch (Lit: to awaken to . . .; to experience . . . for the first time) II
2. _____ de Qn ou Qch (to be born of . . .; to result from . . . Ex: *un crime né du désespoir*, a crime born of despair) IV
3. être né pour Qch (to be born for . . . *e.g.,* success) V

nantir
1. _____ Qn (to coddle . . .; to give security to . . .) I
2. se _____ de Qch (to provide oneself with . . .) IV
3. _____ Qn de Qch (to provide . . . with . . .) VI

napper
1. _____ Qch (to cover . . . with a cloth; to nap . . . with a sauce) I
2. _____ Qch de Qch (to cover, nap . . . with . . .) VI

narrer
1. _____ Qch (to narrate . . .) I
2. _____ Qch à Qn (to narrate . . . to . . .) VI

négliger
1. _____ Qn ou Qch (to neglect . . .) I
2. _____ de *Inf.* (to fail to . . .) IX-A
3. *ne rien négliger pour Inf.* (to try every means to . . . Ex: *Il n'a rien négligé pour nous aider*, he did everything he could to help us) X

négocier
1. _____ Qch (to negotiate . . .) I
2. _____ avec Qn (to trade with . . .; to negotiate with . . .) V

nicher
1. _____ Qn ou Qch (to nest, lodge . . .) I
2. se _____ dans Qch (to nest, roost in . . .) V
3. _____ Qn ou Qch dans Qch (to put, nest, lodge . . . in . . .) VI

nommer
1. _____ Qn ou Qch (to name, appoint . . .) I
2. _____ Qn à Qch (to appoint . . . to . . .) VI

notifier
1. _____ Qch (to signify . . . Ex: *Le juge a notifié son approbation*, the judge indicated his approval) I
2. _____ Qch à Qn (to inform someone of something) VI

nouer
1. _____ Qch (to knot . . .) I
2. _____ Qch dans Qch (to knot, tie . . . in . . .) VI
3. _____ Qch avec Qn (to strike up, establish . . . with . . . Ex: *nouer conversation avec quelqu'un*, to strike up a conversation with someone) VI

nourrir
1. _____ Qn ou Qch (to feed, nourish . . .; to foster . . . *e.g.*, hopes) I
2. se _____ de Qch (to subsist on . . .; to sustain oneself with . . .) IV
3. _____ Qn ou Qch de Qch (to feed, nourish, foster . . . with, on . . .) VI

noyer
1. _____ Qn ou Qch (to drown . . .) I
2. être noyé de Qch (to be drowned in . . . *e.g.*, tears, sorrow) IV
3. se _____ dans Qch (to drown oneself in . . .) V
4. _____ Qn ou Qch dans Qch (to drown . . . in . . .) VI

nuancer
1. _____ Qch (to shade, color . . .) I
2. _____ Qch de Qch (to shade, color . . . with . . .) VI

nuire
1. _____ à Qn ou Qch (to harm . . .) II

O

obéir
1. _____ à Qn ou Qch (to obey . . .) II

objecter
1. _____ Qch (to raise . . . as an objection; to use . . . as an excuse) I
2. _____ Qch à Qn (to hold . . . against . . . Ex: *On lui a objecté sa jeunesse*, his youth was held against him) VI

obliger
1. _____ Qn (to be of service to . . .; to bind . . . legally) I
2. être obligé à Qn (to be grateful to . . .) II
3. _____ Qn ou Qch à Qch (to force something on . . .; to limit . . . to . . . Ex: *Sa faible santé l'oblige à une vie sédentaire*, his poor health limits him to a sedentary life) VI
4. s'_____ à ou de *Inf.* (to make oneself . . .; to undertake to . . . *À* is more common; *de* is more literary) VIII-A, IX-A
5. _____ Qn à ou de *Inf.* (to oblige . . . to . . . *À* is more common; *de* is more literary) VIII-B, IX-B
6. être obligé de *Inf.* (to be obliged to . . .) IX-A

obliquer
1. _____ sur, vers Qch (to edge, slant towards . . .) V

obséder
1. _____ Qn (to obsess . . .) I
2. être obsédé de Qch (to be obsessed with . . .) IV
3. être obsédé par Qn ou Qch (to be obsessed by, driven mad by . . .) V

obstiner (s')
1. s'_____ à, dans Qch (to persist in . . .) III, V
2. s'_____ à *Inf.* (to persist in ---*ing*) VIII-A

obtenir
1. _____ Qch (to obtain . . .) I
2. _____ Qch de Qn (to obtain . . . from . . .) VI
3. _____ de *Inf.* (to succeed in ---*ing*; to arrange to . . . Ex: *Elle a obtenu de voir le président,* she succeeded in seeing the president) IX-A

obvier
1. _____ à Qch (to obviate . . .) II

occuper
1. _____ Qn ou Qch (to occupy, busy . . .) I
2. s'_____ de Qn ou Qch (to be interested in . . .; to take care of, see to . . .; to bother about . . .) IV
3. _____ Qn à *Inf.* (to busy, to put . . . to work ---*ing*) VIII-B
4. _____ Qch à *Inf.* (to spend . . . ---*ing*, Ex: *Il occupe ses heures de loisir à lire,* he spends his spare time reading) VIII-B

octroyer
1. _____ Qch (to grant, bestow . . .) I
2. _____ Qch à Qn (to bestow . . . on . . .; to grant . . . to . . .) VI

offenser
1. _____ Qn (to offend . . .; to give offense to . . .) I
2. s'_____ de Qch (to take offense at . . .) IV

offrir
1. _____ Qch (to offer, give . . .) I
2. s'_____ à Qn ou Qch (to offer, volunteer oneself to . . .; to expose oneself to . . . *e.g.*, *à un danger*, to a danger; to make advances to . . .) III
3. _____ Qch à Qn ou Qch (to offer, give . . . to . . .; to expose . . . to . . .) VI
4. s'_____ à *Inf.* (to offer, volunteer to . . .) VIII-A
5. _____ de *Inf.* (to offer to . . .) IX-A

offusquer
1. _____ Qn (to irritate, displease . . .) I
2. s'_____ de Qch (to be offended at, by . . .) IV

oindre
1. _____ Qn (to anoint . . .) I
2. _____ Qn de Qch (to anoint . . . with . . .) VI

ombrager
1. _____ Qch (to shade, shadow . . .) I
2. _____ Qn ou Qch de Qch (to shade, protect . . . from . . . *e.g.*, *du soleil*, from the sun) VI

omettre
1. _____ Qn ou Qch (to omit . . .) I
2. _____ de *Inf.* (to neglect to . . .) IX-A

opérer
1. _____ Qn (to operate on . . .) I
2. _____ Qch (to effect . . .) I
3. _____ Qn de Qch (to operate on . . . for . . .) VI

opiniâtrer (s')
1. s'_____ dans Qch (to persist stubbornly in . . .) V
2. s'_____ à *Inf.* (to persist stubbornly in ---*ing*) VIII-A

opposer
1. ———— Qn ou Qch (to divide, separate, contrast . . .) I
2. s'———— à Qn ou Qch (to oppose, resist . . .) III
3. ———— Qn ou Qch à Qn ou Qch (to set . . . against . . .;
to contrast . . . with . . .; to offer . . . in opposition to . . . Ex: *Il ne trouva pas de réponse à
opposer à mon argument,* he could find no answer to counter my argument) VI

opter
1. ———— entre Qch (to choose between . . .) V
2. ———— pour, contre Qch (to opt for, against . . .) V

ordonner
1. ———— Qch (to arrange . . .; to put . . . in order) I
2. ———— Qn (to ordain . . .) I
3. ———— Qch à Qn (to prescribe . . . for . . . Ex: *ordonner
un remède à un malade,* to prescribe a remedy
for a patient; to sentence someone to . . .; to
mete out . . . to someone, Ex: *ordonner un
travail à un ouvrier,* to give a worker a job) VI
4. ———— à Qn de *Inf.* (to order . . . to . . .) IX-B

orner
1. ———— Qn ou Qch (to adorn, decorate . . .) I
2. s'———— de Qch (to adorn oneself with . . .) IV
3. ———— Qn ou Qch de Qch (to adorn, decorate . . . with
. . .) VI

oser
1. ———— Qch (to dare . . .) I
2. ———— *Inf.* (to dare to . . .) VII-A

ôter
1. ———— Qch (to remove . . .) I
2. ———— Qn ou Qch à Qn (to take . . . away from . . .) VI
3. ———— Qn ou Qch de Qch (to remove . . . from . . .) VI

ouater
1. _____ Qch (to wad, pad . . .) I
2. _____ Qch de Qch (to wad, pad . . . with . . .) VI

oublier
1. _____ Qn ou Qch (to forget . . .) I
2. _____ de *Inf.* (to forget to . . .) IX-A

ouvrir
1. _____ Qch (to open . . .) I
2. s'_____ à Qn (to speak freely to . . .) III
3. _____ Qch à Qn (to open . . . for . . .) VI

P

pactiser
1. _____ avec Qn ou Qch (to deal with, make a pact with . . . *e.g., avec l'ennemi*, with the enemy; to compromise with . . . *e.g., avec sa conscience*, with one's conscience) V

pailleter
1. _____ Qch (to spangle . . .) I
2. _____ Qch de Qch (to spangle . . . with . . .) VI

palabrer
1. _____ avec Qn (to palaver with . . .) V

pâlir
1. _____ de Qch (to become pale, livid with . . . *e.g., de colère*, with anger) IV

pallier
1. _____ Qch (to palliate . . .) I
2. _____ à Qch (to mitigate . . .) II

palpiter
1. _____ de Qch (to throb with . . . *e.g.*, *d'émotion*, with emotion) IV

pâmer (se)
1. se _____ de Qch (to swoon, pass out with . . . *e.g.*, *de rire*, with laughter; *d'admiration*, with admiration) IV

paraître
1. _____ [+ adjectif] à Qn (to seem . . . to . . . Ex: *La situation parut grave au général*, the situation seemed serious to the general) II
2. *Il paraît à Qn que* (it seems to . . . that . . .) II
3. _____ *Inf.* ou *Inf. passé* (to seem, appear to be ---*ing*, to have . . . Ex: *Il paraissait rêver*, he seemed to be dreaming) VII-A

pardonner
1. _____ Qch (to pardon, excuse . . .) I
2. _____ à Qn (to forgive, pardon . . .) II
3. _____ Qch à Qn (to forgive someone for something) VI
4. _____ à Qn de *Inf.* ou *Inf. passé* (to forgive . . . for ---*ing*, for having . . .) IX-B

parer
1. _____ Qn ou Qch (to adorn, decorate . . .) I
2. se _____ de Qch (to adorn oneself with . . .) IV
3. _____ Qn ou Qch de Qch (to adorn, decorate . . . with . . .) VI

parer
1. _____ Qch (to avoid, avert . . .) I
2. _____ à Qch (to guard against . . .) II

parier
1. _____ Qch (to bet, wager . . .) I
2. _____ à Qn que . . . (to bet someone that . . .) II
3. _____ sur, contre, pour Qn ou Qch (to bet on, against, for . . .) V
4. _____ avec Qn (to bet with . . .) V
5. _____ Qch sur, contre, pour Qn ou Qch (to bet . . . on, against, for . . .) VI

parler
1. _____ [une langue] (to speak . . . *e.g.*, French) I
2. _____ à Qn (to talk to . . .) II
3. _____ de Qn ou Qch (to talk about . . .) IV
4. _____ avec Qn (to talk with . . .) V
5. _____ pour, en faveur de, contre Qn ou Qch (to speak for, in favor of, against . . .) V
6. _____ sur Qn ou Qch (to speak about, on . . .) V
7. _____ de *Inf.* (to talk about --*ing*) IX-A

parsemer
1. être parsemé de Qch (to be strewn, sprinkled with . . .) IV
2. _____ Qn ou Qch de Qch (to strew, sprinkle . . . with . . .) VI

partager
1. _____ Qch (to divide, share . . .) I
2. _____ Qch à, entre Qn ou Qch (to divide, share . . . among . . .) VI
3. _____ Qch en Qch (to divide . . . into . . . Ex: *partager une pièce en deux*, to divide a room in half) VI
4. _____ Qch avec Qn (to share . . . with . . .) VI

participer
1. _____ à Qch (to take part in . . .) II
2. _____ de Qch (to have the characteristics of . . .) IV

partir
1. _____ de Qch (to leave from . . .) IV
2. _____ pour Qch (to leave for . . .) V
3. _____ *Inf.* (to leave in order to . . .) VII-A

parvenir
1. _____ à Qch (to reach, arrive at . . .) II
2. faire parvenir Qch à Qn (to send . . . to . . .; to forward . . . to . . .) VI
3. _____ à *Inf.* (to manage to . . . Ex: *Si tu le lui expliques bien, il parviendra à comprendre*, if you explain it to him well, he will manage to understand) VIII-A

passer
1. _____ Qch (to pass, surpass, pass by, cross . . .; to spend [time]; *passer un examen*, to take a test) I
2. se _____ (to take place, to happen) I
3. _____ à, dans* Qn ou Qch (to go over to, to defect to . . . Ex: *passer à l'ennemi*, to defect to the enemy; *passer dans l'opposition*, to go over to the opposition; to go on to . . . Ex: *Passons à autre chose*, let's go on to something else) II, V
4. se _____ de Qn ou Qch (to do without . . . Ex: *Je ne peux pas me passer d'elle*, I can't do without her) IV
5. _____ pour Qn ou Qch (to appear to be . . .; to pass for . . .) V
6. _____ par Qch (to pass through, by way of . . .) V
7. _____ sur Qch (to skip, pass over . . .) V
8. _____ chez Qn (to drop by someone's house) V
9. _____ Qch à Qn (to pass . . . to . . .) VI
10. _____ *Inf.* (to stop by to . . .) VII-A
11. _____ [un certain temps] à *Inf.* (to spend [time] ---*ing*, Ex: *J'ai passé l'hiver à faire du ski*, I spent the winter skiing) VIII-B
12. se _____ de *Inf.* (to do without ---*ing*) IX-A

---

*See Appendix II: **DANS, EN, À**, p. 298.

passionner
1. ———— Qn (to impassion, arouse great interest in . . . Ex: *Ce film m'a passionné*, I was fascinated by the movie) I
2. être passionné de, pour Qn ou Qch (to be very interested in, enthusiastic about . . .) IV, V
3. se —— pour Qch (to be very interested in . . .) V

pâtir
1. ———— de Qch (to suffer on account of . . .) IV

paver
1. ———— Qch (to pave . . .) I
2. ———— Qch de Qch (to pave . . . with . . .) VI

payer
1. ———— Qn ou Qch (to pay . . .; to pay for . . .) I
2. se —— Qch (Coll: to give oneself . . .; to treat oneself to . . .) I
3. se —— de Qch (to be satisfied with . . . Ex: *se payer de mots*, to be all talk) IV
4. ———— de Qch (to make a show of . . . Ex: *payer d'audace*, to put up a good front) IV
5. être payé pour Qch (to be paid, punished for . . .) V
6. ———— Qch à Qn (to pay . . . to . . .; to treat someone to something, Ex: *Il m'a payé un verre*, he bought me a drink) VI
7. ———— Qn de Qch (to pay . . . for . . .) VI
8. être payé pour *Inf.* (to be paid for ---*ing*, to . . .) X

pécher
1. ———— contre Qn ou Qch (to sin against . . .) V

peiner
1. ———— Qn (to grieve, distress . . .) I
2. être peiné de Qch (to be pained, distressed by, at . . .) IV
3. être peiné de *Inf.* (to be grieved, distressed to . . .) IX-A
4. *Il peine à Qn de Inf.* (it grieves, pains . . . to . . . Ex: *Il me peine de vous le dire*, it pains me to tell you) IX-B

pencher
1. ———— Qch (to tilt, bend . . .) I
2. se ———— sur Qn ou Qch (to bend over, towards . . .; to study closely, take an active interest in . . .) V
3. ———— pour Qn ou Qch (to lean towards, be inclined towards . . .) V

pendre
1. ———— Qn ou Qch (to hang . . .) I
2. ———— à Qch (to hang from . . .) II
3. être pendu à Qch (to be tied to, inseparable from . . .; to be hung from . . .) II
4. se ———— à Qn ou Qch (to hang on to, cling to . . .) III
5. ———— Qn ou Qch à Qch (to hang . . . from . . .) VI

pénétrer
1. ———— Qn ou Qch (to penetrate . . .) I
2. être pénétré de Qch (to be overcome with . . . *e.g., de remords*, with remorse) IV
3. ———— dans Qch (to enter, break into . . .) V
4. ———— Qn ou Qch de Qch (to penetrate, pierce . . . with . . .; to imbue, inspire . . . with . . . Ex: *Il les a pénétrés de son enthousiasme,* he inspired them with his enthusiasm) VI

penser
1. ———— à Qn ou Qch (to think of, about . . .) III
2. ———— Qch de Qn ou Qch (to think . . . about . . .; in questions, to have an opinion about . . . Ex: *Que pensez-vous du nouveau professeur?* What do you think of the new professor?) VI
3. ———— *Inf.* (to intend to . . .; to think that . . . Ex: *Il pense pouvoir le faire,* he thinks that he can do it) VII-A
4. ———— à *Inf.* (to think about, consider ---*ing*) VIII-A

percer
1. _____ Qch (to pierce . . .) I
2. _____ Qch de Qch (to pierce . . . with . . .) VI

percuter
1. _____ Qch (to strike . . .; to crash into . . .) I
2. _____ contre Qn ou Qch (to explode against . . .; to crash into . . .) V

perfectionner
1. _____ Qch (to perfect . . .) I
2. se _____ dans Qch (to perfect oneself in . . .) V

périr
1. _____ de Qch (to die of . . . *e.g., d'inanition*, of starvation; to die from . . . *e.g., d'une blessure grave*, from a serious wound) IV

permettre
1. _____ Qch (to permit, allow . . .) I
2. _____ Qch à Qn (to permit someone something) VI
3. se _____ de *Inf.* (to take the liberty of ---*ing*) IX-A
4. _____ à Qn de *Inf.* (to allow . . . to . . .) IX-B

persévérer
1. _____ dans Qch (to persevere in . . .) V
2. _____ à *Inf.* (to persevere in ---*ing*) VIII-A

persister
1. _____ dans Qch (to persist in . . .) V
2. _____ à *Inf.* (to persist in ---*ing*) VIII-A

persuader
1. _____ Qn (to persuade, convince . . .) I
2. se _____ de Qch (to convince oneself of . . .) IV
3. _____ Qn de Qch (to convince . . . of . . .) VI
4. _____ à Qn de *Inf.* (to persuade . . . to . . .) IX-B

peser
1. _____ Qn ou Qch (to weigh . . .) I
2. _____ à Qn (to lie heavily on . . .; to trouble, be oppressive to . . . Ex: *Ses ennuis lui pèsent*, his problems are troubling him) II
3. _____ sur Qn ou Qch (to weigh upon . . .; to be a burden to . . .) V

pester
1. _____ contre Qn ou Qch (to rant and rave against . . .) V

pétrir
1. _____ Qch (to mold, knead . . .) I
2. être pétri de Qch (to be made of, filled with . . . *e.g., de rancune*, with bitterness; *d'orgueil*, with pride) IV

peupler
1. _____ Qch (to people, populate . . .) I
2. _____ Qch de Qn ou Qch (to people, populate . . . with . . .) VI

philosopher
1. _____ sur Qn ou Qch (to philosophize on . . .) V

picoter
1. être picoté de Qch (to be pock-marked with . . .) IV
2. être picoté par Qch (to be pricked, stung by . . .) V

pincer
1. _____ Qn ou Qch (to pinch . . .) I
2. _____ Qch à Qn (to pinch someone's . . . Ex: *pincer la joue à l'enfant*, to pinch the child's cheek) VI

piquer
1. ———— Qn ou Qch (to prick . . .; to offend . . .) I
2. se ———— de Qch (to pride oneself on . . .; to take offense at . . .) IV
3. se ———— de *Inf.* (to pride oneself on ---*ing*) IX-A

plaider
1. ———— Qch (to plead . . . *e.g.*, innocence) I
2. ———— contre, pour Qn ou Qch (to plead, argue in court against, for . . .) V

plaindre
1. ———— Qn ou Qch (to pity . . .) I
2. se ———— (to complain) I
3. se ———— à Qn (to complain to . . .) III
4. se ———— de Qn ou Qch (to complain about . . .) IV
5. se ———— de *Inf.* ou *Inf. passé* (to complain about ---*ing*, about having . . .) IX-A

plaire
1. ———— à Qn (to please, be pleasing to . . . Ex: *Cette maison me plaît beaucoup*, I like this house a lot) II
2. se ———— à un endroit (to like it in a place, *e.g.*, *se plaire à la montagne*, to like it in the mountains) III
3. se ———— à *Inf.* (to enjoy, like ---*ing*; to amuse oneself by ---*ing*) VIII-A
4. *Il plaît à Qn de Inf.* (to like to . . .; to find . . . a pleasure, Ex: *Il me plaît beaucoup de sortir souvent*, I enjoy going out often) IX-B

plaisanter
1. ———— sur, de Qch (to joke about . . .) V, IV

planer
1. ———— sur Qn ou Qch (to hover over . . .) V

pleurer

1. _____ Qn ou Qch (to mourn, mourn for . . .; to cry . . . *e.g., des larmes de joie*, tears of joy) I
2. _____ de Qch (to weep for, with . . . *e.g., de honte*, with shame) IV
3. _____ sur Qch (to cry over . . .) V

plier

1. _____ Qn ou Qch (to fold, bend . . .) I
2. se _____ à Qn ou Qch (to yield to . . .; to abide by . . .) III
3. _____ sous Qch (to bend under, give way to . . .) V
4. _____ Qn à Qch (to bend, break . . . to . . . Ex: *plier quelqu'un à la discipline*, to make someone be disciplined) VI

plonger

1. _____ dans Qch (to plunge into . . .) V
2. _____ Qn ou Qch dans Qch (to plunge, immerse . . . in . . .) VI

ployer

1. _____ devant Qn ou Qch (to give way before, under . . .) V

poivrer

1. _____ Qch (to pepper . . .) I
2. _____ Qch de Qch (to pepper . . . with . . .) VI

porter

1. _____ Qn ou Qch (to wear, carry . . .) I
2. se _____ *bien, mal* (to be in good, bad health) I
3. se _____ *à une extrémité* (to go to an extreme)
4. être porté sur Qch (to have a weakness for . . .) V
5. _____ sur Qch (to bear on, have bearing on . . .; to fall on . . . Ex: *La discussion porte sur la situation économique*, the economic situation is being discussed) V
6. _____ Qch à Qn (to carry . . . to . . .) VI

7. _____ Qn à Qch (to lead, incite . . . to . . .) VI
8. être porté à *Inf.* (to be inclined, disposed to . . .) VIII-A
9. _____ Qn à *Inf.* (to lead, cause . . . to . . .) VIII-B

poser
1. _____ Qch (to put, put down . . .; to ask [a question]; to pose . . . *e.g.*, a problem) I
2. se _____ (to arise, Ex: *La question ne se pose pas*, the problem does not arise) I
3. _____ pour Qch (to pose for . . .) V
4. se _____ comme, en Qn ou Qch (to pose as . . .) V
5. se _____ sur Qn ou Qch (to alight on, rest on . . .) V
6. _____ Qch à Qn (to ask someone [a question]; to pose . . . for . . .) VI
7. _____ Qch sur, contre Qch (to put, rest . . . on, against . . .) VI

posséder
1. _____ Qn ou Qch (to possess . . .) I
2. être possédé de Qch (to be possessed by . . . *e.g.*, *d'un démon*, by a demon) IV

poudrer
1. _____ Qch (to powder . . .) I
2. _____ Qch de Qch (to powder . . . with . . .) VI

poudroyer
1. _____ Qch (to cover . . . with dust) I
2. _____ Qch de Qch (to dust . . . with . . .) VI

pourvoir
1. _____ à Qch (to provide for, see to . . . *e.g.*, *à ses besoins*, for one's needs) II
2. se _____ de Qch (to provide oneself with . . .) IV
3. _____ Qn de Qch (to provide . . . with . . .) VI

pousser
1. ————— Qn ou Qch (to push . . .; to utter . . . *e.g.*, a cry) I
2. ————— Qn à *Inf.* (to push, urge . . . to . . .) VIII-B

pouvoir
1. ————— *Inf.* (to be able to . . .) VII-A

pratiquer
1. ————— Qch (to practice [a profession]; to go in for . . .
           e.g., a sport) I
2. ————— Qch dans Qch (to cut, work . . . in . . . Ex:
           pratiquer un trou dans un mur, to cut a hole in
           a wall) VI

prêcher
1. ————— Qch (to preach . . .) I
2. ————— à Qn (to preach to . . .) II
3. ————— Qch à Qn (to preach . . . to . . .) VI

précipiter
1. ————— Qch (to throw, hurl . . .) I
2. se ————— dans Qch (to rush into . . .) V
3. se ————— sur Qn ou Qch (to throw oneself onto . . .; to rush
           at . . .) V
4. ————— Qn dans Qch (to rush, hurry . . . into . . .) VI

prédestiner
1. être prédestiné à Qch (to be predestined, born for . . .) II
2. être prédestiné à *Inf.* (to be predestined, born to . . .) VIII-A

prédire
1. ————— Qch (to predict . . .) I
2. ————— Qch à Qn (to predict . . . to, for . . .) VI

prédisposer
1. _____ Qn à Qn ou Qch (to predispose . . . towards . . .) VI
2. _____ Qn contre Qn ou Qch (to prejudice . . . against . . .) VI

prédominer
1. _____ sur Qch (to dominate . . .; to have the upper hand over . . .) V

préexister
1. _____ à Qn ou Qch (to be preexistent to . . .; to predate . . .) II

préférer
1. _____ Qn ou Qch (to prefer . . .) I
2. _____ Qn ou Qch à Qn ou Qch (to prefer . . . to . . .) VI
3. _____ *Inf.* (to prefer to . . .) VII-A

préjuger
1. _____ de Qch (to make a premature judgment on . . .) IV

préluder
1. _____ à Qch (to serve as a prelude to . . .; to precede . . .) II
2. _____ par Qch (to begin with . . .) V

préméditer
1. _____ Qch (to premeditate . . .) I
2. _____ de *Inf.* (to premeditate ---*ing*) IX-A

prémunir
1. se _____ contre Qch (to secure, protect oneself against . . .) V
2. _____ Qn ou Qch contre Qch (to caution, arm . . . against . . .) VI

prendre
1. ———— Qn ou Qch (to take . . .; to catch . . .) I
2. se (laisser) prendre à, dans Qch (to get caught by, in . . .
   Ex: *se (laisser) prendre au piège,* to get caught
   in a trap) III, V
3. s'en —— à Qn [pour Qch] (to blame . . . [for . . .]) III
4. se —— de Qch (to begin to have . . . Ex: *se prendre
   d'amitié pour quelqu'un,* to begin to be friendly
   with someone) IV
5. se —— pour Qn ou Qch (to take oneself for . . .) V
6. être pris dans Qch (to be caught in . . .) V
7. ———— Qch à Qn (to take . . . from . . .) VI
8. ———— Qn ou Qch pour Qn ou Qch (to take, mistake . . .
   for . . . *e.g., pour un voleur,* for a thief; *pour
   un imbécile,* for an idiot) VI
9. ———— Qn ou Qch en Qch (to take a . . . to . . . Ex: *prendre quelqu'un en aversion,* to take a dislike to
   someone) VI
10. ———— Qn comme, pour Qch (to take . . . as . . . *e.g.,
    comme associé,* as a partner) VI
11. ———— *garde* de *Inf.* (to take care to . . .; Lit: to take
    care not to . . .) IX-A
12. ———— *garde* de ne pas *Inf.* (to take care not to . . .)
    IX-A

préparer
1. ———— Qn ou Qch (to prepare . . .) I
2. se —— à Qch (to prepare oneself for . . ., *e.g., à la mort,*
   for death) III
3. se —— pour Qch (to get ready for . . . *e.g., pour le bal,*
   for the dance) V
4. ———— Qn ou Qch à Qch (to prepare . . . for . . .) VI
5. ———— Qch à Qn (to prepare . . . for . . .; to have . . .
   [*e.g.,* a surprise] in store for . . .) VI
6. être préparé à *Inf.* (to be prepared to . . .) VIII-A
7. ———— Qn ou Qch à *Inf.* (to prepare . . . to . . .) VIII-B

préoccuper
1. _____ Qn (to preoccupy . . .) I
2. se _____ de Qn ou Qch (to give one's attention to . . .; to be concerned about . . .) IV

préposer
1. _____ Qn à Qch (to appoint . . . to . . .; to put someone in charge of . . .) VI

prescrire
1. _____ Qch (to prescribe . . .) I
2. _____ Qch à Qn (to prescribe . . . to, for . . . Ex: *prescrire un remède à un malade*, to prescribe a remedy to, for a patient) VI
3. _____ à Qn de *Inf.* (to strongly advise . . . to . . .; to stipulate that someone . . .) IX-B

présenter
1. _____ Qn ou Qch (to present . . .) I
2. se _____ [à Qn] (to introduce oneself [to . . .]) III
3. se _____ à Qch (to report for . . . *e.g.*, *à un examen*, for a test) III
4. se _____ pour Qch (to apply for . . . *e.g.*, a job) V
5. _____ Qn à Qn (to introduce . . . to . . .) VI

préserver
1. _____ Qn ou Qch (to preserve . . .) I
2. se _____ de Qn ou Qch (to protect oneself from . . .) IV
3. _____ Qn ou Qch de Qn ou Qch (to protect . . . from . . .) VI

présider
1. _____ Qch (to chair . . .) I
2. _____ à Qch (to preside over . . .) II

pressentir

1. _____ Qch (to have a premonition of . . .; to foresee . . .) I
2. faire pressentir Qch à Qn (to give someone a hint of something) VI
3. _____ Qn sur Qch (to sound someone out on something) VI

presser

1. _____ Qn ou Qch (to press, hurry . . .) I
2. _____ Qn de Qch (to assail, ply . . . with . . .) VI
3. se _____ de *Inf.* (to hasten to . . .) IX-A
4. _____ Qn de *Inf.* (to urge . . . to . . .) IX-B

présumer

1. _____ Qn ou Qch (to presume . . . Ex: *présumer le pire*, to presume the worst; *présumer quelqu'un innocent*, to presume someone innocent) I
2. _____ de Qch (to overestimate . . . e.g., *de sa force*, one's strength) IV
3. _____ de *Inf.* (to presume to . . .) IX-A

prétendre

1. _____ Qch (to claim, affirm . . .) I
2. _____ à Qch (to lay claim to . . .; to pretend to . . . e.g., *au trône*, to the throne) II
3. _____ *Inf.* ou *Inf. passé* (to claim to . . ., to have . . .) VII-A

prêter

1. _____ Qch (to loan . . .) I
2. _____ à Qch (to give rise to . . .; to give occasion for . . . e.g., *à la censure*, to criticism; *prêter à rire*, to give rise to laughter; *prêter à sourire*, to make people smile) II

3. se ____ à Qch (to agree to . . .; to comply with, go along with . . . Ex: *Elle s'est prêtée à cette plaisanterie,* she went along with the joke) III

4. _____ Qch à Qn ou Qch (to loan . . . to . . .; to attribute . . . to . . .) VI

prévaloir

1. se ____ de Qch (to avail oneself of . . .; to pride oneself on . . .) IV

2. _____ sur, contre Qn ou Qch (to prevail over, against . . .) V

prévenir

1. _____ Qn ou Qch (to warn, notify . . .) I

2. _____ Qn de Qch (to notify, warn . . . about, of . . .) VI

3. _____ Qn contre Qn ou Qch (to prejudice . . . against . . .) VI

4. _____ Qn en faveur de Qn ou Qch (to bias . . . in favor of . . .) VI

prier

1. _____ Qn (to pray to . . .) I

2. _____ pour Qn ou Qch (to pray for . . .) V

3. _____ Qn à Qch (to invite . . . to . . .) VI

4. _____ Qn de *Inf.* (to beg, ask . . . to . . .) IX-B

primer

1. _____ Qn ou Qch (to take precedence over . . .; to excel over . . .) I

priver

1. se ____ de Qch (to deprive oneself of . . .; to abstain from . . .) IV

2. _____ Qn de Qch (to deprive . . . of . . .) VI

procéder
1. _____ à Qch (to proceed to . . .) II
2. _____ de Qch (to originate from . . .) IV
3. _____ avec Qch (to proceed with . . . *e.g.*, *avec précau-tion*, with caution) V
4. _____ par Qch (to proceed by . . . *e.g.*, *par élimination*, by elimination) V

procurer
1. se _____ Qch (to procure, acquire . . .) I
2. _____ Qch à Qn (to get, provide . . . for . . .) VI
3. se _____ Qch de Qn (to get . . . from . . .) VI

prodiguer
1. _____ Qch (to be lavish with . . .) I
2. se _____ (to be unsparing of oneself; to show off) I
3. se _____ pour Qn (to outdo oneself for . . .) V
4. _____ Qch à Qn (to shower someone with something) VI

profiler
1. se _____ sur, à Qch (to be outlined on . . .) V, III
2. se _____ contre Qch (to be outlined against . . .) V

profiter
1. _____ à Qn ou Qch (to be useful, profitable to . . .) II
2. _____ de Qn ou Qch (to take advantage of . .) IV

prohiber
1. _____ Qch (to prohibit . . .) I
2. _____ Qch à Qn (to prohibit, forbid someone some-thing) VI
3. _____ à Qn de *Inf.* (to prohibit . . . from ---*ing*) IX-B

projeter
1. _____ Qch (to throw, cast . . . *e.g.*, a shadow; to plan . . .; to project . . .) I
2. _____ de *Inf.* (to plan to . . .) IX-A

prolonger
1. _____ Qch (to prolong . . .) I
2. _____ Qch de Qch (to lengthen . . . by . . .) VI

promettre
1. _____ Qch (to promise . . .) I
2. se _____ Qch (to count on . . .; to look forward to . . .) I
3. _____ Qn ou Qch à Qn (to promise . . . to . . .) VI
4. se _____ de *Inf.* (to resolve to . . .) IX-A
5. _____ [à Qn] de *Inf.* (to promise [someone] to . . .) IX-B

prononcer
1. _____ Qch (to pronounce . . .) I
2. _____ sur Qn ou Qch (to pass judgment on . . .) V
3. _____ Qch à Qn (to pronounce . . . to . . .) VI

proportionner
1. _____ Qch (to proportion, adjust . . .) I
2. _____ Qch à, avec Qch (to proportion, adjust . . . to . . .) VI

proposer
1. _____ Qn ou Qch (to propose, suggest . . .) I
2. se _____ Qch (to have . . . in mind) I
3. se _____ comme Qn ou Qch (to run for . . .; to offer one's services as . . . *e.g., comme interprète,* as an interpreter) V
4. _____ Qch à Qn (to propose . . . to . . .) VI
5. _____ Qn ou Qch comme Qch (to hold up . . . as . . . *e.g., comme modèle,* as a model) VI
6. _____ Qn ou Qch pour Qch (to suggest . . . for . . . *e.g., pour un poste,* for a job) VI
7. _____ de *Inf.* (to suggest ---*ing*) IX-A
8. se _____ de *Inf.* (to intend to . . .) IX-A
9. _____ à Qn de *Inf.* (to suggest to . . . that . . . Ex: *Je lui ai proposé de m'accompagner,* I suggested that he, she accompany me) IX-B

proscrire
1. _____ Qn ou Qch (to proscribe, outlaw . . .) I
2. _____ Qn ou Qch de Qch (to ostracize, outlaw, banish . . . from . . .) VI

prosterner

1. se _____ devant Qn ou Qch (to prostrate oneself before
...) V

protéger

1. _____ Qn ou Qch (to protect . . .) I
2. se _____ de Qch (to guard against . . .; to protect oneself
from, against . . .) IV
3. _____ Qn ou Qch contre Qn ou Qch (to protect . . . from,
against . . .) VI

protester

1. _____ Qch (to protest . . .) I
2. _____ de Qch (to affirm . . . Ex: *protester de son innocence*, to affirm one's innocence) IV
3. _____ contre Qn ou Qch (to protest against . . .) V

prouver

1. _____ Qch (to prove . . .) I
2. _____ Qch à Qn (to prove . . . to . . .) VI

provenir

1. _____ de Qch (to come, originate from . . .) IV

provoquer

1. _____ Qn ou Qch (to cause, provoke . . .) I
2. _____ Qn à Qch (to incite, provoke . . . to . . .) VI
3. _____ Qn à *Inf.* (to induce, provoke . . . to . . .) VIII-B

puer

1. _____ Qch (to stink of . . . Ex: *puer l'ail*, to stink of
garlic) I

puiser

1. _____ Qch (to draw [water]) I
2. _____ Qch à, dans Qch (to draw . . . from . . . Ex:
puiser une cruche d'eau à la fontaine, to draw
a pitcher of water from the fountain) VI
3. _____ Qch chez Qn (to draw, derive one's . . . from . . .
Ex: *puiser ses thèmes chez un auteur*, to take
one's themes from an author) VI

punir
1. ———— Qn (to punish . . .) I
2. ———— Qn de, par Qch (to punish . . . with . . . *e.g., de mort*, with death) VI
3. ———— Qn pour, de Qch (to punish . . . for . . .) VI
4. Qn de *Inf. passé* (to punish . . . for having . . .) IX-B

purger
1. ———— Qn ou Qch (to purge, cleanse . . .) I
2. se ———— de Qch (to purge, rid oneself of . . .) IV
3. ———— Qn ou Qch de Qch (to purge, rid . . . of . . .) VI

purifier
1. ———— Qn ou Qch (to purify . . .) I
2. ———— Qn ou Qch de Qch (to cleanse, purify . . . of . . .) VI

Q

qualifier
1. ———— Qn ou Qch (to qualify, designate, call . . .) I
2. être qualifié [de] Qch (to be considered, called a . . .) IV, I
3. se ———— pour Qch (to qualify for . . .) V
4. ———— Qn ou Qch [de] Qch (to consider . . . a . . . Ex: *qualifier le vol de crime*, to consider theft a crime) VI
5. ———— Qn ou Qch pour Qch (to qualify . . . for . . .) VI

quémander
1. ———— Qch (to solicit . . .) I
2. ———— Qch de Qn (to solicit someone's . . .; to beg someone for something) VI

quereller
1. se ———— avec Qn (to quarrel with . . .) V

questionner
1. ———— Qn (to question . . .) I
2. ———— Qn de Qch (to question . . . about . . .) VI

R

rabâcher
1. ———— Qch (to harp on . . .) I
2. ———— Qch à Qn (to drum . . . into . . .) VI

rabattre
1. ———— Qch (to lower . . .; to pull . . . down; to turn . . . back) I
2. se ———— sur Qch (to fall back on . . .; to have recourse to . . .) V

raccomoder
1. ———— Qch (to mend . . .) I
2. se ———— avec Qn (to make up with . . .; to be reconciled with . . .) V
3. ———— Qn avec Qn (to reconcile . . . with . . .) VI

raccorder
1. ———— Qch (to join, coordinate . . .) I
2. se ———— à Qch (to join, link up with . . .) III
3. ———— Qn ou Qch à, avec Qn ou Qch (to link, connect . . . with . . .) VI

raccrocher
1. ———— Qch (to hang up . . . again) I
2. se ———— à Qn ou Qch (to clutch hold of . . .) III

racheter
1. ———— Qn ou Qch (to redeem . . .; to buy back . . .; to compensate for [a deficiency]) I
2. se ———— (to redeem oneself) I
3. ———— Qn ou Qch à Qn (to ransom, buy back . . . from . . .) VI

raconter
1. _____ Qch (to relate, narrate . . .) I
2. _____ Qch à Qn (to relate, narrate . . . to . . .) VI

radier
1. _____ Qn ou Qch (to erase, cross off, eliminate . . .) I
2. _____ Qn ou Qch de Qch (to erase, cross off . . . from . . .) VI

raffiner
1. _____ Qch (to refine . . .) I
2. _____ sur Qch (to exaggerate, overdo . . .; to split hairs, Ex: *Il raffine sur l'étiquette*, he is overly fussy about etiquette) V

raffoler
1. _____ de Qn ou Qch (to adore, be crazy about . . .) IV

raidir
1. _____ Qn ou Qch (to stiffen . . .) I
2. se _____ contre Qn ou Qch (to brace oneself against . . .) V

raisonner
1. _____ Qch (to consider, study . . .) I
2. _____ Qn (to reason with . . .) I
3. _____ avec Qn (to have a discussion with . . .) V
4. _____ sur Qch (to speculate on, argue about . . .) V

rallier
1. _____ Qn (to win over . . .) I
2. se _____ à Qn ou Qch (to rally to . . .; to join . . .) III
3. _____ Qn à Qch (to win . . . over to . . .) VI

ramener

1. ———— Qn (to bring . . . back) I
2. se ———— à Qch (to be reduced to . . .; to amount to . . . Ex: *Son argument se ramenait à une idée très simple*, his argument boiled down to a very simple idea) III
3. ———— Qn à Qch (to bring, take . . . back to . . . Ex: *ramener quelqu'un chez lui, à la maison*, to bring, take someone home; *ramener quelqu'un à la raison*, to bring someone back to his senses) VI

ramper

1. ———— devant Qn ou Qch (to grovel to . . .) V

rappeler

1. ———— Qn ou Qch (to call . . . back; to summon up . . .; to repeal . . .) I
2. se ———— Qn ou Qch (to remember, recall . . .) I
3. ———— Qch à Qn (to remind someone of something) VI
4. ———— Qn à Qch (to call . . . back to . . . Ex: *rappeler quelqu'un à son devoir*, to remind someone of his duty) VI
5. se ———— de *Inf.* ou *Inf. passé* (to remember to . . .; to remember having . . .) IX-A
6. ———— à Qn de *Inf.* (to remind . . . to . . .) IX-B

rapporter

1. ———— Qch (to relate, report . . .; to bring . . . back) I
2. se ———— à Qch ou Qn (to relate to . . .; to have reference to . . . Ex: *Cette idée ne se rapporte pas au texte*, this idea has no relation to the text) III
3. s'en ———— à Qn ou Qch (to leave it up to . . .; to rely on . . .) III
4. ———— Qch à Qch (to relate . . . to . . .; to refer . . . to . . . Ex: *Il faut rapporter la cause à l'effet*, one must relate the cause to the effect) VI

rapprocher
1. ———— Qn ou Qch (to compare . . .; to bring . . . together) I
2. se ———— de Qn ou Qch (to draw near to . . .; to resemble . . .) IV
3. ———— Qn ou Qch de Qn ou Qch (to bring . . . near to . . .; to make . . . approach . . . Ex: *rapprocher l'art à la vie*, to make art imitate life) VI

rassasier
1. ———— Qn ou Qch (to sate, satisfy . . .) I
2. se ———— de Qch (to have one's fill of . . .) IV
3. être rassasié de Qch (to have one's fill of . . .; to be fed up with . . .) IV
4. ———— Qn ou Qch de Qch (to satisfy, sate . . . with . . .) VI

rassurer
1. ———— Qn (to reassure . . .) I
2. se ———— sur Qch (to reassure oneself about . . .) V
3. ———— Qn sur Qch (to reassure . . . about . . .) VI

ratiboiser
1. ———— Qn (Coll: to swindle . . .; to clean . . . out) I
2. ———— Qch à Qn (Coll: to cheat, do someone out of something) VI

rattacher
1. ———— Qn ou Qch (to fasten, to reattach . . .) I
2. se ———— à Qch (to be connected with . . .) III
3. ———— Qn ou Qch à Qch (to fasten . . . to . . .; to connect . . . with . . .) VI

rattraper
1. ———— Qn ou Qch (to overtake . . .; to catch up with . . .; to make up for [a deficiency]) I
2. se ———— (to catch up) I
3. se ———— à Qch (to catch hold of . . .) III

ravaler
1. _____ Qn ou Qch (to cut down, debase . . .) I
2. _____ Qch (to choke down, swallow . . .) I
3. se _____ à Qch (to lower, debase oneself to . . .) III
4. _____ Qn ou Qch à Qch (to reduce . . . to . . .) VI

ravir
1. _____ Qn ou Qch (to delight . . .; to carry off . . .) I
2. être ravi de Qn ou Qch (to be delighted by, with . . .) IV
3. _____ Qn ou Qch à Qn (to steal . . . from . . .) VI
4. être ravi de *Inf.* (to be delighted to . . .) IX-A

ravitailler
1. _____ Qn ou Qch (to supply . . . [with food, munitions])
   I
2. se _____ en Qch (to stock up on . . . *e.g., en blé,* on
   wheat) V
3. _____ Qn ou Qch en Qch (to supply . . . with . . .) VI

rayer
1. _____ Qch (to rule, stripe, cross off . . .) I
2. _____ Qn ou Qch de Qch (to cross . . . off . . .; to remove . . . from . . .)VI

rayonner
1. _____ de Qch (Lit: to radiate with . . . *e.g., de joie,* with
   joy) IV

réaccoutumer
1. _____ Qn à Qch (to reaccustom . . . to . . .) VI

réagir
1. _____ à Qch (to react, respond to . . .) II
2. _____ contre Qch (to react against . . .) V
3. _____ sur Qch (to react with . . . [chemically]; to have
   a reciprocal influence on . . .) V

rebeller (se)
1. se —— contre Qn ou Qch (to rebel against . . .) V

rebiffer (se)
1. se —— contre Qn ou Qch (to bristle, bridle at . . .) V

rebuter
1. —— Qn (to discourage, put off . .) I
2. être rebuté par Qch (to be dismayed, put off, disgusted by . . .) V
3. se —— de *Inf.* (to be dismayed, disgusted at ---*ing*) IX-A

recevoir
1. —— Qn ou Qch (to receive . . .; to admit . . . [to a school]) I
2. être reçu à Qch (to be admitted to . . . *e.g.,* à *l'université,* to the university; to pass [an exam]) II
3. —— Qch de Qn (to receive . . . from . . .) VI
4. —— Qch dans Qch (to catch . . . in . . . Ex: *Le chien a reçu la balle dans sa bouche,* the dog caught the ball in his mouth) VI

réchapper
1. —— de, à Qch (to escape from . . .; to make it through . . . Ex: *réchapper d'une maladie,* to recover from, make it through an illness) IV, II
2. en —— (to make it through)

rechigner
1. —— à Qch (to lack enthusiasm for . . .) II
2. —— à *Inf.* (to be unwilling to . . .) VIII-A

réciter
1. —— Qch (to recite . . .) I
2. —— Qch à Qn (to recite . . . to . . .) VI

réclamer

1. ———— Qn ou Qch (to clamor for . . .; to require . . .
       e.g., beaucoup de patience, much patience) I
2. se ———— de Qn (to appeal to . . .; to take . . . as an authority) IV
3. ———— contre Qn ou Qch (to protest against . . .) V
4. ———— Qch à Qn (to ask for, demand . . . from . . .) VI

recommander

1. ———— Qn ou Qch (to recommend . . .) I
2. se ———— à Qn (to commend oneself to . . .; to seek the protection of . . .) III
3. se ———— de Qn (to use, give . . . as a reference) IV
4. se ———— par Qch (to show one's merit by . . .) V
5. ———— Qn à Qn (to commend, recommend . . . to . . .) VI
6. ———— Qch à Qn (to recommend . . . to . . .; to enjoin someone to . . . *e.g., le secret,* to secrecy) VI
7. ———— à Qn de *Inf.* (to recommend that someone . . .) IX-B

recommencer

1. ———— Qch (to begin . . . again) I
2. ———— à ou de *Inf.* (to begin to . . . again) VIII-A, IX-A

récompenser

1. ———— Qn ou Qch (to reward . . .) I
2. ———— Qn de Qch (to reward . . . for . . .) VI

réconcilier

1. ———— Qn ou Qch (to reconcile, reconciliate . . .) I
2. se ———— avec, à Qn ou Qch (to make up with . . .; to reconcile oneself to . . .) V, III
3. ———— Qn ou Qch avec, à Qn ou Qch (to reconcile . . . with . . .) VI

reconnaître

1. _____ Qn ou Qch (to recognize . . .) I
2. se _____ (to recognize oneself; to know, make out where one is) I
3. se _____ *coupable* (to acknowledge one's guilt) I
4. _____ Qn à Qch (to recognize . . . by . . . Ex: *Je l'ai reconnue à sa voix*, I recognized her by her voice) VI
5. _____ Qch à Qn (to admit, recognize that someone possesses . . . Ex: *Il faut lui reconnaître du talent*, you must admit that he has talent) VI

recourir

1. _____ à Qn ou Qch (to have recourse to . . .) III

recouvrir

1. _____ Qn ou Qch (to cover . . . completely; to cover up . . .) I
2. se _____ de Qch (to cover oneself up with . . .; to mask oneself with . . .) IV
3. _____ Qn ou Qch de Qch (to cover up, mask . . . with . . .) VI

récrier (se)

1. se _____ de Qch (Lit: to cry out with, in . . . *e.g.*, *d'admiration*, in admiration) IV
2. se _____ contre Qch (to cry out at . . .; to protest against . . .) V

récrire

1. _____ Qch (to rewrite . . .) I
2. _____ à Qn (to write to . . . again) II
3. _____ Qch à Qn (to write . . . to . . . again) VI

récriminer

1. _____ contre Qn ou Qch (to criticize . . . bitterly; to take recriminations against . . .) V

reculer
1. _____ devant Qn ou Qch (to shrink, retreat from . . .) V

redemander
1. _____ Qch (to ask for . . . again; to ask for more . . .;
to ask for . . . back) I
2. _____ Qch à Qn (to ask someone something again; to
ask someone for something again; to ask someone to give something back; to ask someone for
more . . .) VI

redevoir
1. _____ Qch (to owe a balance of . . .) I
2. _____ Qch à Qn (to owe a balance of . . . to . . .) VI

redire
1. _____ Qch (to tell . . . again) I
2. avoir, trouver [Qch] à redire à Qch (to find fault with . . .;
to take exception to . . . Ex: *Je ne trouve rien à
redire à sa façon d'agir*, I can find no fault with
his actions) II
3. _____ Qch à Qn (to tell someone something again) VI

redoubler
1. _____ Qch (to redouble, increase . . .; to put a lining in
. . .) I
2. _____ de Qch (to strengthen, increase . . . Ex: *redoubler
de force, d'énergie*, to increase one's strength,
one's zeal) IV

redouter
1. _____ Qn ou Qch (to dread . . .) I
2. _____ de *Inf.* (to dread ---*ing*) IX-A

réduire

1. ———— Qch (to reduce . . .) I
2. se ———— à Qch (to restrict oneself to . . .; to be reduced to . . .) III
3. se ———— en Qch (Of things: to turn into, be reduced to . . .) V
4. ———— Qch en Qch (to turn . . . into . . .; to reduce . . . to . . . Ex: *réduire une ville en ruines*, to reduce a city to ruins) VI
5. ———— Qn ou Qch à, en Qch (to reduce, demote, drive . . . to . . . *e.g., en esclavage*, to slavery; *au désespoir*, to despair) VI
6. ———— Qn à *Inf.* (to reduce, drive . . . to . . .) VIII-B

réexpédier

1. ———— Qch (to forward . . .; to return . . . to the sender) I
2. ———— Qch à Qn (to forward . . . to . . .) VI

référer

1. se ———— à Qn (to refer to . . . as an authority) III
2. se ———— à Qch (to refer to . . .) III
3. en ———— à Qn (to refer the matter to . . .) II
4. ———— Qch à Qch (to ascribe . . . to . . .) VI

refiler

1. ———— Qch à Qn (Coll: to palm off . . . on . . .) VI

réfléchir

1. ———— Qn ou Qch (to reflect . . .) I
2. ———— à, sur Qch (to meditate on . . .; to think about . . .) II, V

refouler

1. ———— Qn ou Qch (to repulse . . .; to drive, force, hold . . . back, Ex: *refouler l'ennemi*, to drive back the enemy; *refouler ses larmes*, to hold back one's tears) I

refroidir
1. être refroidi par Qn ou Qch (to be turned off by . . .; to react negatively to . . .) V

réfugier (se)
1. se _____ à, dans, en* Qch (to take refuge in . . .) II, V
2. se _____ chez Qn (to take refuge with . . .) V

refuser
1. _____ Qn ou Qch (to refuse . . .) I
2. se _____ Qch (to deny oneself . . .) I
3. se _____ à Qch (to object to . . .; to refuse to accept . . .) III
4. _____ Qch à Qn (to deny . . . to . . . Ex: *refuser une permission à un soldat*, to deny a leave to a soldier) VI
5. se _____ à *Inf.* (to refuse to . . . [as a matter of principle]) VIII-A
6. _____ de *Inf.* (to refuse to . . .) IX-A

régaler
1. _____ Qn (to regale, entertain . . .) I
2. se _____ de Qch (to feast on . . .; to treat oneself to . . .) IV
3. _____ Qn de Qch (to treat . . . to . . .) VI

regarder
1. _____ Qn ou Qch (to look at . . .) I
2. _____ Qn (to concern . . . Ex: *cela ne vous regarde pas*, that's none of your business) I
3. _____ à Qch (to pay close attention to . . .; to consider . . . Ex: *regarder à ses dépenses*, to watch what one spends) II
4. se _____ comme Qch (to consider oneself . . .) V
5. _____ Qn ou Qch comme Qch (to consider . . . a . . .) VI
6. _____ *Inf.* Qn ou Qch (to watch someone or something . . . Ex: *regarder tomber la pluie*, to watch the rain fall) VII-B

See Appendix I: **PREPOSITIONS OF GEOGRAPHICAL LOCATION**, p. 289 and Appendix II: **DANS, EN, À**, p. 298.

regimber
1. _____ contre Qch (to balk, kick at, against . . .) V

régler
1. _____ Qch (to rule, regulate . . .; to settle, *e.g.*, a bill) I
2. se _____ sur Qn ou Qch (to go by . . .; to take . . . as an example) V
3. _____ Qch sur Qn ou Qch (to model . . . on . . .; to use someone or something as an example for . . .) VI
4. _____ *son compte* à Qn (Coll: to get even with . . .) VI

régner
1. _____ sur Qn ou Qch (to rule over . . .) V

regorger
1. _____ Qch (to regurgitate . . .) I
2. _____ de Qn ou Qch (to overflow with . . .; to be packed with . . .) IV

regretter
1. _____ Qn ou Qch (to regret, to miss . . .) I
2. _____ de *Inf.* ou *Inf. passé* (to be sorry to . . ., to have . . .) IX-A

réintégrer
1. _____ Qch (to regain possession of . . .) I
2. _____ Qn dans Qch (to reinstate . . . in . . .; to restore . . . to . . .) VI

rejaillir
1. _____ sur Qn ou Qch (to splash, splatter on . . .; to reflect on . . . Ex: *Son succès rejaillit sur sa famille*, her success was reflected on her family) V

rejeter

1. _____ Qn ou Qch (to reject . . .; to throw . . . back) I
2. _____ Qch sur Qn ou Qch (to cast . . . on . . .; to transfer . . . to . . . Ex: *rejeter la faute sur d'autres*, to cast the blame on others) VI

réjouir

1. _____ Qn ou Qch (to delight . . .; to cheer up . . .) I
2. se _____ à Qch (to be delighted at . . .) III
3. se _____ de Qch (to be delighted by . . .) IV
4. _____ Qn de Qch (to delight, cheer up . . . with . . .) VI
5. se _____ à *Inf.* (to be delighted to . . .) VIII-A
6. se _____ de *Inf.* (to be glad, thankful to . . .) IX-A

relater

1. _____ Qch (to relate, state . . .) I
2. _____ Qch à Qn (to relate, state . . . to . . .) VI

reléguer

1. _____ Qn ou Qch à Qch (to relegate . . . to . . .) VI

relever

1. _____ Qn ou Qch (to raise, pick up, heighten . . .) I
2. se _____ de Qch (to get over . . .; to recover from . . .) IV
3. _____ de Qch (to stem from . . .; to depend on . . .) IV
4. _____ Qn de Qch (to release . . . from . . . Ex: *relever un religieux de ses voeux*, to release a monk from his vows) VI
5. _____ Qch de Qch (to heighten, emphasize . . . with . . . Ex: *relever une étude sérieuse d'anecdotes amusantes*, to spark a serious study with amusing anecdotes) VI

relier

1. _____ Qn ou Qch (to bind, tie, connect . . .) I
2. _____ Qn ou Qch à, avec Qn ou Qch (to link, connect . . . with . . . Ex: *relier une oeuvre à la tradition*, to link a work with tradition) VI
3. _____ Qch en Qch (to bind . . . in . . . Ex: *relier un livre en cuir*, to bind a book in leather) VI

remarquer
1. _____ Qn ou Qch (to notice . . .) I
2. se faire remarquer (to draw attention to oneself) I
3. faire remarquer Qn ou Qch à Qn (to point out . . . to . . .) VI

rembourser
1. _____ Qn ou Qch (to reimburse . . .) I
2. _____ Qch à Qn (to pay back . . . to . . .) VI
3. _____ Qn de Qch (to reimburse . . . for . . .) VI

remédier
1. _____ à Qch (to remedy, cure . . .) II

remercier
1. _____ Qn (to thank . . .) I
2. _____ Qn de, pour Qch (to thank . . . for . . . *e.g., de sa bonté,* for his kindness. *Pour* is often used for concrete objects, Ex: *remercier quelqu'un pour un cadeau,* to thank someone for a present) VI
3. _____ Qn de *Inf.* ou *Inf. passé* (to thank . . . for ---*ing,* for having . . .) IX-B

remettre
1. _____ Qn ou Qch (to put, set . . . back; to put on . . . again; to put off . . .) I
2. se _____ à Qch (to begin . . . again) III
3. s'en _____ à Qn [de Qch] (to rely on . . . [for . . .]) III
4. se _____ de Qch (to recover from . . .) IV
5. _____ Qch à Qn (to deliver, hand over . . . to . . .) VI
6. _____ Qch à Qch (to postpone . . . until . . . Ex: *remettre la conférence au lendemain,* to postpone the lecture until the next day) VI
7. se _____ à *Inf.* (to begin to . . . again) VIII-A

remonter
1. _____   Qn ou Qch (to take . . . upstairs again) I
2. _____   à Qch (to date back to . . .; to go back to . . . *e.g.*, *à la source*, to the source) II

remontrer
1. _____   Qch (to show . . . again) I
2. en _____   à Qn (to outdo . . .; to be superior to . . .) II

remplacer
1. _____   Qn ou Qch (to replace . . .; to substitute for . . .) I
2. _____   Qn ou Qch par Qn ou Qch (to replace . . . with, by . . .) VI

remplir
1. _____   Qch (to fill, fill up, in, out . . .) I
2. se _____   de Qch (to be filled with . . .) IV
3. _____   Qn ou Qch de Qch (to fill . . . with . .) VI

rémunérer
1. _____   Qn ou Qch (to remunerate . . .) I
2. _____   Qn de Qch (to remunerate . . . for . . .) VI

renâcler
1. _____   à, sur Qch (Coll: to sniff, snort at . . .; to disdain . . .) II, V

renaître
1. _____   à Qch (to be reborn to . . .; to feel . . . anew) II

renchérir
1. _____   Qch (to increase something's value) I
2. _____   sur Qn ou Qch (to outdo, outbid . . .; to improve on . . .) V

rencogner
1. _____   Qn (to drive . . . into a corner) I
2. se _____   dans Qch (to retreat into . . .; to ensconce oneself in . . . *e.g.*, *dans un fauteuil*, in an armchair) V

rendre

1. _____ Qn ou Qch (to return, give back . . .) I
2. _____ Qn ou Qch [+ adjectif] (to make . . . Ex: *rendre quelqu'un malade*, to make someone sick) I
3. se _____ *compte* de Qch (to realize . . .) IV
4. se _____ à Qn ou Qch (to yield, surrender to . . .) III
5. se _____ à Qch (to go to, report to . . .) III
6. _____ Qch à Qn (to return . . . to . . .) VI
7. _____ Qn ou Qch à Qch (to restore . . . to . . . *e.g., à la santé*, to health) VI

renfermer

1. _____ Qn ou Qch (to close up . . . again; to enclose . . .) I
2. se _____ dans Qch (to confine oneself to . . .; to withdraw into . . .) V
3. _____ Qn ou Qch dans Qch (to shut up . . . in . . .; to enclose . . . in . . .) VI

renfoncer

1. _____ Qch (to drive, knock . . . in further; to pull, push . . . down) I
2. se _____ dans Qch (to sink, settle into . . . *e.g., dans un coussin*, into a cushion) V

renoncer

1. _____ Qch (to renounce . . . *e.g.,* one's country) I
2. _____ à Qch (to renounce, waive, give up . . . Ex: *renoncer à ses droits*, to waive one's rights) II
3. _____ à *Inf.* (to forego, give up ---*ing*; to stop trying to . . .) VIII-A

renouer

1. _____ Qch (to tie up . . . again; to resume, renew . . .) I
2. _____ avec Qn ou Qch (to resume ties, relations with . . .) V

renseigner
1. _____ Qn (to inform . . .) I
2. se _____ sur Qn ou Qch (to find out about . . .) V
3. _____ Qn sur Qn ou Qch (to inform . . . about . . .) VI

rentrer
1. _____ Qch (to bring, take . . . in) I
2. _____ dans Qch (to fit into . . .) V
3. _____ *Inf.* (to come home, return in order to . . .) VII-A

renverser
1. _____ Qn ou Qch (to overthrow, overturn . . .; to lean . . . back) I
2. se _____ sur Qch (to fall back, lean back on . . .) V

renvoyer
1. _____ Qn ou Qch (to return . . .; to send . . . back; to fire [an employee]) I
2. _____ Qn ou Qch à Qn ou Qch (to send . . . back to . . .; to refer . . . to . . . Ex: *La note renvoie le lecteur à l'appendice*, the note refers the reader to the appendix) VI

repaître
1. se _____ de Qch (Of animals: to eat one's fill of . . .; Lit: to feast on, fill oneself with . . . Ex: *se repaître de sang*, to feed on, revel in blood; *se repaître d'illusions*, to fill oneself with illusions) IV

répandre
1. _____ Qch (to pour out, shed, spread . . .) I
2. se _____ (to flow, spread out) I
3. se _____ en Qch (to overflow with . . .; to spew . . . Ex: *se répandre en invectives*, to hurl abuse; to be lavish with . . . Ex: *se répandre en éloges*, to give lavish praise) V

repartir
1. ———— de Qch (to depart from . . . again) IV
2. ———— pour Qch (to set off for . . . again) V

répartir
1. ———— Qch (to distribute, share . . .) I
2. ———— Qch en Qch (to separate, divide . . . into . . .) VI
3. ———— Qch entre Qn ou Qch (to distribute . . . among . . .) VI

repentir (se)
1. se ———— de Qch (to be sorry for, repent for . . .) IV
2. se ———— de *Inf. passé* (to repent for having . . .) IX-A

répéter
1. ———— Qch (to repeat, rehearse . . .) I
2. se ———— (to repeat oneself; to reoccur) I
3. se ———— Qch (to repeat something to oneself) I
4. ———— Qch à Qn (to repeat . . . to . . .) VI

replier
1. ———— Qch (to fold up . . .) I
2. se ———— sur Qn ou Qch (to fold up into . . . Ex: *un couteau qui se replie sur le manche*, a knife that folds into the handle; to retreat to . . .; to withdraw into . . . Ex: *se replier sur soi-même*, to withdraw into oneself) V

répliquer
1. ———— à Qch (to respond to, answer . . .) II
2. ———— Qch à Qn (to retort . . . to . . . Usually used in questions, Ex: *Que pouvait-il répliquer à cet homme?* what could he answer that man) VI

replonger
1. ———— Qn ou Qch (to plunge, immerse . . . again) I
2. se ———— dans Qch (to immerse oneself in . . . again) V
3. ———— Qn ou Qch dans Qch (to plunge, immerse . . . in . . . again) VI

répondre

1. ——— Qch (to answer . . . *e.g.*, *la vérité*, the truth. Usually used in questions, Ex: *Qu'a-t-il répondu?* what did he answer?) I

2. ——— à Qn ou Qch (to answer . . . *e.g.*, *à une question*, a question; *au professeur*, the teacher) II

3. ——— à Qch (to correspond to . . ., to fit . . . Ex: *Le suspect ne répond pas au signalement*, the suspect does not fit the description) II

4. ——— de Qn ou Qch (to answer for . . .; to be responsible for . . .) IV

5. ——— par Qch (to answer by, in . . . *e.g.*, *par écrit*, in writing; *par télégramme*, by a telegram) V

6. ——— pour Qn (to answer for, in the place of . . .) V

7. ——— Qch à Qn (to answer . . . to . . .) VI

reporter

1. ——— Qch (to carry, take . . . back) I

2. se ——— à Qch (to refer to . . . Ex: *Reportons-nous au texte*, let us refer to the text) III

3. se ——— sur Qn ou Qch (to be given, transferred to [an undeserving object], Ex: *Tout son amour se reportait sur son chien*, he lavished all his love on his dog) V

4. ——— Qch à Qn ou Qch (to carry, take . . . back to . . .; to postpone . . . until . . .) VI

5. ——— Qch sur Qn ou Qch (to give, transfer . . . to . . .) VI

reposer

1. ——— Qch (to rest . . .) I

2. se ——— (to rest) I

3. se ——— Qch (to rest one's . . . Ex: *se reposer les pieds*, to rest one's feet) I

4. se ——— de Qch (to rest from . . .) IV

5. ——— sur Qch (to rest on, be based on . . .) V

6. se ——— sur Qn ou Qch [de Qch] (to rely on . . . [for . . .]) V

7. _____ Qch sur Qch (to lean, rest . . . against . . .; to base . . . on . . .) VI
8. se _____ de *Inf.* (to rest from ---*ing*) IX-A

reprendre
1. _____ Qch (to retake, recapture, resume . . .; to take . . . back) I
2. _____ Qn (to criticize . . .) I
3. se _____ (to recover one's wits; to correct oneself) I
4. se _____ à Qch (to take new interest in . . .; to take up . . . again) III
5. _____ de Qch (to help oneself to more . . .) IV
6. se _____ à *Inf.* (to begin to . . . again) VIII-A

représenter
1. _____ Qn ou Qch (to represent, depict . . .) I
2. se _____ Qch (to imagine . . .) I
3. _____ Qn ou Qch comme Qch (to describe, depict . . . as . . .) VI

reprocher
1. se _____ Qch (to blame oneself for . . .) I
2. _____ Qch à Qn ou Qch (to find something wrong with . . .; to begrudge someone something; to criticize someone or something for something, Ex: *On lui a reproché sa candeur*, his, her frankness was criticized) VI
3. se _____ de *Inf.* ou *Inf. passé* (to blame oneself for ---*ing*, for having . . .) IX-A
4. _____ à Qn de *Inf.* ou *Inf. passé* (to criticize, blame . . . for ---*ing*, for having . . .) IX-B

répugner
1. _____ Qn (to repulse, revolt . . .) I
2. _____ à Qn (to be repugnant, revolting to . . .) II
3. _____ à Qch (to be revolted by . . .; to find . . . distasteful) II
4. _____ à *Inf.* (to be loath to . . .) VIII-A
5. *Il répugne à Qn de Inf.* (to be loath to . . . Ex: *Il me répugne de faire cela*, I am loath to do that) IX-B

réputer

1. être réputé [pour] Qch (to be known as, considered to be
   . . . *e.g., le meilleur*, the best) V, I
2. être réputé *Inf.* ou *Inf. passé* (to be considered, reputed to
   . . ., to have . . .) VII-A

réserver

1. _____ Qch (to reserve . . .) I
2. se _____ pour Qn ou Qch (to wait for, save oneself for
   . . .) V
3. être réservé sur Qch (to be discreet about . . .) V
4. _____ Qn ou Qch à, pour Qn (to reserve . . . for . . .; to
   hold . . . in store for . . . Ex: *La nuit réservait
   des dangers aux voyageurs*, the night held dangers in store for the travelers) VI
5. se _____ [le droit] de *Inf.* (to reserve the right to . . .) IX-A

résider

1. _____ à, dans, en* [un endroit] (to reside in . . . *e.g., à
   Paris*, in Paris; *en France*, in France) II, V
2. _____ dans, en** Qch (Figurative: to lie, reside in . . .
   Ex: *La difficulté réside en ceci*, the problem
   lies in this; *le danger réside dans l'extrême hau-
   teur*, the danger lies in the extreme height) V

résigner

1. _____ Qch (to give up . . .) I
2. se _____ à Qn ou Qch (to resign oneself to, submit to . . .)
   III
3. se _____ à *Inf.* (to resign oneself to ---*ing*) VIII-A

résister

1. _____ à Qn ou Qch (to resist, withstand . . .) II

---

*See Appendix I: **PREPOSITIONS OF GEOGRAPHICAL LOCA-
TION**, p. 289.

See Appendix II: **DANS, EN, À, p. 298.

résoudre
1. ———— Qch (to solve, resolve . . .) I
2. se ———— en Qch (to dissolve, turn into . . .) V
3. être résolu en Qch (Of things: to be dissolved, turned into . . .) V
4. ———— Qch en Qch (to dissolve, reduce, transform . . . into . . . Ex: *résoudre la vapeur en eau*, to turn steam into water) VI
5. se ———— à *Inf.* (to make up one's mind to . . .) VIII-A
6. être résolu à, de *Inf.* (to be resolved to . . .) VIII-A, IX-A
7. ———— Qn à *Inf.* (to persuade . . . to . . .) VIII-B
8. ———— de *Inf.* (to resolve to . . .) IX-A

resplendir
1. ———— de Qch (to glow, shine with . . . *e.g.*, *de santé*, with health) IV

ressembler
1. ———— à Qn ou Qch (to resemble . . .) II

ressentir
1. ———— Qch (to feel . . . *e.g.*, *du chagrin*, sorrow) I
2. se ———— de Qch (to feel . . . deeply; to feel the effect of . . .) IV

ressortir
1. ———— Qch (to bring out . . . again) I
2. faire ressortir Qch (to emphasize, bring out . . . Ex: *Cette robe fait ressortir la couleur de ses yeux*, that dress brings out the color of her eyes) I
3. ———— à Qn ou Qch (to come under the jurisdiction of . . .; to be derived from . . .) II
4. ———— de Qch (to be the result of . . .; to result from . . .) IV

ressouvenir
1. se _____ de Qn ou Qch (to have a faint memory of . . .) IV
2. faire ressouvenir Qn de Qn ou Qch (to remind . . . of . . .) VI
3. se _____ de *Inf. passé* (to remember having . . .) IX-A

rester
1. *Il reste Qch ou Qn* (to be left, remain, Ex: *Il reste une bouteille*, there is one bottle left) I
2. en _____ à Qch (to remain at . . .; to go no further than . . . Ex: *Nous en sommes restés aux préliminaires*, we didn't get past the preliminaries) II
3. _____ de Qn ou Qch (to remain, be left of . . . Ex: *C'est tout ce qui reste de sa fortune*, that's all that's left of his, her fortune) IV
4. *Il reste Qch à Qn ou Qch* (to have . . . left, Ex: *Il ne lui reste que cinq dollars*, he, she only has five dollars left) VI
5. _____ (à, pour) *Inf.* (to stay, remain to, in order to . . . Ex: *Il reste à dîner avec nous*, he is staying to have dinner with us. Omission of preposition is more colloquial) VIII-A, X, VII-A
6. _____ à *Inf.* (to remain, keep on ---*ing*, to continue to . . . Ex: *Après son repas, il restait à fumer en regardant passer les gens*, after his meal, he sat smoking as he watched the people go by) VIII-A
7. _____ à *Inf.* (to be left, to remain to . . . Ex: *La vaisselle reste à faire*, the dishes still have to be done) VIII-A
8. *Il reste à Qn à Inf.* (to still have to . . . . Ex: *Il me reste à finir mon travail*, I still have to finish my work) VIII-B
9. *Il reste Qch à Inf.* (there are still, there remain . . . to . . . Ex: *Il reste deux villages à traverser*, there are still two villages to pass through) VIII-B
10. *Il reste à Qn Qch à Inf.* (to still have . . . to . . . Ex: *Il nous reste deux devoirs à faire*, we still have two assignments to do) VIII-B

restituer
1. _____ Qch (to restore, return, make restitution of . . .) I
2. _____ Qch à Qn (to return, make restitution of . . . to . . .) VI

restreindre
1. _____ Qn ou Qch (to restrain, limit . . .) I
2. se _____ à Qch (Of things: to be limited to . . .) III
3. _____ Qch à Qch (to limit . . . to . . .) VI

résulter
[Only in Third Person]
1. _____ de Qch (to result from . . .) IV

résumer
1. _____ Qch (to summarize, sum up . . .) I
2. se _____ à Qch (Coll: to boil down to . . .) III

retarder
1. _____ Qn ou Qch (to delay . . .) I
2. _____ de [un certain temps] (Of clocks: to be . . . slow, Ex: *Ma montre retarde de cinq minutes*, my watch is five minutes slow) IV

retenir
1. _____ Qn ou Qch (to keep, hold . . .; to keep, hold . . . back, in, up, Ex: *retenir ses larmes*, to hold back one's tears; to reserve . . . *e.g.*, a table; to remember . . . *e.g.*, a number) I
2. se _____ à Qch (to catch hold of . . .) III
3. _____ Qch sur, de Qch (to retain, withhold . . . from . . . Ex: *On a retenu dix dollars sur ses gages*, ten dollars were withheld from his wages) VI
4. _____ Qn à, pour *Inf.* (to keep, detain . . . to . . . Ex: *Nous avons retenu le professeur à dîner*, we asked the professor to stay for dinner) VIII-B, X
5. se _____ de *Inf.* (to refrain from, keep oneself from ---*ing*) IX-A
6. _____ Qn ou Qch de *Inf.* (to prevent, keep . . . from ---*ing*) IX-B

retentir

1. _____ de Qch (to ring out, peal with . . . Ex: *La maison retentit de leurs rires*, the house rang out with their laughter) IV

retirer

1. _____ Qch (to withdraw . . .; to take . . . off, out) I
2. se _____ de Qch (to leave . . .; to withdraw from . . .) IV
3. _____ Qch à Qn (to take . . . away from . . .; to take . . . back from . . .) VI
4. _____ Qn ou Qch de Qch (to take . . . out of, away from . . . Ex: *retirer un lapin d'un chapeau*, to take a rabbit out of a hat; *retirer un enfant de l'école*, to take a child out of school; *retirer de l'argent de la banque*, to withdraw money from the bank) VI

retomber

1. _____ dans Qch (to relapse into . . . *e.g., de mauvaises habitudes*, bad habits; to sink back into . . . *e.g., dans l'oubli*, into oblivion) V
2. _____ sur Qch (to fall back, down onto . . .) V
3. _____ sur Qn ou Qch (to fall to, be the responsibility of . . . Ex: *Le blâme retombera sur lui*, the blame will fall on him) V

retourner

1. _____ Qch (to turn . . . over, inside out; to return . . . *e.g.*, a gift) I
2. se _____ (to turn around, over) I
3. _____ à Qch (to return to . . .; to revert to . . .) II
4. se _____ contre Qn ou Qch (to turn against . . .) V
5. _____ Qch à Qn (to return, counter someone's . . . Ex: *retourner sa critique à quelqu'un*, to counter someone's criticism) VI
6. _____ Qch à Qn ou Qch (to return . . . to . . . Ex: *retourner un cadeau au magasin*, to take a gift back to the store) VI
7. _____ Qch contre Qn ou Qch (to turn . . . against . . .) VI
8. _____ *Inf.* (to return, to go back in order to . . .) VII-A

retrancher

1. _____ Qch (to cut . . . out; to expurgate, eliminate . . .) I
2. se _____ derrière Qn ou Qch (to take refuge behind . . .) V
3. se _____ dans Qch (to entrench oneself in . . . Ex: *Il s'est retranché dans cette attitude hostile*, he stubbornly maintained that hostile attitude) V
4. _____ Qch de Qch (to expurgate . . . from . . .; to cut . . . out, off from . . . Ex: *Le maire a retranché quelques remarques de son discours*, the mayor cut out several remarks from his speech) VI
5. _____ Qch sur Qch (to deduct . . . from . . .; to withhold . . . from . . .) VI

retremper

1. _____ Qn ou Qch (to dip, wet . . . again) I
2. se _____ à Qch (to draw renewed vigor from . . .) III
3. se _____ dans Qch (to immerse oneself in . . . again) V
4. _____ Qn ou Qch dans Qch (to dip, immerse . . . in . . . again) VI

réunir

1. _____ Qn ou Qch (to convene . . .; to join, unite, reunite . . .) I
2. se _____ (to meet, Ex: *se réunir une fois par mois*, to meet once a month) I
3. se _____ contre Qn ou Qch (to join together against . . .) V
4. se _____ avec Qn (to gather, meet with . . .) V
5. se _____ en Qch (to join together, unite in . . .) V
6. _____ Qch à Qch (to attach, join . . . to, with . . .) VI
7. se _____ pour *Inf.* to gather, join together to . . .) X

réussir

1. _____ Qch (to complete . . . successfully, Ex: *J'ai réussi mon expérience*, my experiment was a success) I
2. _____ à Qch (to succeed at . . . Ex: *réussir à un examen*, to pass a test) II
3. _____ à Qn (to turn out well for . . . Ex: *Tout lui réussit*, everything turns out well for him, her) II

4. ———— dans Qch (to be successful in . . . *e.g., dans son travail*, in one's work) V

5. ———— à *Inf.* (to succeed in ---*ing*; to manage to . . .) VIII-A

revaloir

1. ———— Qch à Qn (to pay someone back in kind for something, Ex: *Je vous revaudrai ces paroles-là*, I'll get even with you for those words!) VI

réveiller

1. ———— Qn ou Qch (to awaken . . .) I

2. se ———— de Qch (to awaken from . . . *e.g., d'un rêve*, from a dream) IV

3. ———— Qn de Qch (to awaken . . . from . . .) VI

révéler

1. ———— Qch (to reveal . . .) I

2. ———— Qch à Qn (to reveal . . . to . . .) VI

revenir

1. ———— à Qch (to come back to . . .; to amount to . . . Ex: *Le repas revient à six dollars*, the meal comes to six dollars; *cela revient au même*, that amounts to the same thing) II

2. en ———— à Qch (to revert to, go back to . . . Ex: *Il en revient toujours à ses manières-là*, he always reverts to that way of behavior) II

3. ———— à Qn (to return, come back to . . .) II

4. ———— de Qch (to come back from . . . *e.g., de Paris*, from Paris; to get over, recover from . . . Ex: *revenir de sa peur*, to get over one's fright; to be disabused of . . . *e.g., de ses illusions*, of one's illusions) IV

5. ———— sur Qch (to retrace . . . Ex: *revenir sur ses pas*, to retrace one's steps; to go back on . . . *e.g., sur sa parole*, on one's word; to harp on . . . Ex: *revenir sur le même sujet*, to harp on the same subject) V

6. ———— *Inf.* (to come back in order to . . .) VII-A

rêver
1. _____ Qch (to dream . . .) I
2. _____ à Qn ou Qch (to muse about, daydream about . . .)
   III
3. _____ de Qn ou Qch (to dream about . . .) IV
4. _____ de *Inf.* (to dream of ---*ing*) IX-A

revêtir
1. _____ Qn ou Qch (to clothe, cover . . .; to put on . . .) I
2. se _____ de Qch (to put on . . .; to clothe oneself in . . .) IV
3. _____ Qn ou Qch de Qch (to clothe . . . in . . .; to cover
   . . . with . . .) VI

révolter
1. _____ Qn ou Qch (to revolt, disgust . . .) I
2. se _____ contre Qn ou Qch (to rebel, revolt against . . .) V

rigoler
1. _____ de Qn ou Qch (Coll: to joke, kid about . . .) IV

rimer
1. _____ Qch (to versify . . .; to set . . . to verse) I
2. _____ à Qch (to jibe, be in accord with . . . Ex: *Cela ne
   rime à rien*, that doesn't make any sense) II
3. _____ avec Qch (to rhyme with . . .) V

riposter
1. _____ Qch (to retort . . .) I
2. _____ à Qn ou Qch (to give a sharp answer to . . .) II
3. _____ Qch à Qn (to retort . . . to . . .) VI

rire
1. _____ à Qn ou Qch (Lit: to greet . . . with a smile; to
   smile on . . .) II
2. _____ de Qn ou Qch (to laugh at . . .) IV

risquer
1. _____ Qch (to risk . . .) I
2. se _____ à Qch (to take a chance at . . . *e.g., au jeu,* at gambling) III
3. se _____ dans Qch (to venture in, into . . .) V
4. se _____ à *Inf.* (to venture to, dare to . . .) VIII-A
5. _____ de *Inf.* (to have a chance of ---*ing*, Ex: *Il risque de tomber,* he might fall; *La situation risque de devenir grave,* the situation may well become serious) IX-A

rivaliser
1. _____ avec Qn ou Qch (to rival . . .) V
2. _____ avec Qn ou Qch de Qch (to rival . . . in . . . *e.g., d'élégance,* in elegance) V

rogner
1. _____ Qch (to clip, pare . . .) I
2. se _____ Qch (to clip, pare one's . . . *e.g., les ongles,* one's nails) I
3. _____ *les ailes* à Qn (to clip someone's wings) VI

rompre
1. _____ Qch (to break, break off . . .) I
2. se _____ à Qch (to get used to, broken in to . . .) III
3. être rompu à Qch (to be used to, broken in to . . .) II
4. être rompu de Qch (to be worn out with . . . *e.g., de fatigue,* with fatigue) IV
5. _____ avec Qn ou Qch (to break off with, break up with . . .) V
6. _____ *la tête, les oreilles* à Qn (Coll: to make a deafening noise, to talk someone's ears off) II
7. _____ Qn à Qch (to break in . . . to . . . Ex: *rompre un ouvrier au travail,* to break in a worker to a job) VI

ronger
1. _____ Qch (to gnaw . . .) I
2. se _____ de Qch (to torment oneself with . . . *e.g.*, *de jalousie*, with jealousy) IV
3. être rongé de Qch (to be consumed, eaten away with . . . *e.g.*, *de regret*, with regret; to be riddled with . . . *e.g.*, *de trous*, with holes) IV
4. être rongé par Qn ou Qch (to be gnawed, eaten away by . . . *e.g.*, *par les rats*, by rats) V

rougir
1. _____ Qch (to redden . . .) I
2. _____ de Qch (to flush, blush with . . . *e.g.*, *de honte*, with shame; to be embarrassed by . . ., to be ashamed of . . . *e.g.*, *de ses vêtements râpés*, of one's shabby clothing) IV

rouler
1. _____ Qn (Coll: to swindle, trick . . .) I
2. _____ Qch (to roll, turn over . . .) I
3. _____ sur Qch (to roll along . . .; to run to . . . Ex: *La conversation roulait sur la politique*, the conversation turned to politics; *rouler sur l'or*, to be rolling in money) V
4. se _____ dans, en* Qch (to roll up in, into . . . *e.g.*, *dans une couverture*, in a blanket; *en boule*, into a ball) V
5. _____ Qn ou Qch dans, en* Qch (to roll . . . in, into . . .) VI

ruer
1. se _____ à, vers Qn ou Qch (to rush to, towards . . .) III, V
2. se _____ sur Qn ou Qch (to hurl, fling oneself at, on . . .; to rush at . . .) V

---

*See Appendix II: **DANS, EN, À**, p. 298.

ruisseler

1. _____ de Qch (to stream with . . . *e.g.*, *de sueur*, with perspiration) IV

ruminer

1. _____ Qch (to ruminate on . . .) I

ruser

1. _____ avec Qn (to be wily, crafty with . . .) V

S

sacrifier

1. _____ Qn ou Qch (to sacrifice . . .) I
2. _____ à Qch (to conform to . . ., *e.g.*, *à la mode*, to fashion) II
3. se _____ à Qn ou Qch (to sacrifice oneself to . . .) III
4. se _____ pour Qn ou Qch (to sacrifice oneself for . . .) V
5. _____ Qn ou Qch à Qn ou Qch (to sacrifice . . . to . . .) VI

saigner

1. _____ Qn (to bleed . . .) I
2. _____ de Qch (to bleed from . . . Ex: *Il saigne du nez*, his nose is bleeding) IV
3. se _____ [*aux quatre veines*] pour Qn ou Qch (to bleed oneself [dry] for . . .) V

saisir

1. _____ Qn ou Qch (to seize . . .) I
2. se _____ de Qn ou Qch (to seize upon, grab hold of . . .) IV
3. _____ Qn ou Qch à Qch (to grab . . . by . . . *e.g.*, *au bras*, by the arm; *au collet*, by the collar) VI

sanctionner
1. _____ Qch (to sanction . . .) I
2. être sanctionné par Qch (to be sanctioned by . . .) V

satisfaire
1. _____ Qn ou Qch (to satisfy, content . . .) I
2. _____ à Qch (to carry out . . ., *e.g.,* one's duties; to meet
    . . . *e.g.,* demands) II
3. être satisfait de Qn ou Qch (to be satisfied with . . .) IV
4. être satisfait de *Inf.* ou *Inf. passé* (to be glad, satisfied to
    . . ., to have . . .) IX-A

saturer
1. _____ Qn ou Qch (to saturate . . .) I
2. se _____ de Qch (to become saturated with . . .) IV
3. _____ Qn ou Qch de Qch (to saturate . . . with . . .) VI

saupoudrer
1. _____ Qn ou Qch (to sprinkle . . .) I
2. _____ Qn ou Qch de Qch (to sprinkle . . . with . . .
    Usually culinary, Ex: *saupoudrer un bifteck de
    sel et de poivre,* to sprinkle a steak with salt and
    pepper) VI

sauter
1. _____ Qch (to skip . . .) I
2. faire sauter Qch (to fry . . .; to blow up, explode . . .) I
3. _____ à Qn ou Qch (to jump, leap at . . .; to skip to
    . . .) II
4. _____ de Qch (to jump with, for . . . *e.g., de joie,* for
    joy) IV
5. _____ sur, par, dans Qn ou Qch (to jump on, through,
    in . . .) V

sauver

1. _____ Qn ou Qch (to save . . .) I
2. se _____ (to run away, to get away) I
3. se _____ de Qn ou Qch (to make one's escape from . . .; to run away from . . .) IV
4. _____ Qn ou Qch de Qn ou Qch (to save . . . from . . .) VI
5. _____ Qch pour Qn ou Qch (to save . . . for . . .) VI
6. _____ Qn de *Inf.* (to save . . . from ---*ing*) IX-B

savoir

1. _____ Qch (to know . . .) I
2. faire savoir Qch à Qn (to inform someone of something, Ex: *Il ne m'a pas fait savoir ses projets*, he hasn't informed me of his plans) VI
3. _____ *Inf.* (to know how to . . .) VII-A

scandaliser

1. _____ Qn (to scandalize . . .) I
2. se _____ de Qch (to become shocked at, by . . .) IV
3. être scandalisé de Qch (to be shocked at . . .) IV
4. être scandalisé par Qch (to be shocked by . . .) V

sceller

1. _____ Qch (to seal . . .) I
2. _____ Qch de Qch (to seal . . . with . . .) VI

sculpter

1. _____ Qch (to sculpt, carve . . .) I
2. _____ Qch dans Qch (to carve . . . in, out of . . .) VI

seconder

1. _____ Qn ou Qch (to second . . .; to assist . . .) I
2. être secondé par Qn (to be seconded by . . .) V

sembler

1. _____ [+ adjectif] à Qn (to seem . . . to . . . Ex: *Cela lui semble normal*, that seems normal to him, her) II
2. *Il semble à Qn que* (it seems to . . . that . . . Ex: *Il me semble qu'elle a raison*, it seems to me that she's right) II
3. _____ *Inf. ou Inf. passé* (to seem to . . ., to have . . .) VII-A

semer

1. _____ Qch (to sow . . .) I
2. _____ Qch de Qch (to sow . . . with . . .) VI

sentir

1. _____ Qn ou Qch (to feel, smell . . .) I
2. _____ Qch (to smell of . . . Ex: *sentir la pipe*, to smell of pipe smoke; to taste of . . .) I
3. se _____ *Inf.* (to feel oneself ---*ing*, Ex: *se sentir glisser*, to feel oneself slipping) VII-A
4. _____ *Inf.* Qn ou Qch (to feel someone or something . . . Ex: *J'ai senti s'arrêter la voiture*, I felt the car stop) VII-B

seoir

[Only in third person]

1. _____ à Qn (to suit, become . . . Ex: *Cette robe lui sied*, that dress becomes her) II
2. *Il sied à Qn de Inf.* (it is fitting for . . . to . . .) IX-B

séparer

1. _____ Qn ou Qch (to separate . . .) I
2. se _____ de, d'avec Qn ou Qch (to leave, separate from . . . *e.g., de son mari*, from one's husband) IV, V
3. être séparé de, d'avec Qn (to be separated from . . .) IV, V
4. _____ Qn ou Qch de, d'avec Qn ou Qch (to separate . . . from . . .) VI

seriner

1. ———— Qch (to grind out . . . *e.g.,* a melody) I
2. ———— Qch à Qn (to drum . . . into . . .) VI

servir

1. ———— Qn ou Qch (to serve . . .) I
2. se ——— (to help oneself) I
3. ———— à Qch (to be useful for . . .) II
4. ———— à Qn [pour Qch ou *Inf.*] (to be useful to . . . [for . . ., for --*ing*]) II
5. ———— de Qn ou Qch [à Qn] (to serve, act as . . . [for . . .]) IV
6. se ——— de Qn ou Qch (to use, make use of . . .) IV
7. ———— à *Inf.* (to be used for ---*ing*, to . . . Ex: *Un couteau sert à couper*, a knife is used for cutting, to cut) VIII-A
8. *À quoi* [*ça*] *sert de Inf.* ou *Inf. passé* (What is the use of ---*ing*, of having . . .; what good does it do to, to have . . . Ex: *À quoi sert d'attendre?* What is the use of waiting? Use of *ça* is colloquial) IX-A

sévir

1. ———— contre Qn ou Qch (to deal severely with . . .; to punish . . .) V

sevrer

1. ———— Qn (to wean . . .) I
2. se ——— de Qch (to wean, deprive oneself of . . .) IV
3. ———— Qn de Qch (to wean, deprive . . . of . . .) VI

siéger

1. ———— à Qch (to sit in, on . . . *e.g., au Congrès*, in Congress; *à la Cour suprême*, on the Supreme Court) II

signaler

1. ———— Qn ou Qch (to point out . . .; to signal . . .) I
2. se ——— par Qch (to distinguish oneself, be distinguished by . . .) V
3. ———— Qn oh Qch à Qn ou Qch (to point . . . out to . . .; to draw . . . [*e.g.,* someone's attention] to . . .) VI

signifier
1. _____ Qch (to signify . . .) I
2. _____ Qch à Qn (to indicate . . . to . . .; to inform someone of something) VI

sillonner
1. _____ Qch (to furrow . . .) I
2. _____ Qch de Qch (to furrow . . . with . . .) VI

soigner
1. _____ Qn ou Qch (to take care of . . .; to look after . . .; to polish, be careful of . . . *e.g.*, one's style) I

solidariser
1. se _____ avec Qn ou Qch (to join together with . . .; to support . . .) V

solliciter
1. _____ Qn ou Qch (to solicit, apply for . . .; Lit: to attract, invite . . . *e.g.*, attention) I
2. être sollicité par Qn pour Qch (to be solicited by . . . for . . . *e.g.*, a contribution) V
3. _____ Qn pour Qch (to ask . . . for . . .) VI
4. _____ Qn de *Inf.* (to ask, urge . . . to . . .) IX-B

sombrer
1. _____ sous, dans Qch (to sink under, into . . .) V
2. _____ dans Qch (Figurative: to sink into . . . *e.g.*, *dans la folie*, into madness) V

sommer
1. _____ Qn (to summon . . .) I
2. _____ Qn de, à *Inf.* (to call on . . . to . . .; to summon . . . to . . .) IX-B, VIII-B

songer
1. _____ à Qn ou Qch (to think, muse about . . .) III
2. _____ à *Inf.* (to think of, about ---*ing*) VIII-A

sonner
1. ———— Qch (to ring, sound . . . *e.g.*, a bell) I
2. ———— de Qch (to play [a horn], Ex: *sonner du clairon*, to play the bugle) IV

sortir
1. ———— Qn ou Qch (to take . . . out) I
2. ———— de Qch (to go out of . . .; to come from . . . Ex: *sortir d'une bonne famille*, to come from a good family; *sortir du peuple*, to come from the people) IV
3. se ———— de Qch (to get out of . . . *e.g.*, a bad situation) IV
4. ———— Qch de Qch (to take . . . out of . . .) VI
5. ———— *Inf.* (to go out in order to . . .) VII-A

soucier
1. se ———— de Qn ou Qch (to care about, trouble oneself about . . .) IV
2. ne pas se soucier de *Inf.* (to not care about, not bother to . . . Ex: *Il ne se soucie pas de répondre*, he doesn't bother to answer) IX-A

souder
1. ———— Qch (to solder . . .) I
2. ———— Qch avec Qch (to solder . . . to . . .) VI

souffler
1. ———— Qch to utter, breathe . . . *e.g.*, a word; to snuff [a candle]) I
2. ———— dans, sur Qch (to blow, breathe on, in . . . *e.g.*, *sur sa soupe*, on one's soup; *dans, sur ses mains*, on one's hands [to warm them]) V
3. ———— Qn ou Qch à Qn (to suggest, whisper . . . to . . .; to steal . . . from . . .) VI

souffrir
1. ———— Qn ou Qch (to suffer, put up with . . .; to bear . . .) I

2. _____ de Qch (to suffer from . . . *e.g., du froid,* from the cold; to have a pain in . . . Ex: *souffrir du dos,* to have a backache) IV

3. _____ de *Inf.* (to suffer from, at ---*ing*) IX-A

souhaiter

1. _____ Qch (to wish for, desire . . .) I

2. _____ Qch à Qn (to wish someone something, Ex: *Je vous souhaite une bonne année,* I wish you a happy new year) VI

3. _____ *Inf.* (to hope to . . . Ex: *Nous souhaitons aller en France l'année prochaine,* we hope to go to France next year) VII-A

souiller

1. _____ Qn ou Qch (to soil, dirty, sully . . .) I

2. _____ Qn ou Qch de Qch (to soil, dirty, sully . . . with . . .) VI

soulager

1. _____ Qn ou Qch (to relieve, ease, comfort . . .) I

2. se _____ (to ease one's mind; to relieve oneself) I

3. se _____ de Qch (to ease, relieve one's . . . Ex: *se soulager de sa douleur,* to ease one's pain) IV

4. _____ Qn ou Qch de Qch (to ease someone's . . .; to relieve . . . of . . . *e.g., de sa peine,* of his grief) VI

5. se _____ de *Inf.* ou *Inf. passé* (to be relieved at, eased by ---*ing*, by having . . .) IX-A

soûler

1. _____ Qn (Coll: to get . . . drunk) I

2. se _____ (Coll: to get drunk) I

3. se _____ de Qch (to gorge on . . .; to glut oneself with . . .; to become drunk with . . . *e.g., de pouvoir,* with power) IV

4. _____ Qn de Qch (to intoxicate . . . with . . .) VI

soulever
1. _____ Qn ou Qch (to raise, lift . . .) I
2. se _____ contre Qn ou Qch (to rise up in rebellion against . . .) V
3. _____ Qn contre Qn ou Qch (to arouse . . . against . . .) VI

soumettre
1. _____ Qch (to submit . . .; to control . . .) I
2. se _____ (to yield) I
3. être soumis à Qn ou Qch (to be subject to, under the control of . . .) II
4. se _____ à Qn ou Qch (to yield to : . .; to comply with . . .) III
5. _____ Qn ou Qch à Qn ou Qch (to submit, subject . . . to . . .) VI

soupçonner
1. _____ Qn ou Qch (to suspect . . .) I
2. _____ Qn de Qch (to suspect . . . of . . .) VI
3. _____ Qn de *Inf.* ou *Inf. passé* (to suspect . . . of ---*ing*, of having . . .) IX-B

soupirer
1. _____ après, pour Qn ou Qch (to desire . . .; to yearn, long for . . .) V

sourire
1. _____ à Qn ou Qch (to smile at, on . . .) II
2. _____ de Qn ou Qch (to be amused by . . .) IV

souscrire
1. _____ Qch (to sign, draw . . . *e.g.*, a check; to underwrite . . . *e.g.*, a loan) I
2. _____ à Qch (to contribute to . . .; to consent to, subscribe to . . . *e.g.*, an opinion, a belief) II

soustraire
1. _____ Qch (to subtract, remove . . .; to take . . . away) I
2. se _____ à Qch (to avoid, elude . . .) III
3. _____ Qn ou Qch à, de Qch (to shield, protect . . . from . . .) VI
4. _____ Qch à Qn ou Qch (to remove, steal . . . from . . .) VI

soutirer
1. _____ Qch (to tap, draw off . . .) I
2. _____ Qch à Qn (to get, wheedle . . . out of . . .) VI

souvenir
1. se _____ de Qn ou Qch (to remember . . .) IV
2. *Il souvient à Qn de Qn ou Qch* (Lit: to recall . . . Ex: *Il me souvient d'un incident assez drôle*, I recall a rather funny incident) II
3. faire souvenir Qn de Qn ou Qch (to remind . . . of . . .) VI
4. se _____ de *Inf.* ou *Inf. passé* (to remember to . . .; to remember ---*ing*, having . . .) IX-A

spécialiser (se)
1. se _____ dans Qch (to specialize in . . .) V

spéculer
1. _____ sur Qch (to speculate in, on . . .) V

statuer
1. _____ sur Qch (to pronounce judgment on . . .; to settle . . . *e.g.*, a dispute) V

stigmatiser
1. _____ Qn ou Qch (to brand, stigmatize . . .) I
2. _____ Qn ou Qch de Qch (to brand, stigmatize . . . with, as . . .) VI

stupéfier
1. _____ Qn (to stupefy . . .) I
2. être stupéfié par Qch (to be stupefied, astounded by . . .) V

subdiviser
1. _____ Qch (to subdivide . . .; to split up . . .) I
2. _____ Qch en Qch (to subdivide, split . . . in . . .) VI

subir
1. _____ Qn (to be forced to accept . . .; to bear with, endure . . .) I
2. _____ Qch (to undergo . . . *e.g.*, an operation; to come under . . . *e.g.*, an influence; to suffer . . . *e.g.*, a loss) I
3. faire subir Qch à Qn (to inflict . . . on . . .; to make someone undergo . . . Ex: *faire subir un examen au candidat*, to make the candidate take a test) VI

submerger
1. _____ Qn ou Qch (to submerge . . .) I
2. être submergé de Qch (to be submerged, swamped with . . .) IV
3. _____ Qn ou Qch de Qch (to submerge, swamp . . . with . . .) VI

subordonner
1. _____ Qn ou Qch (to subordinate . . .) I
2. se _____ à Qn ou Qch (to subordinate oneself to . . .) III
3. _____ Qn ou Qch à Qn ou Qch (to subordinate . . . to . . .) VI

subsister
1. _____ de Qch (to subsist on . . .) IV

substituer
1. se _____ à Qn (to substitute for . . .; to take someone's place) III
2. _____ Qn ou Qch à Qn ou Qch (to substitute . . . for . . .) VI

subvenir

1. _____ à Qch (to provide for . . .; to subsidize . . . Ex: *L'Etat subvient aux frais universitaires et sco-laires*, the state subsidizes tuition fees) II

succéder

1. se _____ (to follow one another, Ex: *Les années se succè-dent*, the years follow one another) I
2. _____ à Qn ou Qch (to succeed, follow after . . .) II

succomber

1. _____ à Qch (to yield to, be overcome by . . . *e.g.*, sleep, temptation) II
2. _____ sous Qch (to succomb to, sink under . . . *e.g.*, a weight) V

suffire

1. _____ à Qch (to be adequate, equal to . . . *e.g.*, *à ses besoins*, to one's needs) II
2. *Il suffit de Qch pour Inf.* (. . . is, are sufficient to . . . Ex: *Il suffit de quelques mots pour la faire pleurer*, a few words are enough to make her cry) IV
3. _____ à, pour *Inf.* (to be adequate, suffice to . . .) VIII-A, X
4. *Il suffit de Inf.* (it is sufficient to . . .) IX-A
5. *Il suffit à Qn de Inf.* (to be satisfied with ---*ing*, Ex: *Il suf-fisait aux enfants de regarder*, the children were satisfied with watching) IX-B

suffoquer

1. _____ Qn ou Qch (to suffocate, smother . . .) I
2. _____ de Qch (to choke with . . . *e.g.*, *de colère*, with anger) IV

suggérer

1. _____ Qch (to suggest . . .) I
2. _____ Qch à Qn (to suggest . . . to . . .) VI
3. _____ à Qn de *Inf.* (to suggest that someone . . .) IX-B

suivre

1. _____ Qn ou Qch (to follow . . .) I
2. être suivi de Qn ou Qch (to be followed by . . . Ex: *La voiture du président fut suivie d'un long cortège,* the President's car was followed by a long cortege; *la cérémonie fut suivie d'une réception,* the ceremony was followed by a reception) IV
3. être suivi par Qn ou Qch (to be followed by . . . Indicates greater physical pursuit than #2, Ex: *Le suspect fut suivi par un détective,* the suspect was followed by a detective) V
4. _____ Qn ou Qch *des yeux, du regard* (to follow, look after . . . with one's eyes) I

superposer

1. _____ Qch (to superimpose . . .) I
2. _____ Qch à Qch (to superimpose . . . on . . .) VI

suppléer

1. _____ Qch (to supply . . .; to fill in, make up [a lack]) I
2. _____ Qn (to replace, take the place of . . .) I
3. _____ à Qch [par Qch] (to compensate for . . . [with . . .]) II

supplier

1. _____ Qn (to beg, entreat . . .) I
2. _____ Qn de *Inf.* (to beg, entreat . . . to . . .) IX-B

supprimer

1. _____ Qch (to suppress, put down . . .) I
2. _____ Qn (Coll: to kill, rub out . . .) I
3. _____ Qch à Qn (to deprive someone of something; to take . . . away from . . .) VI
4. _____ Qch de Qch (to eliminate, delete . . . from . . .) VI

surabonder

1. _____ de, en Qch (to overflow with, be glutted with . . ., to have an excess of . . . Ex: *surabonder de blé,* to have an excess of wheat; *surabonder en éloges,* to overflow with praise) IV, V

surcharger
1. _____ Qn ou Qch (to overload, overwork . . .) I
2. se _____ de Qch (to overburden oneself with . . .) IV
3. _____ Qn ou Qch de Qch (to overburden . . . with . . .) VI

surenchérir
1. _____ sur Qn (to bid higher than . . .; to outbid . . .) V

surpasser
1. _____ Qn ou Qch (to surpass . . .) I
2. se _____ (to outdo oneself) I
3. _____ Qn ou Qch en Qch (to surpass . . . in . . .; to be superior to . . . in . . . Ex: *surpasser quelqu'un en beauté, en intelligence*, to be prettier, smarter than someone) VI

surprendre
1. _____ Qn ou Qch (to surprise . . .; to catch . . . unaware; to come across . . . unexpectedly) I
2. être surpris de Qch (to be surprised at, by . . .) IV
3. _____ Qn à *Inf.* (to catch someone ---*ing*) VIII-B
4. être surpris de *Inf.* (to be surprised to . . .) IX-A

surseoir
1. _____ à Qch (to delay, stay, postpone . . .) II

survivre
1. _____ à Qn ou Qch (to survive, outlive . . .) II

survoler
1. _____ Qch (to fly over . . .; to skip over . . .) I

suspecter
1. _____ Qn ou Qch (to suspect, doubt . . .) I
2. _____ Qn ou Qch de Qch (to suspect . . . of . . .) VI
3. _____ Qn ou Qch de *Inf.* ou *Inf. passé* (to suspect . . . of ---*ing*, of having . . .) IX-B

suspendre
1. ———— Qn ou Qch (to suspend, hang . . .) I
2. se ———— à Qch (to hang by, onto, from . . .) III
3. être suspendu sur Qch (to hang over . . . *e.g.*, the edge) V
4. ———— Qn ou Qch à Qch (to hang . . . from, on . . .) VI
5. ———— Qn ou Qch par Qch (to hang . . ., suspend . . . by . . .) VI

sympathiser
1. ———— avec Qn (to get along well with . . .) V

—T—

tabasser
1. ———— Qn (Coll: to beat up . . .) I

tabler
1. ———— sur Qch (to count on, reckon on . . .) V

tâcher
1. ———— de *Inf.* (to try, strive to . . .) IX-A

taire
1. ———— Qch (to hush up, suppress . . .; to keep silent about . . .) I
2. faire taire Qn (to silence . . .) I
3. se ———— (to keep silent) I
4. se ———— sur Qch (to say nothing about . . .) V
5. ———— Qch à Qn (to keep, conceal . . . from . . .) VI

taper
1. ———— Qch (to beat, tap . . .; to type . . .) I
2. ———— *des pieds* (to stamp one's feet)
3. ———— sur Qn ou Qch (Coll: to beat up . . .; to beat down on . . .) V

tarder
1. _____ à *Inf.* (to delay, to be late in ---*ing*, Ex: *Ne tardez pas à venir*, don't put off coming) VIII-A
2. *Il tarde à Qn de Inf.* (to be anxious to . . . Ex: *Il lui tarde de commencer*, he, she is anxious to begin) IX-B

targuer (se)
1. se _____ de Qch (to pride oneself on . . .) IV
2. se _____ de *Inf.* ou *Inf. passé* (to pride oneself on ---*ing*, on having . . .) IX-A

tarir
1. _____ Qch (to dry up . . .) I
2. se _____ (to run dry) I
3. ne _____ pas sur Qch (to be forever talking about . . .) V

tâter
1. _____ Qn ou Qch (to touch, feel . . .; to feel out . . .) I
2. _____ de Qch (to experience . . .; to try one's hand at . . .) IV
3. _____ *le pouls* à Qn (to take someone's pulse) VI

taxer
1. _____ Qch (to tax . . .; to set, regulate . . . *e.g.*, a price) I
2. _____ Qn ou Qch de Qch (to call . . . [a] . . . Ex: *taxer quelqu'un de menteur*, to call someone a liar; *taxer la protestation de trahison*, to call protest treason; to accuse . . . of . . . *e.g.*, *de négligence*, of negligence) VI

teindre
1. _____ Qch (to dye, stain . . .) I
2. être teint de Qch (to be stained, colored with . . .) IV
3. se _____ de Qch (to take on a tinge of . . .) IV
4. _____ Qch en [+ couleur] to dye something . . . Ex: *teindre quelque chose en bleu*, to dye something blue) VI
5. _____ Qch de Qch (to dye, stain . . . with . . .) VI

teinter

1. ———— Qch (to tint . . .) I
2. être teinté de Qch (to be tinted with . . .) IV
3. se ———— de Qch (to have, take on a tint of . . .) IV
4. ———— Qch de Qch (to tint . . . with . . .) VI

télégraphier

1. ———— Qch (to telegraph, wire, cable . . .) I
2. ———— à Qn (to send a telegraph, wire, cable to . . .) II
3. ———— Qch à Qn (to telegraph, wire, cable . . . to . . .) VI
4. ———— à Qn de *Inf.* (to telegraph, wire, cable . . . to . . .) IX-B

téléphoner

1. ———— à Qn (to telephone, call . . .) II
2. ———— Qch à Qn (to tell someone something over the telephone, Ex: *J'ai téléphoné les résultats à Pierre*, I called Pierre with the results) VI
3. ———— à Qn de *Inf.* (to tell someone by telephone to . . .) IX-B

témoigner

1. ———— Qch (to show, manifest . . . Ex: *témoigner sa surprise*, to show one's surprise) I
2. ———— de Qch (to affirm, bear witness to . . ., to give evidence of . . . Ex: *Elle témoigna de sa fidélité*, she affirmed her loyalty) IV
3. ———— en faveur de, contre Qn (to testify, give evidence in favor of, against . . .) V

tempêter

1. ———— contre Qn ou Qch (to storm, rage against . . .) V

tendre

1. ———— Qch (to stretch . . .; to stretch out, hold out . . .) I
2. ———— à Qch (to strive for, towards . . . e.g., *à la perfection*, for perfection) II
3. ———— Qch à Qn (to hold out . . . to . . .) VI
4. ———— *un piège* à Qn (to set a trap for . . .) VI
5. ———— à *Inf.* (to tend to . . .) VIII-A

tenir

1. _____ Qn ou Qch (to hold . . .; to keep . . . *e.g.,* a promise) I

2. se _____ (to remain, to be, Ex: *se tenir debout,* to be standing) I

3. _____ à Qn ou Qch (to be fond of . . . Ex: *Je tiens beaucoup à ce portrait,* I'm very fond of this portrait; With a thing as subject: to be caused by . . . Ex: *Sa mauvaise santé tient à son régime,* his poor health is a result of his diet) III

4. se _____ à Qch (to hang on to . . .; to keep to, abide by . . . Ex: *se tenir aux règles,* to abide by the rules) III

5. s'en _____ à Qch (to limit oneself to . . .) III

6. ne _____ qu'à Qn ou Qch (to be entirely up to . . .; to rest entirely on . . . Ex: *Ma vie ne tient qu'à lui,* my life is entirely in his hands) III

7. _____ de Qn (to take after . . .) IV

8. _____ de Qch (to be of the same nature as . . .) IV

9. _____ contre Qn ou Qch (to resist, hold out against . . .) V

10. en _____ pour Qn (to have a crush on . . .) V

11. _____ Qch de Qn (to have learned . . . from . . .; to have received . . . from . . .; to be indebted to someone for something) VI

12. _____ Qn ou Qch pour Qn ou Qch (to consider . . . a . . .; to take . . . for . . .) VI

13. _____ Qn ou Qch par Qch (to hold . . . by . . . *e.g., par la main,* by the hand) VI

14. _____ à *Inf.* (to be set on --- *ing,* to be eager to . . .) VIII-A

15. être tenu de *Inf.* (to be obliged, expected to . . .) IX-A

tenter

1. _____ Qn (to tempt . . .) I

2. _____ Qch (to undertake, attempt . . .) I

3. _____ de *Inf.* (to attempt to, try to . . .) IX-A

4. être tenté de *Inf.* (to be tempted to . . .) IX-A

terminer

1. _____ Qch (to end, finish, conclude . . .) I
2. se _____ en, par* Qch (to finish, end in . . . Ex: *Quels mots se terminent par un "x"?* What words end in "x"? *Une comédie qui se termine en tragédie,* a comedy that ends in tragedy) V
3. _____ Qch par *Inf.* (to conclude, end . . . by ---*ing*) X

tirer

1. _____ Qn ou Qch (to pull . . .; to draw . . . *e.g.,* a sword) I
2. _____ à [*sa*] *fin* (to be ending, drawing to a close)
3. se _____ de Qch (to extricate oneself from . . .) IV
4. _____ sur, contre Qn ou Qch (to shoot at . . .; to fire on . . .) V
5. _____ vers, sur Qch (to border on . . . Ex: *Un bleu qui tire sur le vert,* a blue that borders on green) V
6. _____ Qn ou Qch de Qn ou Qch (to take . . . from, out of . . .; to draw, derive . . . from . . .; to drag . . . from, out of . . .; to save . . . from . . . Ex: *tirer quelqu'un du danger,* to save someone from danger) VI

tomber

1. faire tomber Qn ou Qch (to knock, push . . . over; to cause . . . to fall) I
2. laisser tomber Qch (to drop . . .) I
3. laisser tomber Qn (Coll: to stand . . . up; to stop seeing . . .) I
4. _____ de Qch (to fall from . . . *e.g., du ciel,* from the sky; to drop with . . . *e.g., de fatigue,* with fatigue) IV
5. _____ dans, en* Qch (to fall in, into . . . Ex: *tomber en disgrâce,* to fall into disgrace; *tomber dans l'oubli,* to sink into oblivion; *tomber dans un trou,* to fall into a hole) V
6. _____ sur Qn ou Qch (to attack . . .; to come across . . .) V

---

*See Appendix II: **DANS, EN, À,** p. 298.

tonner
1. _____ contre Qn (to thunder, inveigh against . . .) V

toquer (se)
1. se _____ de Qn (Coll: to have a crush on . . .) IV

tordre
1. _____ Qch (to twist . . .) I
2. se _____ Qch (to twist one's . . . Ex: *se tordre la cheville*, to twist one's ankle) I
3. se _____ de Qch (to double up with . . . *e.g.*, *de rire*, with laughter; *de douleur*, with pain) IV
4. _____ Qch à Qn (to twist someone's . . . Ex: *tordre le bras à quelqu'un*, to twist someone's arm) VI

toucher
1. _____ Qn ou Qch (to touch . . .; of money: to receive or cash . . .) I
2. _____ à Qch (to tamper, meddle with . . .; to approach, draw near to, approximate . . .; to handle . . . *e.g.*, merchandise; to dabble in . . . Ex: *toucher à la peinture,* to dabble in painting) II
3. être touché de Qch (to be touched, moved by . . .) IV

tourmenter
1. _____ Qn ou Qch (to torment, harass, worry . . .) I
2. se _____ de Qch (to worry, fret about . . .) IV
3. être tourmenté par Qn ou Qch (to be tormented by . . .) V
4. _____ Qn ou Qch de Qch (to torment, harass . . . with . . .) VI
5. se _____ pour *Inf.* (to take the trouble to, bother to . . .) X

tourner

1. ———— Qch (to turn, revolve . . .) I
2. ———— *un film* (to shoot a movie) I
3. ———— autour de Qn ou Qch (to linger, pace around . . .; to revolve around . . .) V
4. ———— sur Qch (to depend on . . . Ex: *Tout tourne sur sa réponse*, everything depends on his, her answer) V
5. se ——— vers, contre Qn ou Qch (to turn towards, against . . .) V
6. ———— Qch en Qch (to turn . . . into . . .) VI
7. ———— Qch autour de Qch (to wind . . . around . . .) VI

traduire

1. ———— Qn ou Qch (to translate . . .) I
2. ———— de Qch (to translate from . . . *e.g., de l'anglais,* from [the] English) IV
3. se ——— par Qch (to become manifest by . . . Ex: *Son désir se traduisit par son regard*, his longing was evident in his expression) V
4. ———— Qn ou Qch en Qch (to translate . . . into . . .; *traduire quelqu'un en justice*, to prosecute someone) VI

trafiquer

1. ———— Qch (to trade, do business in . . .; to tamper with, doctor . . .) I
2. ———— de Qch (to make money on . . .; to sell . . . *e.g.,* one's honor; to traffic in . . . *e.g., de drogues,* in drugs) IV

traiter

1. ———— Qn ou Qch (to treat, deal with . . .) I
2. ———— de Qch (to deal with [a subject]) IV
3. ———— avec Qn (to negotiate with . . .) V
4. ———— Qn de Qch (to call . . . a . . . *e.g.,* a coward) VI

tramer
1. _____ Qch (to weave, to plot . . .) I
2. _____ Qch contre Qn ou Qch (to plot . . . against . . .) VI

trancher
1. _____ Qch (to cut, slice . . .; to settle . . . *e.g.*, an argument) I
2. _____ avec Qch (to contrast strongly with . . .) V
3. _____ sur Qch (to stand out against, from . . .) V
4. _____ Qch à Qn (to cut off someone's . . . *e.g.*, someone's head) VI

tranquilliser
1. _____ Qn (to calm, reassure . . .) I
2. _____ Qn sur Qn ou Qch (to reassure . . . about . . .) VI

transférer
1. _____ Qn ou Qch (to transfer . . .) I
2. _____ Qch à Qn (to transfer . . . to . . .; to sign over . . . to . . .) VI

transformer
1. _____ Qn ou Qch (to transform . . .) I
2. se _____ en Qn ou Qch (to turn into . . .) V
3. _____ Qn ou Qch en Qn ou Qch (to turn, transform . . . into . . .) VI

transiger
1. _____ avec Qn ou Qch (to compromise with . . .; to make concessions to . . .) V

transmettre
1. _____ Qch (to transmit . . .) I
2. _____ Qch à Qn (to transmit . . . to . . .) VI

transmuer
1. _____ Qch en Qch (to transmute . . . into . . .) VI

transpirer
1. _____ de Qch (to perspire, Ex: *Il transpire des mains*, his hands perspire) IV
2. _____ sur Qch (to sweat over . . .; to work hard on . . .) V

travailler
1. _____ Qn ou Qch (to work . . .; to cultivate . . . *e.g.*, the earth; to work on, study . . . *e.g.*, a role) I
2. _____ à Qch (to work for, towards . . .) II
3. _____ pour Qn ou Qch (to work for . . .) V
4. _____ à *Inf.* (to strive to . . .) VIII-A

travestir
1. se _____ en Qn ou Qch (to disguise oneself, dress up as . . .) V
2. _____ Qn ou Qch en Qn ou Qch (to disguise, dress up . . . as . . .) VI

trébucher
1. _____ sur, contre Qch (to stumble over, against . . .) V

trembler
1. _____ de Qch (to tremble with . . . *e.g.*, *de peur*, with fear) IV
2. _____ de *Inf.* ou *Inf. passé* (to tremble at the thought of ---*ing*; to fear that . . . Ex: *Je tremble de lui avoir déplu*, I fear that I displeased him) IX-A

tremper
1. _____ Qch (to dilute, soak, dip . . .) I
2. _____ dans Qch (to be involved in . . .; to have a hand in . . .) V
3. se _____ dans Qch (to be steeped in . . .) V
4. _____ Qch dans Qch (to dip, dunk . . . in . . .) VI

trépigner
1. ———— de Qch (to stamp, dance with . . . *e.g.*, *de rage*, with rage) IV

trinquer
1. ———— à Qch (to drink to . . .) II
2. ———— avec Qn (to have a drink with . . .; to drink a toast with . . .) V

triompher
1. ———— de Qn ou Qch (to triumph over . . .; to get the better of, overcome . . .) IV

tromper
1. ———— Qn (to deceive . . .) I
2. ———— Qch (to disappoint . . . *e.g.*, one's expectations) I
3. se ———— (to be mistaken) I
4. se ———— de Qch (to be mistaken about . . . Ex: *se tromper d'adresse*, to have the wrong address) IV
5. ———— Qn sur Qch (to mislead, deceive . . . about . . .) VI

troquer
1. ———— Qn ou Qch (to trade, barter, swap . . .) I
2. ———— Qn ou Qch contre Qn ou Qch (to swap, exchange . . . for . . .) VI

trouver
1. ———— Qn ou Qch (to find . . .) I
2. se ———— (to be located) I
3. ———— Qch à Qn ou Qch (to consider someone or something to have . . . Ex: *Je ne lui trouve aucun talent*, I don't think he, she has any talent) VI
4. ———— à *Inf.* (to manage to . . . Ex: *Elle trouve à nourrir ses enfants*, she finds a way to feed her children) VIII-A

tuer
1. ———— Qn ou Qch (to kill . . .) I
2. se ———— à, de Qch (to kill oneself with . . . Ex: *se tuer au, de travail*, to kill oneself with work) III, IV
3. se ———— à *Inf.* (to kill, exhaust oneself ---*ing*) VIII-A

U

unir
1. _____ Qn ou Qch (to unite . . .) I
2. s'_____ à Qn ou Qch (to unite with, join with . . .) III
3. _____ Qn ou Qch à, avec Qn ou Qch (to unite . . . with . . .) VI

user
1. _____ Qch (to wear out, use up . . .) I
2. s'_____ (to wear oneself out; to become worn out) I
3. _____ de Qch (to use, make use of . . . *e.g.*, one's power; to avail oneself of . . . *e.g.*, one's rights) IV
4. s'_____ à *Inf.* (to wear oneself out ---*ing*) VIII-A

usurper
1. _____ Qch (to usurp . . .) I
2. _____ sur Qn ou Qch (to encroach on . . .) V

V

vacciner
1. _____ Qn contre Qch (to immunize . . . against . . .) VI

valoir
1. _____ Qch (to be worth . . .) I
2. _____ Qn (to be as good as, worth as much as . . .) I
3. faire valoir Qch (to make the most of . . .; to set . . . to advantage, Ex: *Elle fait valoir ses beaux cheveux*, she makes the most of her pretty hair) I
4. _____ Qch à Qn (to result in, lead to . . . for . . . Ex: *cette action lui a valu un avancement*, that action got him a promotion) VI
5. *Il vaut mieux Inf.* (it is better, a better idea to . . .) VII-A

vanter
1. _____ Qn ou Qch (to praise . . .) I
2. se _____ (to brag, boast) I
3. se _____ de Qch (to boast of, about . . .) IV
4. _____ Qn ou Qch à Qn (to praise . . . to . . .) VI
5. se _____ de *Inf.* ou *Inf. passé* (to claim boastfully to be able to . . ., of having . . .) IX-A

vaquer
1. _____ à Qch (to attend to . . .) II

veiller
1. _____ Qn (to sit up with, keep watch over . . .) I
2. _____ à Qch (to look after, keep an eye on . . . Ex: *veiller à ses intérêts*, to look out for one's interests) II
3. _____ sur Qn ou Qch (to take care of, look after the welfare of . . .) V

vendre
1. _____ Qn (to betray . . .) I
2. _____ Qch (to sell . . .) I
3. _____ Qn ou Qch à Qn (to sell, betray . . . to . . .) VI

venger
1. _____ Qn ou Qch (to avenge . . .) I
2. se _____ de Qch (to take vengeance for . . .) IV
3. se _____ de Qn (to get even with . . .) IV
4. se _____ sur Qn de Qch (to take vengeance on . . . for . . .) V
5. _____ Qn de Qch (to avenge . . . for . . .) VI

venir
1. en _____ à Qch (to come to . . . *e.g., aux coups*, to blows; to be reduced to . . . *e.g., au vol*, to theft) II

2. _____ de Qn ou Qch (to come from . . .) IV

3. _____ *Inf.* (to come in order to . . . Ex: *Elle vient voir les photos*, she is coming to see the pictures) VII

4. _____ à *Inf.* (to happen to . . . Ex. *Si je venais à mourir,* if I happened to die) VIII-A

5. en _____ à *Inf.* (to end up by ---*ing,* Ex: *Il en est venu à mendier,* he ended up by begging) VIII-A

6. _____ de *Inf.* (to have just . . . Ex: *Nous venons de manger,* we have just eaten) IX-A

verbaliser

1. _____ sur Qch (Of police: to write out a report, a summons on, about . . .) V

2. _____ contre Qn (to testify, issue a summons against . . .) V

verser

1. _____ Qch (to pour, spill . . .) I

2. _____ dans Qch (to verge on, fall into . . . Ex: *Cet auteur verse dans le sublime,* that author verges on the sublime) V

3. se _____ dans Qch (to flow into . . .) V

4. _____ Qch dans Qch (to pour . . . into . . .) VI

5. _____ Qch sur Qn ou Qch (to pour, spill . . . on . . .) VI

vêtir

1. _____ Qn ou Qch (to dress, clothe . . .) I

2. _____ Qn ou Qch de Qch (to dress, clothe . . . in . . .) VI

vexer

1. _____ Qn (to vex, annoy . . .) I

2. se _____ de Qch (to get annoyed, vexed at . . .) IV

3. être vexé de Qch (to be annoyed, vexed at, by . . .) IV

4. se _____ de *Inf.* ou *Inf. passé* (to be annoyed, vexed at ---*ing,* at having . . .) IX-A

vider

1. _____ Qn ou Qch (to empty, drain . . .) I

2. se _____ dans Qch (to empty into . . .) V

3. ———— Qn ou Qch de Qch (to empty, drain . . . of . . .) VI

4. ———— Qch dans, sur Qn ou Qch (to empty, pour . . . into, onto . . .) VI

virer

1. ———— à Qch (to curve, turn to . . . Ex: *virer à droite*, to turn, curve to the right; *virer au tragique*, to turn to tragedy) II

viser

1. ———— Qn ou Qch (to take aim at . . .) I

2. ———— à Qch (to aim for . . . e.g., *à la perfection*, for perfection) II

3. ———— à *Inf.* (to aspire to . . .; to set one's sights on ---*ing*) VIII-A

vivre

1. ———— de Qch (to live on, by . . .) IV

vociférer

1. ———— Qch contre Qn ou Qch (to shout, yell . . . at . . .) VI

voiler

1. ———— Qn ou Qch (to veil, hide . . .) I

2. ———— Qch à Qn (to veil, hide . . . from . . .) VI

3. ———— Qn ou Qch de Qch (to veil, obscure . . . with . . .) VI

voir

1. ———— Qn ou Qch (to see . . .) I

2. ———— *Inf.* Qn ou Qch (to see someone or something . . . Ex: *J'ai vu arriver le train*, I saw the train arrive) VII-B

3. ———— à *Inf.* (to see to, to take care to . . . Ex: *Voyez à tout préparer*, see to it that everything is ready) VIII-A

voler
1. _____ Qn (to rob . . .) I
2. _____ Qch (to steal . . .) I
3. _____ Qch à Qn (to steal . . . from . . .) VI

voter
1. _____ Qch (to pass . . . *e.g.*, a law; to carry . . . *e.g.*, a motion; to vote . . . *e.g.*, appropriations) I
2. _____ pour, contre Qn ou Qch (to vote for, against . . .) V

vouer
1. se _____ à Qn ou Qch (to dedicate oneself to . . .) III
2. _____ Qn ou Qch à Qn ou Qch (to dedicate, consecrate . . . to . . .) VI

vouloir
1. _____ Qn ou Qch (to want, desire . . .) I
2. s'en _____ (to be angry with oneself) I
3. en _____ à Qn [de Qch] (to be angry with . . ., to have a grudge against . . . [about . . .]) II
4. _____ de Qn ou Qch (to want some of something, Ex: *Veux-tu de ces bonbons?* do you want any of this candy?; to want something to do with . . . Ex: *Ils ne veulent pas de lui*, they want nothing to do with him) IV
5. _____ Qch de Qn (to want . . . from . . .) VI
6. _____ *Inf.* (to want to . . .) VII-A
7. s'en _____ de *Inf. passé* (to be angry with oneself for having . . .) IX-A
8. en _____ à Qn de *Inf.* ou *Inf. passé* (to be angry with . . . for ---*ing*, for having . .) IX-B

Prepositions of Geographical Location

A. Prepositions used with names of Cities and Countries

Various prepositions are used, with or without a definite article, with verbs of coming (e.g., *venir*), going (e.g., *aller*), being (e.g., *être*), or doing (e.g., *habiter*), depending on whether the object of the preposition is a feminine country, a masculine country, or a city.

Feminine countries end in *e*, for example, *la France, l'Italie, l'Argentine.* (Exceptions: *le Mexique, le Cambodge*). Masculine countries end in a consonant or a vowel other than *e*, for example, *l'Irak, le Canada, les États-Unis.*

	Feminine Countries	Masculine Countries	Cities
Place In Which	en	au, aux	à
Place To Which	en	au, aux	à
Place From Which	de, d'	du, des	de

Examples:

Place In Which

Tu habites *en* Italie?	Do you live *in* Italy?
Elle a vu beaucoup de choses *au* Canada.	She saw a lot *in* Canada.
Nous avons passé six semaines *à* Rome.	We spent six weeks *in* Rome.

Place To Which

Il est allé *en* France l'été passé.	He went *to* France last summer.
Nous irons *au* Brésil pour le Mardi gras.	We will go *to* Brazil for the Mardi gras.
Je dois aller *à* Chicago la semaine prochaine.	I have to go *to* Chicago next week.

Place From Which

Je suis arrivé *de* France hier.	I arrived *from* France yesterday.
Il faut traverser la frontière pour aller *du* Canada aux États-Unis.	You have to cross the border to go *from* Canada to the United States.
Êtes-vous venu *de* Paris?	Did you come *from* Paris?

Note 1: Masculine countries beginning with a vowel follow the rules for feminine countries, e.g., *Je vais* **en** *Iran.* I am going *to* Iran; *Je viens* **d'***Irak.* I am coming *from* Iraq.

Three masculine countries can take either *en* or *au.* One can say: *en Danemark* or *au Danemark*; *en Portugal* or *au Portugal*; *en Luxembourg* or *au Luxembourg.*

Note 2: When a definite article is part of the city's name, e.g., *Le Havre, La Nouvelle-Orléans*, the article is kept and a contraction is made with the preposition when necessary. The contraction is not capitalized.

Je viens *du* Havre.	I am coming *from* Le Havre.
Elle a débarqué *au* Havre.	She landed *at* Le Havre.
Nous habitons *à La* Nouvelle-Orléans.	We live *in* New Orleans.

Note 3: When the name of a city or country is modified, e.g., *le vieux Paris, la France méridionale*, the preposition *dans* is used with the definite article in place of *en.*

J'aurais aimé vivre *dans le* vieux Paris.	I would have liked to live *in* (*the*) old Paris.
Il a passé l'été *dans la* France méridionale.	He spent the summer *in* southern France.

B. Prepositions used with names of Continents

Continents that are modified (e.g., *l'Amérique du Sud, l'Afrique du Nord*) take a preposition plus a definite article. Continents that are not modified take no definite article. *For example*:

Elle a passé plusieurs années dans *l'*Amérique du Sud.	She spent several years *in* South America.
Il a beaucoup voyagé *en* Asie.	He has traveled extensively *in* Asia.
Le bateau vient *d'*Afrique.	The boat is coming *from* Africa.

	Modified Continent	Unmodified Continent
Place In Which	dans l'*	en
Place To Which	dans l'*	en
Place From Which	de l'	d'

*In spoken French, *en* is often used instead of *dans l'*.

C. Prepositions used with names of Provinces and States

French Provinces

Note that feminine provinces (i.e., those ending in *e*) follow the rules for feminine countries.

	Feminine Provinces	*Masculine Provinces*
Place In Which	en	dans le, l'
Place To Which	en	dans le, l'
Place From Which	de, d'	du, de l'

Examples:

Nous avons bu de la bière *en* Alsace.

We drank beer *in* Alsace.

As-tu cherché des truffes *dans le* Périgord?

Did you hunt for truffles *in* Perigord?

Ils sont allés en voiture *de* Normandie *en* Bretagne.

They drove *from* Normandy *to* Brittany.

Note: In spoken French, masculine provinces can be used with the same prepositions as feminine provinces:

J'ai passé mes vacances *en* Poitou.

I spent my vacation *in* Poitou.

American States

Some American states have French forms. Most of these forms are feminine:

la Californie

la Floride

la Georgie

la Louisiane

la Pennsylvanie

la Virginie

la Virginie occidentale

States which are feminine in French follow the rules for feminine countries.

Two states have French forms and are masculine:

le Maine
le Nouveau Mexique

The other states have no French form, e.g., *le Nebraska.* These states are masculine.

	Feminine States*	Masculine States
Place In Which	en	au**, dans le, l' (dans l'état de)
Place To Which	en	au**, dans le, l' (dans l'état de)
Place From Which	de	du, de l' (de l'état de)

*Even though they are feminine, the two states *la Caroline du Nord* and *la Caroline du Sud* take the same prepositions as masculine states.
**Note that *au* is used with a masculine state beginning with a consonant (*e.g., Texas*). However, for masculine states beginning with a vowel, *à l'* is NOT used. Either *dans l'* or *dans l'état d'* is used.

Examples:

Je suis né *en* Virginie.　　　I was born *in* Virginia.

La ville de New York se trouve *dans* l'état de New York.　　　New York City is located *in* New York State.

Pour aller *du* Colorado *en* Californie, il faut traverser les Montagnes Rocheuses.	To go *from* Colorado *to* California, you have to cross the Rocky Mountains.

D. Prepositions used with Street Names

Street names are frequently used *without* a preposition in French where the preposition *on* would be used in English.

J'habite rue Cambon.	I live *on* Cambon Street.
Il travaille boulevard St-Michel.	He works *on* St-Michel Boulevard.

There are French prepositions, however, which correspond to the English preposition *on*. The preposition varies according to the type of thoroughfare and is used with a definite article.

Examples:

Il habite *dans la* rue Cambon.	He lives *on* Cambon Street.
Il habite *dans l'*avenue Foch.	He lives *on* Foch Avenue.
Il habite *sur le* boulevard St-Michel.	He lives *on* St-Michel Boulevard.
Il habite *sur la* route nationale N7.	He lives *on* Highway N7.

The prepositions *de* or *à* are used along with a definite article with verbs of coming from or going to a street name.

Vas-tu *à la* Cinquième avenue?	Are you going *to* Fifth Avenue?
Il est venu *du* boulevard Raspail.	He came *from* Raspail Boulevard.

E. Prepositions used with names of Islands

The use of prepositions with names of islands is somewhat complex. The preposition varies according to the gender, size, and geographic location of the island. There are five major categories:

1. *Masculine Islands* (e.g., *Cuba, Madagascar*)

2. *Large Feminine Islands* (e.g., *la Sardaigne, l'Islande, la Corse, la Sicile*)

3. *Small Feminine Islands Near Europe* (e.g., *Chypre, Malte*)

4. *Small Feminine Islands Far From Europe* (e.g., *la Martinique, la Réunion, la Guadeloupe*)

5. *Very Small Islands* (usually with the word *île* in their name, e.g., *l'île de la Cité, l'île Maurice, l'île d'Yeu*)

	Masculine	Large* Feminine	Small Feminine Near	Small Feminine Far	Very Small
Place In Which	à	en	à	à la, l'	dans l'
Place To Which	à	en	à	à la, l'	dans l'
Place From Which	de, d'	de, d'	de, d'	de la, l'	de l'

*Exception: *la Terre-Neuve*, Newfoundland. This large feminine island takes the same prepositions as masculine islands.

Examples:

On cultive le sucre *à* Cuba.

Sugar is grown *in* Cuba.

Beaucoup de Français passent leurs vacances *en* Corse.

Many French people spend their vacation *in* Corsica.

La guerre a éclaté *à* Chypre.

War has broken out *on* Cyprus.

Ils ont fait une croisière *à la* Martinique.

They took a cruise *to* Martinique.

Ce restaurant se trouve *dans* l'Île de la Cité, en face de Notre-Dame.

That restaurant is *on the* Île de la Cité, across from Notre Dame.

APPENDIX II

Dans, En, À

A. When to Use DANS, EN and À

The prepositions *dans* and *à* are generally used when the noun is preceded by some type of modifier: a definite article, an indefinite article, a demonstrative adjective, or a possessive adjective.*

Examples:

Il a passé deux années *dans la* prison d'Alcatraz.	He spent two years *at* Alcatraz.
Nous avons dîné *dans un* restaurant français.	We ate dinner *in a* French restaurant.
Marie étudie *dans sa* chambre.	Marie is studying *in her* room.
Il s'est jeté *à l'*eau.	He jumped *into the* water.
On l'avait logé *à un* très mauvais hôtel.	They put him up *at a* very bad hotel.

---

*With the exception of geographical place names: See Appendix I.

The preposition *en* is generally used when the noun is NOT preceded by a definite article, an indefinite article, a demonstrative adjective, or a possessive adjective.

Examples:

On l'a jeté *en* prison.	They threw him *in* jail.
Ils ont fait des courses *en* ville.	They did some shopping *in* town.
Je suis venu *en* classe sans avoir préparé ma leçon.	I came *to* class without having prepared my lesson.

Exceptions: The following expressions take *en* with a definite article:

en l'absence de	in the absence of
en l'honneur de	in honor of
en l'espace de	in the space of
en l'air	in the air
en l'an	in the year

B. Differences in Meaning Between DANS, EN and À

The preposition *dans* often has a more physical or precise meaning than the prepositions *à* or *en*. *Dans* frequently has the sense of *inside* or *into*. Compare the following sentences:

Elle est montée *dans* la voiture.

She got *into* the car.

Nous sommes venus *en* voiture.

We came *by* car.

Je ne veux pas entrer *dans* ce bar.

I don't want to go *into* this bar.

On a applaudi quand il est entré *en* scène.

They applauded when he came *on* stage.

Elle est entrée *au* couvent à l'âge de dix-huit ans.

She entered the convent at the age of eighteen.

Ne faites pas tant de bruit *dans* la maison!

Don't make so much noise *in* the house!

Est-ce que ta mère est *à* la maison?

Is your mother *at* home?

On a mis les bouteilles au frais *dans* la rivière.

They put the bottles to cool *in* the river.

Ne reste pas *au* soleil; mets-toi *à* l'ombre.

Don't stay *in* the sun; go sit *in* the shade.

C. The Use of DANS, EN and À with Vehicles of Transportation

1. To go somewhere by . . .

   On va quelque part:

en autobus	à bicyclette
en auto(mobile)	à cheval
en avion	à moto(cyclette)
en bateau	à pied
en scooter	
en taxi	par le train
en vélo	
en voiture	

2. To get on, get in . . .

   On monte:

   dans un autobus
   dans un avion
   à bord d'un bateau, sur un bateau
   dans un taxi
   dans un train
   dans une voiture

3. To be in, be on . . .

   On est:

   dans un autobus

dans un avion
à bord d'un bateau, sur un bateau
dans un taxi
dans un train
dans une voiture

Notes

Notes

Notes

Notes

Notes